My Story

www.**rbooks**.co.uk

My Story: Building Beyond *Big Brother*

CRAIG PHILLIPS

BANTAM PRESS

LONDON · TORONTO · SYDNEY · AUCKLAND · JOHANNESBURG

TRANSWORLD PUBLISHERS
61–63 Uxbridge Road, London W5 5SA
A Random House Group Company
www.rbooks.co.uk

First published in Great Britain
in 2009 by Bantam Press
an imprint of Transworld Publishers

This book is a work of non-fiction based on the life, experiences and recollections of
the author. In some cases names of people, places, dates, sequences or the detail
of events have been changed solely to protect the privacy of others. The author
has stated to the publishers that, except in such minor respects not affecting the
substantial accuracy of the work, the contents of this book are true.

A CIP catalogue record for this book
is available from the British Library.

ISBN 9780593063736

Addresses for Random House Group Ltd companies outside the UK
can be found at: www.randomhouse.co.uk
The Random House Group Ltd Reg. No. 954009

The Random House Group Limited supports The Forest Stewardship
Council (FSC), the leading international forest-certification organization. All our
titles that are printed on Greenpeace-approved FSC-certified paper carry the FSC logo.
Our paper procurement policy can be found at
www.rbooks.co.uk/environment

Typeset in 11/16.5pt Sabon by
Falcon Oast Graphic Art Ltd.
Printed and bound in Great Britain by
CPI Mackays, Chatham, ME5 8TD

2 4 6 8 10 9 7 5 3 1

All images courtesy of the author except where otherwise stated. Section one, p. 8:
Phillips family © Ian Simpson. Section two, p. 1: Craig entering *BB* house courtesy
Shropshire Star; Craig with Davina © Ken McKay/Rex Features; *TV Quick* awards
© Myung Jung Kim/PA Archive/Press Association Images. P. 2: all images ©
Mirrorpix. P. 3: Craig with Victoria Beckham © Richard Young/Rex Features; Craig
with Barbara Windsor © Fiona Hanson/PA Archive/Press Association Images. P. 4:
Craig with Linda Robson © ITV/Rex Features; *Ready Steady Cook*, *The Weakest
Link*, Craig with Colin and Justin and *Big Strong Boys* team all © BBC Photograph
Library. P. 5: Craig with Avid Merrion © Steve Finn/Getty Images; Craig canoeing ©
Trinity Mirror/Mirrorpix/Alamy. P. 6: Craig getting head shaved courtesy *Shropshire
Star*; Craig launching drink-drive campaign © Torbay Council. P. 7: Craig diving
with sharks © Mike White. P. 8: Craig with Cherie Blair and group shot © Craig
Phillips/Ian Simpson; Craig with Tony Blair © Barrie Grunewald.

Every effort has been made to obtain the necessary permissions with reference to
copyright material, both illustrative and quoted. We apologize for any omissions
in this respect and will be pleased to make the appropriate acknowledgements
in any future edition.

I'd like to dedicate this book to my entire family for always being there, and most of all to my mum and dad who I thank sincerely for bringing me into this weird and wonderful world. RIP Dad (1936–1985).

Contents

Acknowledgements

Writing a list of acknowledgements for this book has been as hard as writing the book itself. So, if I leave anybody out, you know who you are, and thanks for your love, friendship and support. There are so many friends, family, work and business colleagues from the past, the present – some ever-present – whom I thank sincerely but sadly just haven't been able to mention in the book, so here goes . . .

Firstly to my family: to my mum and Robbie for all their love and constant support. Mum, I hope I always make you proud, and Robbie, thanks for always being there for Mum and making her happy. My only sister Beverley, where do I start, I can't thank you enough for the countless times you've been there through the good times and the bad, and for all your support in my work and everything I've done. You're an amazing mum, sister and friend; you make me so proud.

To my gorgeous nieces, Lauren and Kelly, I'm so proud of you. You're very talented, bright and beautiful and do your mum credit. I really know you'll both do well in your chosen careers – sorry for nagging, it's because I care too much. I'm always proud of you both, follow your dreams.

To the entire ever-growing Maddocks and Everett families, there are too many relatives to mention and too many good times to recall! Thank you all for the love and support, especially Stephen for sharing the first night after leaving *Big Brother* with me (not in that way though!).

To the McCarthey and Harris families – just like my immediate family, we're as close but there are too many to mention you all! Thank you all for welcoming me as one of your own. Lee, Viv and Sam – I'll never forget the many wonderful holidays we shared together. Lee, it was an honour to be your best man – hopefully one day you'll be mine – and to be godfather to your children (I wish I could spend more time with you guys). Marion – Joanne's lovely smile and personality will always be in my memory. If it wasn't for Jo, I may not have even considered applying for *Big Brother*.

To Andy Bennett – thanks for being a great friend and business partner, I've enjoyed travelling the world and filming some amazing projects together. Let's hope there are many more to come, you're always top of my team sheet.

To Newport and the Midlands' finest: Simon and Tina Anderson, Barry Tongue, Kev Turner, Rod Butler, Dale Pain, Ian 'Hodgy' Hodgkinson, Ben Martin, Simon Lane, Tony Chan, Stan Yam, Stef Brotherton, Matt Thurstfield, Patrick O'Connell, Nick Hewittson, Gary Price, Pete Hurst and big Roy, Seth and Dan from the Physical Sculpture gym (Dan, RIP buddy) . . . and all the regulars at the Shakespeare Inn – you're barred!

To the good old Northern lads: Barry Myerscough, Barry Roberts, Bobby Roach, the Watson family, Pete Casey, Tommy Doyle and Frankie Dettori (my little brother, I'll teach you how to ride a horse one day or next time we're in Ibiza), John Aldridge (when are we next getting in the boxing ring?), Wayne, Steve and Sam – the Vegas and Puerto Banus boys. Julian Flanagan and all his family for so many good nights in the Newz bar and for being a great pal – hope the golf's getting better.

To the soap studs: Scott Wright, Ricky Tomlinson, Dean Gaffney, Jack Marsden, Ryan Thomas, Philip Olivier, Dan Jillings. To the builder boys: Tim Butler, Mick Baker, Keith Cadwallader for work and support at the building school and on my property developments. To the good old Southern chaps: Roger and Dan Walker, James aka 'Fletcher', Adam, Jason, and to all their families . . . Don't blame them, it's never their fault, it's always mine!

Steve Rotheram – where do I start? A fantastic ambassador for Liverpool and clearly the best Lord Mayor, I thank you for all the support for the skills centre and for the honour of asking me to be an appeal ambassador. Thanks even for the dodgy brickwork you did on my extension, but most of all for being a good friend. Elaine Bowker, thanks for your support and trust via the Learning & Skills Council for the skills centre. Thanks to Paul Crawford and all the staff at the skills centre. Thanks also to my architect Jon Moorehouse at Constructive Thinking.

Thanks to John at John Noel Management; Debbie Catchpole at Fresh Partners; Diana Mackay and Chris Kirby at

Melcombe International for their assistance on this book, ongoing support and continual kind hospitality at their home; Lucy Bridle at IAS Smarts; David Seymour and his team at Everbuild; Andy Acton; Derek Royall; Avis Robinson; Rob Gladwin; Rippleffect and Ampersand teams. A big thank you of course goes to my co-writer Rebecca Cripps, who I'm sure you'll agree captured my voice and my words really well, along with Doug Young, Becky Jones and all the patient team at Bantam Press to whom I'm most grateful for their assistance in compiling and publishing this book, and helping to make it happen.

The *Big Brother* thanks: I'd like to thank all the production team from Bazal and Endemol who were involved from the selection stage to Brett Kahr's final psychoanalysis interview with me. Neil Higgins and his security team: Panos, Tony and Mar, when I think back, boy, you had your hands full looking after me! My fellow housemates Sada, Nichola, Caroline, Tom, Andy, Darren, Nick, Melanie, Anna and Claire – thanks for an amazing sixty-four days in the house, hope you are all well and happy wherever you may be, not forgetting Davina and Dermot. Thanks most of all to Peter Bazalgette for the amazing aftercare and support, as well as matching my donation of £70,000 for Joanne's appeal.

Thanks to Chris Anderson and Steve Lee for writing 'At This Time Of Year' and to all at Warner Music involved in the recording and the video production, it was great fun. For all the stick I get about it, I'm still glad I did it.

A big thank you of course goes to all the various TV professionals, broadcasters and production companies I've worked with over the years; from commissioners to executives, producers, directors, on-screen talent: all those involved in front of and behind the camera. To mention just a few who have become close friends, having worked so closely with them and spent countless nights in hotels on some great productions together: Terri Dwyer, Gordon Whistance, Colin McAllister and Justin Ryan, James Martin, Suzi Perry, Linda Robson, Debra Veal, Stewart Castledine, Jason Godwin and all the *60 Minute Makeover* handymen, John, Jeff and the boys, Carolyn Eeles, Kate Silverton, Jenny Powell, Laura Stevens, Ko Chohan, Simon Paintin. Leigh Francis aka Avid Merrion (or should I say Mr Keith Lemon Businessman of the Year 1993), thank you please for letting me out of the cupboard, you still have the face!

The panto pals . . . a fairytale dream come true and great fun to work with you all. Long but fun months with custard pies galore! Simon Barry, Jane Brown, Steve Boden and Richard Chandler – thanks for providing me with great roles to play in some great shows which have helped me become great friends with Lisa Riley, Dean Sullivan, Syd Little, Frank Williams, Richard DeVere, Pete Price, Matt Milburn, Diane Youdale, Alex Hall, Tony Adams, John Cooper, Jane Omorogbe and Lara Sacher. Thanks to all my other co-stars and crew in all the shows.

Thanks to Alan Hamilton my PA, who fits in all of the above categories, as good as family, the closest friend and the best, most dedicated, work colleague, who has always put me in front of his family and friends. Without him I'd probably be on the dole.

To the many members of the public who chose to vote for me to win *Big Brother* and who have supported me in my television and charity activities, a huge thanks from the bottom of my heart – without you all it wouldn't have been possible.

Tony, Cherie and Euan Blair – thanks for having belief and support in me, best to the family.

In no particular order, thanks to Shelley, Laura, Sharon and Celena. These are four very special, amazing ladies in my life who've shared their hearts with me. I love you all.

To the Wilson family, your daughter is one of the longest and most true friends of mine, lots of love to you all.

As for the hundreds of wonderful charities and good causes I've been honoured and had pleasure to support, I wish I could name you all. Please keep up the good work, I will always be there for you all.

To all the serving British and international forces personnel across the world I've met and had the honour of working with – thanks for making me feel so welcome, respect to you all for the job you do.

1
Famous, Me?

Saturday 16 September 2000, 2 a.m.

'Listen carefully, Craig,' the psychiatrist said. 'It is very important that you digest everything I say. Do you understand?'

'OK,' I said. 'Fire away.'

'When you wake up tomorrow, you will be on the front page of every newspaper in the country.'

'Really?' I said, swallowing hard.

'And for the next forty-eight hours at least, you will be the most talked-about person in Britain.'

Oh my God! I thought. Am I hearing this right?

'Why is that, then?' I asked.

'*Big Brother* has exceeded everyone's expectations,' he explained. 'It's broken world records for telephone voting and viewing figures for Channel 4.'

'I see,' I said, as if his words made any sort of sense to me.

'Over the weekend, every TV and radio news bulletin will be discussing the show,' he went on. 'Every newspaper and magazine will want the winner – that's you – on the cover.'

Me? Craig Phillips, the builder from Liverpool?

'Because you're famous now, Craig. You're famous.'

Famous?

'Do you understand?'

I gulped. 'I think so,' I said.

He leaned forward. 'So how does that make you feel?'

I thought about it for a moment. 'I hear and understand what you're saying,' I said hesitantly, 'but it's not making me feel *anything*. I don't feel excited. I don't feel nervous or scared. I'm just numb, I think.'

He smiled warmly. 'That's to be expected,' he assured me, leaning back in his chair. 'At the moment you're having a delayed reaction. It will sink in soon.'

It was reassuring to have someone there to explain things calmly, because for the past hour or so I'd encountered nothing but mayhem and madness. I'd only just come out of the *Big Brother* house, so how was I to know that the show had become a nationwide phenomenon over the last nine weeks? Or that 7.5 million people had called in their votes during the final week of the show, making it the biggest phone poll in history?

I had absolutely no idea about any of it. I'd been out of contact with the world for sixty-four days, locked up in the *Big Brother* house at Bow Studios in east London. To me, Big Brother was a voice that came over the loudspeakers. But to the rest of Britain, it was a TV sensation that had gripped the nation.

I cast my mind back to what had happened over the last few

hours. It seemed ages since I had been sitting in the house, waiting, waiting for the final verdict. The hour before Davina McCall revealed the winner of Britain's first *Big Brother* had definitely been the longest hour of my life . . .

Friday 15 September 2000, 9 p.m.

I glanced over to the exit door. I could hear shouts and shrieks in the distance and I strained my ears to make out any voices I recognized – was my mum there? My sister? I hoped so. I couldn't wait to see them. My heart leaped at the thought of being free to spend time with my family and friends, of putting all this madness, boredom and lethargy behind me.

Winning mattered to me less, right then, than simply getting out of the house. I was absolutely desperate to get away; I was so sick of the place. It felt overpoweringly claustrophobic.

Beside me on the sofa was Anna Nolan, the only other housemate remaining in the *Big Brother* house. I liked Anna, but by now we had nothing to say to each other. After nine long weeks of being cooped up together, we had simply run out of things to talk about. So we sat there in silence. The time dragged as never before.

9.53 p.m.

Suddenly the silence was shattered. Davina's voice came booming through the house speakers.

'*Big Brother* house!' she said. 'This is Davina!'

'Hello, Davina!' we replied, suddenly alert.

'Hello, guys!' she said. 'I just want to say good luck to you both.'

We grinned up at the speakers.

'The nation has been voting for the last seven days to decide the winner of *Big Brother*,' she continued. 'The total number of calls has now been counted and verified by an independent adjudicator. I can now reveal the final result.'

I gripped Anna's hand and closed my eyes. Anna was shaking; I put my arm around her. The adrenalin was pumping round my body. I was terrified, but I was trying my hardest to keep calm.

'The winner of *Big Brother* is . . .' There was an agonizing pause. Come on, I thought. Just say it! '. . . Craig!'

Relief washed over me as I heard Davina's words. I took a deep breath. Stay calm, I told myself. Focus!

'Anna's still a winner as well,' I remember saying. I think I hugged her, too, but the next moments are blurred in my memory. Then suddenly she was gone, whisked out of the house. I was alone.

I was thrilled to be the winner, not that I had really taken it in: nothing seemed real. All I could think was, When will they let me out? I just wanted to get out of the house, to walk away, because by now I was close to exploding. I needed to be free.

Then I was called to the diary room. Apparently, I wouldn't be leaving for another hour. Even worse, instead of me going out, Davina was coming in. Oh God, I can't bear it! I thought. But there was nothing I could do about it.

My mind turned to practical matters as I walked back into the main living room. The place was a right mess and I couldn't help thinking that I'd be horribly ashamed if my mum suddenly walked in and saw it like that. Davina's coming in here, I thought, so I'd better tidy up! I'd never met her before and wanted to make a good impression.

For the next half an hour or so, I ran around frantically, doing the dishes and clearing things away. It was all pretty pointless, really, because the house was a temporary construction that was due to be demolished, and it was already falling to pieces. The décor was tired and the garden looked extremely shabby. What difference did it make if there was rubbish lying around?

What's more, the whole place stank. The floor had been rolled down without the joins being sealed correctly and all sorts of muck had gone down the cracks. We'd had numerous food fights and spilled everything from wine to suntan cream over the nine weeks, and although we'd done our best to clean it all up, we couldn't reach down between those cracks. So, as time went on, we'd walk across the floor and feel a squelching beneath our feet, and then little bits of food would emerge, stuff that we'd been trying to mop up a couple of days before. So it's not surprising that, after about six weeks, parts of the house had begun to smell – and after nine weeks, it was completely rancid. I guessed it was too much to hope that Davina wouldn't notice . . .

10.40 p.m.

Finally Davina arrived, with about twenty people following her: cameramen and sound and lighting technicians with assistants, all of them running here and there, pulling cables, positioning cameras and talking into radios. I found all the activity very distracting and could barely concentrate on what Davina was asking me. Over the weeks the other housemates and I had become quite territorial about our little environment, so it felt as if my house had been invaded.

Davina congratulated me and gave me a big hug and a kiss. She asked me to show her around the house, so I walked her through into the living area. We sat down on the sofa for a chat. 'How many people do you think voted for you?' she asked at one point.

'Let's see,' I said. 'I've got about thirty friends and family, but I think they would probably have voted twice for me. That makes maybe sixty votes?'

'Craig, three and a half million people voted for you to win tonight!' she said. How many? I was gobsmacked.

'How many times did you think you would be evicted?'

'I thought I'd go every week,' I said.

'And what are you going to miss about the house?'

'Big Brother!' I said, laughing. 'I'm going to miss Big Brother. I'm going to miss Big Brother telling me off, shouting at me, morning, noon and night in there.'

'Did you kind of talk to Big Brother? Did you try and bond?'

'I tried to, yeah.'

'Awww, Big Brother's always watching you, Craig,' she said.

'I know. That's what worries me,' I replied, laughing again.

She turned on the television in the living area. Suddenly my pals at my gym in Telford filled the screen, shouting and screeching. It looked as if there was a huge crowd there, all keyed up and watching the show live. It was significant, I realized, that the programme makers had gone to the extent of throwing a party for hundreds of my friends and people I knew to cheer me on. Although I had no notion of just how significant it really was, I began to feel quite excited.

We continued the tour of the house. I took Davina into the bedrooms and she pointed to where another housemate, Claire, who replaced Nick, had slept. The next thing I knew, she was telling me to jump into the bed with her, so we got under the duvet and carried on chatting there. To this day, I don't know why!

Next, we made our way to the kitchen. 'This is the table where you argued with Nasty Nick!' Davina said with relish.

Who's 'nasty' Nick? I wondered silently, before she swept me on to the next thing. Does she mean Nick Bateman? If so, why is she calling him 'nasty' Nick? I couldn't specifically remember arguing with Nick at the table, because all the housemates regularly had arguments there. And as far as I remembered, there had been more arguments with Caroline than with Nick . . .

I think Davina mentioned at that point that 8.5 million people had watched live online as I confronted Nick for cheating, which had led to him being expelled from the house five weeks previously. I still couldn't take any of it in. All the big figures and statistics she was coming out with were meaningless to me at that point.

Finally, it was time to leave. 'I'm going to hang back so you can enjoy this moment,' Davina said as she escorted me to the door. 'Go out there and see your family. You've won *Big Brother*. Enjoy the rest of your life!'

10.45 p.m.

At last! As I stepped out of the door, I felt like a huge bubble pushing up through the water until all of a sudden it bursts out at the surface. It was a great feeling, as if I could finally breathe again.

Fireworks exploded in the night sky as I walked down a long grid walkway towards freedom. Suddenly I saw my mum and my sister, Bev, push past a line of security men. As they raced towards me, I ran to meet them and we collided in a huge hug. I was so, so happy to see them. It felt like a lifetime since we'd last met.

A line of dazzling flares shot up behind me on the walkway. At that point I was supposed to keep on walking. But, overcome by excitement, we hugged and jumped up and down and veered off to the side of the grid. As a result, the pyrotechnics guys had to cut off the fireworks as they were racing up behind us. I heard later that there was panic in the control room as they contemplated this fantastic moment ending in disaster!

Just then Davina appeared again. She led me along to where some more family members were waiting. My nieces, Kelly and Lauren, and my cousin, Steven, went frantic when they saw me, screeching and trying to pick me up, which was a little bit disconcerting. I couldn't work out why everyone was so excited.

I could hardly hear what they were saying over the din of the crowd and the fireworks. Either way, they weren't making any sense at all.

'Everyone loves you, Craig!' they were shouting as they crowded round me.

'Why, what have I done?' I was trying to say.

Before I could get a straight answer out of anyone, Davina was pulling me another 100 metres along the way to where little Joanne Harris and her family were waiting. Davina was acutely aware that there was only a two-minute window for me to explain Joanne's situation.

I felt overwhelmed with emotion as I hugged little Jo and her mother, Marion.

'Craig, tell us who you're going to give the money to,' Davina said.

Amid the roar of the crowd, I looked Joanne in the eyes and said, 'I'm going to give all the money to you, Joanne! You're going to have it all! Didn't I promise I would get it for you? We're going to America!'

'Can you just explain the story,' Davina prompted, 'because people might not know it?'

I said, 'Joanne needs a heart and lung transplant, but un-fortunately they won't put her on the waiting list in England, because she has Down's syndrome. So we've got to take her to America and pay for it privately, and obviously this is going to cost a lot of money – two hundred and fifty thousand pounds.'

I took a deep breath, fighting back tears,. It was great to be able to talk about what had been on my mind since I had entered the house. I had deliberately chosen not to talk about Jo's situation and try to gain sympathy votes. None of the housemates had any idea what I was intending to do with the prize money if I won it. Every time they had a conversation about it, I walked away.

'We've been saving for a number of years and we've got absolutely nowhere near the target amount. But all the money I've earned here is going towards it, and we need more help!' I yelled. 'We need help!'

Jo seemed overcome by the emotion of the moment. There were tears rolling down her lovely little face. She didn't really have any idea of the scale of the money or the importance of it – she was just happy to see me. Weeks later, Marion told me that Jo had been voting me out of the house every week, as she was missing me and wanted me to come home!

Davina left me with Joanne and my family for just a moment or two, and there was more squealing and leaping about. It was crazy. My sister had arranged two coachloads of family and friends to come down and it was fantastic to see them, if only for a split second. But at the same time I felt completely wowed. I remember one bloke I didn't recognize grabbing at me and saying, 'Craig! I'm your second cousin!' I looked around at everyone going frantic and thought, Who the bloody hell are half these people?

Davina took my hand and led me across a bridge to the studio, where a big stage was set up, shaped like the *Big Brother* eye. Huge crowds lined the walkways and a sea of people surrounded the stage. It was overwhelming to hear them all shouting my name and screaming. Some of them were holding up posters and banners that said 'GOOD LUCK, CRAIG' and 'WE LOVE YOU, CRAIG', with pictures of me on them. I tried to home in on them all, but it was very strange seeing all these strangers' faces as they leaned across the railings trying to grab me. It was completely mind-blowing; overpowering, in fact.

I followed Davina onstage and she introduced me to the hundreds of shouting spectators, before announcing that the other housemates were coming out to join me. I certainly hadn't been expecting that.

One by one, Claire, Darren, Tom, Mel, Caroline, Nichola, Andrew, Sada and Anna arrived onstage – to bounce around and give me a big hug and kiss and act as if they were really pleased for me. Ooh, I thought, a couple of these people are being just a bit false now, because we didn't part on very good terms. They're making out that they're happy for me, but I could just feel that some weren't. It was nice to see most of them, though.

As Tom came to give me a hug, he put his hand over the microphone on my shirt and said, 'F*** Keith Woodall off!' The name meant nothing to me at first, but I could sense the warning note in his voice.

'OK, mate,' I whispered.

Then Nick Bateman bounded onstage, making his entrance to the sound of pantomime boos and hisses from the audience. He was dressed in black from head to toe. Davina introduced him as 'Nasty Nick' and announced that he would be presenting me with the *Big Brother* prize money. He hugged me and we watched a diagram on a big screen show £70,000 being transferred digitally from the *Big Brother* bank account into my account.

I did it! I thought with amazement. The crowd started singing the Liverpool anthem 'You'll Never Walk Alone'.

In no time, I was being led away by a group of security guards and a couple of policemen. As I left, the whole audience was singing 'You'll Never Walk Alone' to me. I was flattered, but still numb. When would it start to feel real?

Suddenly I was being rushed down a network of corridors, surrounded by guards, trying to find a way of getting out of the studios unseen. I could hear shrieking people behind us, trying to catch us up. They were after us. It was like being in some kind of whirlwind.

Finally we squashed into a lift. 'That's better!' I said. 'We can relax now.' Nobody spoke. The only noise was the sound of the guards catching their breath and voices talking in their earpieces.

Somebody pressed the wrong button and we went up two floors instead of down to the basement. As a result, when the lift doors opened, we stepped out into a lobby where loads of people were milling around. 'Aaaaah! It's Craig!' they yelled when they saw me. 'It's him!'

I was totally taken aback. The security guys closed around me and started pushing the people away as they fought to get into the lift with me. There was a proper struggle going on. It was very weird – and scary.

The lift doors closed eventually and shut everyone out. 'I wasn't expecting that!' I said, breathing a sigh of relief. It was the kind of thing I'd seen on television happening to the Beatles, so it seemed a strange way for adults to react when they saw me. It wasn't as if they were kids. I felt quite shaken up.

'That was mad, wasn't it?' I said to the security guards. But still no one said a word and we went down in the lift in silence.

What's going on here? I thought. Why isn't anyone speaking

to me? Where am I going? I wanted to be with my friends and family at the party outside, but instead I was being rushed away from them by a group of burly, silent bodyguards.

When we got to the basement, I was hustled out of the lift and through an exit, and then bundled into a people carrier that was flanked by a police van and police cars. Two security guards jumped in the front of the car and two climbed in the back with me, along with a producer.

In an instant the police cars whizzed away, blue lights flashing, and we went with them. Bloody hell! I thought. Should this be happening? Things were getting scarier. It felt as if I was being kidnapped.

Still no one had explained where I was going or what was happening. 'Why are we leaving?' I asked the producer.

'We just need to take you to a hotel so that a psychiatrist can check you over to see if you're OK,' she said.

'I don't need to see a psychiatrist, you know,' I replied. 'I'm fine. I just want to see my friends and family again.' I was desperate to see them, in fact.

'I'm so sorry. I'm afraid we've got to take you to this hotel,' she persisted. 'You'll see your friends and family soon. We'll bring them over to the hotel later.'

OK, I thought. No problem, as long as I get to see my family soon. A short while later we pulled up in front of one of those big posh hotels on Park Lane, looking over Hyde Park. A couple of security guards got out of the car and ran in the front entrance. The car started up again and we drove around the back, so that I could be smuggled in through the fire exit. The police cars sped off into the night.

The hotel's manager met us at the back of the hotel and took us up to an enormous penthouse suite. It was like nothing I'd ever seen or experienced before – there were three beautifully decorated bedrooms, a huge living and dining area, and an office. The bathroom was the size of a small apartment.

Who's paying for this? I wondered. I knew that a suite like this would cost a couple of thousand pounds a night at least, which I definitely couldn't afford. God, what's happening? I thought. Am I going to be staying here for a long time?

I learned something at this moment that I still swear by today. All the money and material things in the world don't mean a thing if you don't have your close friends and family around to enjoy them with you.

Another producer was waiting for me in the suite, along with the writer of the *Big Brother* book and the *Big Brother* psychiatrist Brett Kahr. 'Congratulations!' they said.

Before I could even say thank you, I was sitting down with the writer of the *Big Brother* book to talk about my experiences in the house. 'I've got to have this written up by the morning, because the book is going to be sent off to print in twenty-four hours, hence the rush,' she said apologetically before she left, fifteen minutes later. The rest of the text had been written and proofed, she added. There was just this last little section to complete.

Next I spent an hour with Brett. It was a nice, calming time, as it happened. Brett explained my situation in depth, which was exactly what I needed. I had met him before, during the *Big Brother* selection process, so he already knew quite a bit about my life and background. He had also watched me in the house from the studio gallery for up to ten hours in a row some days.

'From now on, Craig, your life is going to change. You won't just be able to go back to being a normal builder on a site.'

I was surprised to hear this, as I was expecting to be back on site within a week. Still, this was turning out to be a night of surprises, so I simply tried to listen and digest what he was saying.

'Your life is going to be completely different, but I don't want you to worry about it,' he continued. 'A wonderful thing has happened and I'm sure there will be loads of great opportunities for you.'

'In what way?' I asked.

'Well, there is already an agent lined up for you, and he's in discussions about different types of media work for you; things that will earn you a lot of money and possibly open another career pathway.'

OK! I thought. I don't mind the sound of that!

'But first you have to be mentally prepared to go out there. It will take time to adjust to how the public reacts to you and how you are treated. Even your friends and family are likely to be different initially,' he warned.

Hmm. I didn't know whether that sounded OK or not . . .

Finally Brett left, leaving me alone with a bunch of security guards posted outside my door – in case I decided to wander off. One of them introduced himself as Neil Higgins. 'Are you OK?' he asked. 'Do you need a beer or something to eat?'

By now it was half three in the morning and I hadn't eaten for hours and hours. 'I could do with a good meal, like a steak or something,' I said. 'I've been living on one pound a day food rationing for a while!'

'Anything you want,' he said genially.

'The producer said that they were going to bring my family and friends here . . .' I added.

He frowned. 'Yes, I've been speaking to our other security lads about that. It seems they've tried to bring them over, but there are about six press cars following them, and we can't let anyone know where you're staying. I'm afraid this means we're not going to be able to get your mum and sister here.'

'OK, well, can I go back to the party, then?'

'I'm afraid not,' he said.

'I'm stuck?'

'That's right.'

'But I can't stay here on my own!' I begged. It seemed ironic that I was the only person who couldn't enjoy the celebrations. 'They've given me a little taste of what's happening and I've had a psychiatrist explain it all . . . Now you're telling me I can't do anything about it?'

There was a pause. 'Let's see what we can do about getting someone else over here,' he conceded.

About half an hour later, I heard a familiar voice and my cousin Steven walked into the room with a weird smirk on his face. Oh no, I thought. What does this mean? As he shut the door, his face lit up and he ran towards me, shaking his head and smiling the biggest smile I'd ever seen. He looked so, so pleased, but I started feeling a bit shaky. What is he going to tell me? I wondered. Is it good or bad news?

Now we were face to face. Suddenly Steven started yelling,

'Craig, you're famous! It's fantastic! The whole country loves you!' Then I started screaming too. By the time Neil had popped his head around the door to see if we were OK, we were on the nearest king-size four-poster bed, holding on to each other and bouncing up and down like two big kids. Steven is about six foot four and he kept picking me up, shouting, 'Everyone in the country loves you! You're going to have a brilliant life!'

Only now, as I heard it spelled out by someone I knew so well, did it all suddenly begin to seem real to me. 'Waaaay!' I shouted back, adrenalin pumping through me. We carried on bouncing and bouncing until we were exhausted. It was a rare and brilliant few minutes.

We heard the security guards laughing outside. Then Neil poked his head around the door again and asked, 'Do you guys want to order something, then? Do you want some champagne? I think you deserve it.'

'Yes, please!' we yelled. So they ordered us a bottle of champagne and two big steaks, then some beers and another bottle of champagne followed shortly after. We sat up all night talking and didn't get a wink of sleep. Steve told me all about the show and the build-up to the final night, and how our families had been rallying round to get as many people as possible to vote for me. He explained how some of the other housemates' supporters had been sending out emails saying, 'If you want a free holiday, ring this number,' and the number would turn out to be a vote for their favourite housemate, not me.

'All sorts of schemes were getting cooked up!' he said. He

told me one thing after another; it was hard to believe it all or take in the scale of the show.

We went on drinking and chatting until about 7 a.m., when Neil said, 'I should warn you guys that at some point today we're taking you to a press call, where you'll be questioned and people will be taking photographs of you. So do you think you should get yourself some sleep now? Should you even drink any more?'

'We'll be fine,' I said. Why wouldn't we be?

Some time later we ordered breakfast and tried to sober up with a few strong cups of coffee. Then it was time to go back to Bow Studios for the press conference, at which point I thought for the first time about what it might entail – and I began to feel a little intimidated. Perhaps Neil was right and I shouldn't have drunk all that champagne and beer: instead I should have got some kip.

As we arrived at the studio, there were loads of workmen derigging the big stage. They all came rushing over when they saw me. 'Can we have your autograph and take a picture?' they asked, very excitedly.

'Of course you can!' I said, amazed that anyone would want to.

But the security guards wouldn't let them near me and hurried me past. 'Sorry, lads,' I called back as we left the area. 'They're the bosses at the moment and they won't let me!'

I was shown to a section of the studio that had been set up for the press conference. As I walked through the door, there was a loud cheer and hundreds of cameras started flashing. Shit! I thought. Sober up, sober up! Don't trip up! I kept my head down as I walked towards a long table where the other *Big Brother* finalists – Darren and Anna – and a few other people were sitting. I didn't dare look up at the photographers and trigger their flashes.

I sat down and turned to the people alongside me. As well as Darren and Anna, there were representatives from Endemol, Peter Bazalgette, head of Bazal Productions, along with Matt Baker, the press officer for Channel 4, and a woman I didn't recognize.

Finally I looked up to see a bank of about two hundred journalists, photographers and TV cameramen in front of me, rising five tiers above the ground on a specially constructed stand. It was an overwhelming sight. As soon as I raised my head, all their cameras flashed like crazy. The light was blinding.

I smiled nervously and the wall of cameras lit up again. I put my hand up to my eyes and there was more frantic flashing. In fact, every tiny movement I made seemed to set the cameras off again.

Bloody hell, all these people have come to see us and I'm still a little drunk! I thought. *I need to compose myself. This is really important. They're going to ask me questions and I need to be able to answer them coherently.*

The woman next to me opened the proceedings. 'As you're aware, Craig has been locked away for sixty-four days,' she said. 'He's had no contact with the outside world or with any media. We know you're all eager to ask him questions, so here's how it's going to work. You direct all your questions to me. If I feel a question is appropriate to ask Craig, I will. And if he feels he'd like to answer, he will.'

She looked directly at me. 'If you don't want to answer the question, just say no and we stop it there. If people ask the same question again, we stop the conference.' She was very firm and clear, like a judge.

By way of introduction, she read out some of the statistics about *Big Brother*, including the record-breaking viewing figures for Channel 4. Somebody from Channel 4 read out some stats about the phone calls and internet activity: the highest volume of calls to a live TV programme; the greatest number of hits online. As I heard all these numbers again, the enormity of what had happened began to sink in even deeper. I began to feel even more intimidated. I was sobering up by the minute.

'OK, what's the first question?' the lady asked.

'Craig, you filled in an application form for the show six months ago and were asked to answer in no less than fifty words what you would most miss in the house,' one reporter said.

Oh, shit, I thought. These journalists have done their home-work. I knew exactly what was coming next and I was dreading it.

'And you wrote only one word, and that word was "Sex"!' he went on. A loud ripple of amusement passed through the room.

Suddenly I was stone-cold sober. Be careful! I told myself. Focus.

'So, did you miss it as much as you thought you would?' he continued.

Oh God, I thought. What do I say now?

2

Dear Big Brother

I first heard about *Big Brother* in January 2000, about a month after the first-ever series had aired in Holland at the end of 1999.

I was at home watching TV when a documentary came on showing highlights of the goings-on in the Dutch *Big Brother* house. From the start, the clips of what the original housemates got up to transfixed me. There was a lot of footage of them hanging out and having fun; there were also some emotional scenes that showed them getting upset and arguing.

Despite the tears and the dramas, these people looked as if they were having the time of their lives. It was the kind of existence I imagined university students to have: lots of drinking and sleeping and messing about. It struck a chord with me because I'd have liked to experience the social life students enjoy and I sometimes felt that I had missed out by not going to university.

It intrigued me to think that the *Big Brother* housemates

were stuck inside a house being filmed for every second of the day. The whole idea just seemed really new and exciting. I'd never seen anything like it before. Watching them lark around, I became convinced that I'd have a great time in their situation. The group games and tasks were right up my street. What attracted my attention most of all, though, was the size of the prize money. Seventy thousand pounds was a hell of a lot of cash to walk away with!

The Dutch company that had produced the show was considering an English version. Hey, I thought, that looks like an easy way of winning a big sum of money! Perhaps this could be the solution to my fundraising woes.

It just so happened that I was feeling slightly disheartened that day, after meeting up with my mate Lee McCarthey and some of his family the evening before. We'd all gathered in Lee's mum's pub in Shrewsbury to discuss how best to go about raising more money for Lee's cousin Joanne Harris's life-saving heart and lung transplant. Although we had tried to stay optimistic, things weren't looking good for our campaign.

We'd been arranging fundraising stunts and events for some years. In fact, we'd done everything we could think of. Lee and I had shaved our heads to raise money in my mum's pub in Newport. Joanne's family had organized collections in Telford town centre. Loads of us had got together to appeal for donated goods and auction them off. We'd even made things ourselves to bulk up the auctions.

In the process we had raised the profile of our campaign and drawn quite a bit of attention in Shropshire. Yet whatever we did and however hard we tried, our efforts weren't stacking up to more than a few thousand pounds each year, which was just a drop in the ocean. And we were running out of ideas.

Now, here was a ray of hope. We desperately needed a lump sum like £70,000 to boost the campaign, not to mention our morale. It was a long shot, but I wrote off to the address listed at the end of the Dutch *Big Brother* documentary, saying, 'I like the idea of *Big Brother* and would like to participate in the show. So, if you do *Big Brother* in England, please consider me as an applicant.'

I didn't go into my reasons for wanting to be a part of it just then. I didn't mention Joanne; nor did I say anything to Lee or Joanne's family. After all, what were my chances of being interviewed for a place in the house? I didn't rate them highly. Perhaps I would never even hear back, but it was worth a try. Nothing ventured, nothing gained, as they say.

I had known Lee's little cousin Joanne all her life. Her family and mine had been connected since before we were born. My mum and Lee's mum, Viv, had already known each other for years when Lee and I became pals in our infant year at Rawson Road Primary School.

Lee was quite cheeky like myself, and we had a lot of things in common. We loved birdwatching and the *Star Wars* movies; we lived down the road from one other in Seaforth, Liverpool. He was and still is a great friend to me.

Lee was an only child, so his mum and dad liked his mates coming over to keep him company. Our other close friend was my cousin Steven, who was the same age as us. Together we formed a close trio and often spent weekends staying at each other's houses.

Everyone enjoyed going to Lee's house because it was so big, four storeys high, with masses of rooms. You could play hide and seek for hours and Lee's mum and dad wouldn't even know you were there. Lee had great parties at his house, too. There was one fancy dress party that was the talk of the whole school for weeks, where we all went dressed as pirates. Lee and his dad wore capes and masks and stalked the house as phantom flan-flingers, attacking us.

When we were nine, Lee and his parents moved from Liverpool to Shropshire. I was really upset when I heard he was going. It was only about 70 miles away, but that's like another country when you can't drive! Still, living apart wasn't going to stop us being friends. Being as close as we were, we were determined to keep in touch. We didn't have mobile phones back then, so we had to rely on the home phone (expensive in those days!) and writing letters.

Lee and his parents came back to Liverpool quite regularly and Viv kept in touch with my mum. I often went to visit Lee in the school holidays, too, and sometimes Steven came as well. Lee's dad, Sam, who ran a small supermarket in Harmer Hill, near Shrewsbury, would pick us up in his van when he drove to the wholesalers and abattoir in Liverpool. It was always a great adventure and I loved it. The journey to Lee's house only took an hour and a half, but it felt like a lifetime at that age.

Lee's mum and dad were extremely good to me. Their whole family was lovely and welcoming. They took me on trips around Shropshire and on holiday to Wales, where they had a static caravan. One of the highlights of staying with them was being allowed to go round the aisles of their supermarket after closing time and pick out anything we wanted. It was such a contrast to shopping with my mum. She was always saying, 'Put that down! You can't have it. It's not good for you,' or, 'Forget it, it's too expensive,' so it was a real thrill to ring everything up on the till with Lee in the empty shop. We felt dead grown up. Crisps, ting! Sweets, ting! Biscuits, ting! 'That'll be zero pence in total.' Afterwards we took the receipts upstairs to Viv and Sam to be tallied up for the accounts.

I was nearly eleven when Viv's sister Marion gave birth to baby Joanne on 4 August 1982. Jo had Down's syndrome and was born with a hole in her heart, a condition that is more common in people with Down's syndrome. I remember hearing that she wasn't too well when she was born, but at the time I didn't fully understand the depth of the problem.

It didn't take the doctors long to work out that Jo would eventually need a heart transplant. When that time came, though, she probably wouldn't be able to have it on the NHS, because many hospitals excluded people with Down's syndrome from major operations. It was a horribly unfair policy and the Down's Syndrome Association were lobbying hard to reverse it, but so far their pleas were falling on deaf ears.

Baby Jo inspired a fierce, protective love in everyone from the very beginning. Everybody was extra careful around her, especially when they were holding her. She was a really sweet, precious baby.

As she got older – when she was six or seven – the signs of Down's syndrome became evident in her face and speech, but we treated her just like any other kid, although we were always aware that her health was delicate. She was very cheeky, but so cute and loving that she got away with murder, much more so than the other kids. She absolutely loved Tina Turner and impersonated her endlessly. She learned all the songs and used to sing and dance to them all the time, and she was totally thrilled when she actually met her idol backstage at a concert, at an event organized by the Down's Syndrome Association.

All in all, Jo was a happy little girl. However, there was always the threat of the future hanging in the air. At some point, when she became too ill to carry on, she would need a heart transplant – or, as it became increasingly clear, a heart and lung transplant. What's more, the transplant would have to take place in America, because that's where the specialists were. Since the NHS discriminated against people with Down's syndrome and weren't even putting them on the waiting lists for transplants, surgeons in Britain were inexperienced when it came to operating in this specialist area.

Of course, it would be unbelievably expensive for Jo to have the operation in America. It seemed like an impossible situation. We had to do something about it.

Jo would probably be OK for the time being, as she was mostly in good health. The problem was that her condition could deteriorate at any time. So, since there was no government help, the only answer was to start fundraising privately.

Marion's family set to in the Shrewsbury area to drum up support. Lots of local shops got involved and people started to spread the word that young Jo needed a transplant. They did really well and raised thousands of pounds, but the cost of the operation was still a long way out of reach.

What made things harder was that, as the years went by, the price of Jo's operation was constantly increasing. We'd raise £5,000 one year, but the operation would go up by £10,000: it was always a case of one step forward and two steps back. We now needed a quarter of a million pounds: in other words, an absolute bloody fortune. That was why the documentary about *Big Brother* interested me so much. If I could get myself accepted as a contestant, perhaps I could win that lump sum for Jo.

I forgot all about *Big Brother* in the days and weeks after I wrote off to the production company. Then one day a producer from Bazal Productions (an offshoot of the Dutch company behind the series) phoned me at work, which was a surprise. As a builder, the only calls I usually received were from people asking for quotes!

'You wrote to us about applying to be a TV contestant on *Big Brother* . . .' she said.

'That's right!' I replied eagerly.

'We've decided to go ahead with an English version of the show,' she explained.

Brilliant! I thought.

'We'll be advertising for other applicants in various ways, but in the meantime, we're going to send you an official application form. Just fill it in and send it back to us.'

'OK,' I said. 'I'll do that.'

So I filled in a basic two- or three-page application form and sent it off.

A week later, the same producer phoned again and asked if I

would send her some photos of myself, which I did. A couple of weeks after that, she asked me to send in a three-minute video in which I talked about myself and the reasons why I'd like to go on *Big Brother*.

It was time to go and see Marion. 'Have you heard of *Big Brother*?' I asked her.

'No, what is it?' she said.

Almost no one in England had heard of the show at that point, so it's hard to know how the first series in England managed to attract 45,500 applicants. I think the production company must have advertised online, because I never saw anything about it on TV or in print after watching the documentary about it, and neither did anyone I knew.

'I don't know if anything will come of it,' I told Marion, 'but if I win the prize money, I'll put it in Jo's kitty. Hopefully we'll also be able to spread some awareness about our campaign and start getting closer to the target.'

I borrowed a camcorder and did the filming at Marion's house. Jo was in the video as well; I introduced us both and talked about the campaign, then messed about a bit. I found a small production company and paid them to cut the footage together for me. They turned it into a nice little three-minute piece and I sent it off to Bazal Productions.

Not long afterwards, a letter arrived inviting me to a hotel in Birmingham, where I would be asked to participate in some group activities and meet and mingle with other *Big Brother* applicants. This is saying something, I thought excitedly. But what did they mean about group activities? Would it be the kind of thing I had seen on the documentary about the Dutch house? Intrigued, I rang up Bazal Productions to ask more. It was now about two months since I had originally written off to them and obediently filled in the forms, yet I knew next to nothing about the selection process for picking the people who would be in the house.

The following weekend I took the train to Birmingham, none the wiser. The woman I'd spoken to at Bazal had been very, very vague about what I was going to be doing and why. She barely told me anything about the programme, which I found strange. Why was she keeping me in the dark? I wasn't exactly suspicious, but she had definitely aroused my curiosity.

'It's got to be top secret,' she'd told me. 'It's crucial that the people we put in the house don't know each other and don't know what to expect. The element of surprise is all part of the show.'

OK, I thought, I'll just go along with it and see what happens.

In Birmingham, I found my way to the hotel and was directed to a massive conference room filled with hundreds of other people. With TV cameras capturing our every move, we were put into groups of six and asked to perform various tasks. These were mostly very basic, practical challenges. For instance, the group would be told to stand around a circle marked out on the floor, of about a 2-metre radius, at the centre of which there was a plastic bin. We were told to work as a team with two pieces of rope and lift the bin out of the circle without entering it.

I instantly started thinking up a solution. All that was needed was common sense and a bit of lateral thinking. 'If you two grab hold of that side and we stretch that rope around it, we'll make a star shape,' I said. 'Then, if we hold it this way, we'll be able to loop it around and pick the bin up without anyone crossing the circle.' Straightaway I could feel the cameras homing in on me as I directed the other applicants.

I wasn't being bossy. It was just that I'd been running my own building company for eight years, so I was used to giving people directions at work. Every day on site I'd be saying to the builders working for me, 'You do this and you do that, and once that's finished, move on to this.' So I more or less went into work mode, guiding the group through the task. I felt I must have been doing something right, because I realized the cameras were zooming in on me more than on anyone else.

The groups changed throughout the day, from six people to ten people and back again. The tasks kept to the same kind of format, though. We'd be given a challenge and left to talk it through as a group for a minute or two. Then there would be four or five minutes allotted to complete the task, which mainly involved building or balancing things. It was obvious that the researchers wanted to see how people would mix together in a group and work as a team, and also see who the natural leaders were.

As the day progressed, I felt I was doing quite well. I threw myself into each challenge, bouncing suggestions off the group: 'Let's try this, let's try that!' I worked out the solutions quite easily. The others seemed to be a lot more hesitant about what to do and how to do it and tended just to follow my lead.

I've noticed over the years, from watching the people I've taken on in my building business, that about one person in twenty is a leader. The other nineteen are followers. The leader is the one who thinks ahead, acts independently and directs others. The rest sit around and wait to be told what to do and when and how to do it.

I'm the type of person that starts trying to find a solution to a problem before I'm even told to, and I think that made me stand out in the conference hall. By the end of the day I felt I'd done well, so I wasn't too surprised when, a few days later, I had a call from the producers inviting me to another day of tasks in another major hotel in Birmingham. I asked whether they would pay my travel expenses this time. No deal.

Once again I took the train down to the Midlands and tackled a range of challenges and obstacles in another big conference hall, along with hundreds of other applicants. I felt I did well again; the cameras were following me once again and I was hopeful I was giving them what they were looking for. I thought I was in with a good chance of getting a callback.

It came a couple of days later. 'Well done, we want to take you through to the next stage now,' a producer told me. I was so pleased. Every step felt like a big achievement.

The next stage turned out to be more difficult than expected, though: a fifty-page application form arrived in the post, headed with the words: 'Answer each question in no less than fifty words.'

Fifty pages! Hundreds of questions! Fifty words each! It was like the worst homework you could imagine. There was no way I could do it all in one go, so every night for the next two weeks I sat down and spent about half an hour on it – or until I was bored and threw it down, exasperated. I tried to answer each question as honestly I could, in as much detail as possible. But I was finding it a struggle to go into depth about myself and use fifty words where just a sentence would do. I was a pretty straightforward guy, after all.

There were lots of questions about hobbies, likes and dislikes.

'Do you have any tattoos on your body?'

'If so, where are they?'

'Describe them.'

'Why did you have them done?'

'If you haven't got any, why not?'

'What would you have done if you got one?'

Luckily, I didn't have any tattoos anywhere, but I wasn't too pleased with some of the other questions. They just seemed pointless. Why did anyone need to know all these personal things about me?

'When did you first have sex? With whom?'

I'll go back to this tomorrow, I'd say to myself as I tossed the form aside for the umpteenth time. I didn't exactly have heaps of time to spare, either. It was coming up to the time of year when I had to complete my tax and VAT returns for my accountant, and they were really playing on my mind. If I didn't get the figures and forms in on time, I would face a fine, and my accountant was already chasing me.

The night before it was due to be sent off, I sat down to do my usual half-hour on the *Big Brother* application form. After a few minutes, I came to a set of questions that absolutely really didn't appeal to me:

'How often do you masturbate?'

'What do you think about when you masturbate?'

'When and where do you do it?'

This is totally irrelevant! I thought. Forget it! They were stretching the boundary between public and private too far. I couldn't see why this kind of information would be appropriate for a TV programme. I dropped the form on the floor, deciding instead to focus on getting my tax returns done.

About an hour later, as I was coming to the end of my tax returns, the phone rang. It was a producer from Bazal Productions. 'Why haven't you sent back your application form?' she asked, a bit crossly.

I sighed. 'I've pretty much thrown in the towel, I'm afraid,' I explained. 'The form's lying on the floor. I just don't think these questions are relevant.'

'Oh, no!' she said, sounding very concerned. 'You can't let this go. Please, please fill it in and send it back.'

'But some of the questions are really stupid and in-appropriate,' I said.

'Listen,' she pleaded, 'I shouldn't tell you this, but you're down to the last fifty people.'

I sat up in my seat.

'Only fifty people were sent this application form,' she continued, 'and forty-nine of them have sent it back on time completed. You're the only one who's still outstanding. Please don't give up now.'

'All right,' I said reluctantly. 'I'll fill it in. But I won't be answering some of these questions at length, that's for sure.'

'OK,' she agreed. 'Just put down what you can and send it off by recorded delivery tomorrow morning. Will you do that for me?'

'All right, then.'

This must be fate! I thought. It was a real coincidence that she had called on the very night I'd decided to give the whole thing up. Sighing, I begrudgingly put down my tax returns and picked the application form off the floor. OK, I would answer the questions, but I'd answer them how I wanted, in as many words as I wanted.

I thought back to an article I'd read in a newspaper a few days before. A university student in his final year had apparently been given an essay to write on the subject of risk. All he had written was, 'This is', and submitted it as his complete essay.

I admired his courage. It obviously paid to be arrogant and blunt sometimes. He had passed his degree by taking a major risk, which is why the story had stuck in my mind. I decided to follow his example, because I've always been a risk-taker. Plus, in those days, I thought everything you read in the newspapers was true, when perhaps it was just an urban myth!

The next question I came to was: 'Describe in fifty words what you'd most miss in sixty-four days if you were locked in the *Big Brother* house.'

'Sex', I wrote. Just the one word, nothing more. It was the first thing that jumped into my mind: after all, I was young and male and I had a very high sex drive!

I fired off the rest of the answers and was finished with the form in about ten minutes. The next morning I sent it off recorded delivery.

Three weeks later, Bazal Productions wanted to do a police check on me to make sure I didn't have a criminal record. I had no idea how to go about this, so I got in touch with my family solicitor, who arranged for the police to send out a certificate. After that, there was a medical: a doctor was sent to my house to take blood and urine samples and give me a general all-over health check: breathing, blood pressure, eyes, etc.

Finally, I was invited to the head office in London. Would I come along to meet some of the producers and have psychiatric screening? In other words, I'd spend a couple of hours talking to a psychiatrist.

'Yeah, I've got no objections to that,' I said, feeling slightly unnerved. I had never been to see a psychiatrist before and I never thought I would. Still, I thought, it's their choice, not mine.

Brett Kahr turned out to be a nice fella and I found it easy to talk to him. I spent two or three hours with him, chatting about my life, from my time at school up to the present day. All the while someone was filming us, using a small camera on a tripod, which was fine with me. I've never felt self-conscious in front of cameras. Also, Brett had a really comforting, soothing voice and I instinctively trusted him. He had an almost hypnotic effect on me and I found myself being more open with him than I normally would be with a stranger.

'What would you say was the most significant moment in your childhood, Craig?' Brett asked me.

I took a deep breath. 'The night my father was killed by a drunk driver,' I replied.

3

The Worst Day of My Life

20 April 1985

'Wake up, Craig, and come downstairs quickly, will you? Your mum's here and she needs to have a word.'

I didn't have to be told twice. As I opened my eyes and saw the look on my mate Andrew's dad's face, I knew immediately that something was very wrong.

I jumped out of bed and scrambled to get dressed. In the distance, I could faintly hear someone crying. Who was it? My mum? I rushed downstairs. There was a chill in the air.

Andrew's mum and dad, their faces pale and blank, were standing awkwardly by the front door, which was half open. Their house had been full of sadness since before Christmas Eve, when their fifteen-year-old daughter, Sharon, had died from a brain tumour. Now sorrow had come knocking again, although this time it was another family's tragedy.

I heard the sound of crying again. It was coming from the other side of the door. As I walked outside, my mum and sister, Beverley, reached out to hug me. Their eyes were red-rimmed, their cheeks puffy from crying.

'What is it, Mum?' I asked. 'What's happened?'

'It's your dad, Craig. He's dead, I'm afraid,' Mum whispered. 'He was killed in a road accident last night. I'm sorry, love, he's gone. I'm so, so sorry.'

My body went cold. My dad? Dead? I tried to absorb her words but they did not seem to make any sense.

In a state of complete shock, we walked from Andrew's house back to our house. It was only a few hundred metres away, but we had to pass the exact spot where my father was killed, as it was the only route home. I wasn't aware of that at the time, though. The police cars were long gone, the blood washed away.

Soon family members and friends started to arrive. Everyone was appalled and upset. Yet amidst the crying and grieving and sadness around me, I felt utterly numb. Although I could see and hear everything that was happening, I couldn't engage with any of it, or digest it in any way. It was almost as if I wasn't there.

After a while, though, I began to feel scared at how upset my mum was. I'd never seen her like that before. She was sobbing so much that people were holding her up, because she couldn't support herself. It really terrified me to think that she might not be able to cope. How was she going to manage without my dad? How would any of us manage? I was only thirteen. Life without him was unthinkable.

My dad, Leslie Phillips, was a typical Scouse man: very

proud, very hard-working, very loyal, and my mum, Brenda, was like him in many ways. They brought me up to be honest, genuine and straight down the line, and never to mislead anyone. We were a happy, tight-knit family and I was very close to them both.

A manual labourer for most of his working life – a pipe-fitter for British Gas – my dad also liked his sports and was a very physical person. He had a similar build to myself, short and quite muscular, and he was renowned for his film-star good looks, especially in the 1960s. Apparently, Mum chased him all over town for ten years before she finally caught him!

Dad was also a skilled bricklayer, an all-round builder in fact, and I vividly remember helping him to build the back extension on to our house. I was only small, but I happily carried bricks and tools around for him. Like most little boys with their dads, I hero-worshipped him.

I was always eager to help, but things didn't always go to plan. When Dad did some work on Beverley's wardrobe once, he told me to clear out the old wood and rubbish, make a bonfire and burn it. Unfortunately, what I didn't realize was that Bev had put all her clothes into bin bags, to protect them while the work was being done. I mistook the bags for rubbish and burned her clothes! She was furious, as you can imagine. She wanted to kill me! But Bev's a lovely person and a fantastic sister; she could never be cross with me for long.

Some of the happiest memories I have of Dad are of when we played pool together on Sundays. He often played pool at the Seaforth Social Club and I started going down there when I was about twelve. He really liked a Sunday afternoon drink, so we'd get to the pub at midday when it opened and stay there until 3 p.m. when it had to close because of the licensing laws at the time.

I instantly took to the game of pool. I loved playing so much that I'd be the first to get my ten pence down on the table every Sunday. I used to say to Mum, 'For every ten-pence coin you give me now, I'll give you back a ten-pound note one day – because I'm going to be world snooker champion!'

I was so good at the game that I was a bit of a novelty attraction at first. Everyone was amazed when they saw me go through thirty-five fellas in a day without being beaten by a single one of them. Eventually, though, it started annoying the other players. I think it was partly because they were spending a lot more money than I was; I was drinking nothing but orange juice. Maybe the fact is that they didn't like being beaten by a kid!

So they had a committee meeting and voted to bar me from the pool table, which upset me enormously at the time. I felt rejected. It was a horrible feeling. Most of all, I missed spending that time with my dad and his pals Shaun and Keith, although I tried not to take it too hard. It was out of my dad's hands, but whenever he could, he took me to another social club, the Star of the Sea.

For some reason, Bev, who's two years older than me, always had in her mind that I was Dad's favourite, even though I was the naughty one, always sagging off school and getting into trouble, while she was well behaved, did her homework on time and passed all her exams.

I wasn't aware of Dad showing either of us favouritism. I

think it's just down to the way children sometimes perceive things. Now Bev's got her own kids, both in their late teens – Kelly and Lauren – there's the same kind of jostling for position, the typical sibling thing. But there is also deep love and affection there, just as there was between Bev and Dad. She just didn't notice it at the time.

Perhaps her view of their relationship was coloured by the different ways we were treated. Because I was a lad, I could stay out late; half the time Mum and Dad didn't know where I was or what I was getting up to. 'He'll be all right!' they used to say. 'He's a fella.'

But that wasn't the case with Beverley: she always had to be back on time; she had to be walked to and from the bus stop; and if she was going to someone's house, my parents had to meet their parents first ... Her life was monitored and restricted in a way that mine never was, just because she was a girl. I was happy to accept things that way, as I had the easiest life!

Holidays were of course a special time. The family holiday that stands out most in my mind was the week the four of us spent at Butlins. My dad was a real sun-worshipper. He loved to feel the sun on his skin, to frazzle in the heat if he could. So while Bev and I swam and dived and played in the swimming pool, and Mum kept a watchful eye out for us, Dad would slap castor oil all over his body, knot up a hankie and put it on his head, then stretch out in a deckchair and read his newspaper, a pint of beer by his side. Heaven! He was a really laid-back guy.

Sadly, in the last four or five years of Dad's life, he developed severe rheumatoid arthritis. It got so bad that sometimes he could hardly make a fist; he could barely pick up a cup of tea.

It was a horrible disease and he suffered a lot. As part of his treatment, he'd go to hospital for injections in his spine that would cripple him for days afterwards. He would have to sit in the same chair until the drugs had worked their way into his system and began to relieve his symptoms. Being so active, it was very hard for him. As he was no longer able to jump in and out of trenches, laying pipes, his role became more supervisory: he was one of the people overseeing the day-to-day running of the huge main gas storage container facility in Bootle that provided power for the city.

Dad was always a source of great strength in our family, despite his health problems. We knew we would be lost without him.

Over the course of the day following his death, I began to piece together what had happened the night before. It was a Friday evening and Mum, Dad and Bev had been at the Seaforth Social Club, where Mum sometimes worked behind the bar. The night out was a treat for Bev, who'd had her wisdom teeth removed a few days before. Meanwhile, I was staying at my pal Andrew's house just around the corner on the Seaforth Road.

Mum, Dad and Bev walked home just after closing time, around quarter to midnight. Then, since it was a lovely quiet night, Dad decided to take our boxer, Rocky, for a walk. He often took Rocky out at that time, because it was nice and peaceful and it settled the dog for the night.

As he was walking Rocky around the edge of Seaforth Park, the dog spotted something across the road and started to pull on his lead. This was bad news for Dad because of his weak grip; he struggled to keep a firm hold of the lead. Then Rocky suddenly bolted and Dad stumbled forward into the road, knocked his head and fell to his knees, disorientated.

There was a young lad walking along behind Dad on the other side of the road. When he saw Dad stumble, he trotted over to see if he was OK. By now Dad had let go of Rocky, who was running around, biting his lead and generally being boisterous. Rocky had a lovely nature, but he was really hyperactive. Ignoring the dog, the young lad started to help Dad to his feet.

Suddenly a car came screaming up the road, with its headlights on full. It was bombing straight towards Dad and the young lad. The lad stood up, waved and shouted, 'Stop! Stop!' but the car just seemed to speed up. Without a moment to spare or pull Dad out of the way, the lad had to jump off the road. The car roared forward and hit my dad, dragging him several metres up the road.

The driver was four times over the legal limit. He was so drunk that he wasn't even aware that he had hit somebody, even though the road was well lit and pedestrians were clearly visible to motorists, even at night. It wasn't until he finally came to a stop that he realized, but even then he didn't actually know what it was he had hit.

The young lad who had tried to help Dad – now the chief witness to the accident – rushed to the nearest phone box to call an ambulance. Dad was still alive when the ambulance arrived, but the injuries to his head, shoulder and neck were very severe. It was only two miles to Walton Hospital, but he was pronounced dead on arrival. He was only forty-nine.

It was about 12.30 a.m. by that time. Someone – we never found out who it was – told the witness that they knew Rocky's owners and where they lived. So when the police arrived at the scene of the accident, they knew immediately to go our house.

Bev answered the door. There was a policewoman on the doorstep. 'Do you own a boxer called Rocky?' she asked.

'Yes,' said Beverley.

'Is your mum in?' the policewoman asked hurriedly. 'Can you go and get her? I'm afraid your dad's been involved in a car accident.'

'But we haven't got a car,' Bev said. 'And my dad doesn't drive.'

Ignoring this information, the policewoman said firmly, 'We need to get your mum straight to the hospital, so please go and get her now.'

Bev was fifteen at the time, so it seems strange that the police decided to leave her at the house on her own. She had a little make-up on because she'd been out that night, so perhaps she looked older than she actually was. Of course, these days it would be completely different and the police would make sure that she wasn't left alone.

As Mum left to go to the hospital, the policewoman asked Bev if she could go out and try to get the dog back, despite the fact that it was one in the morning. 'He's running around at the top of the road,' she said. Not knowing how bad the situation was, Bev agreed to go.

My mum was in total shock, so she just did what the police told her to do. They didn't give her any more information about what had happened. They simply said that they had been sent to collect Mum and take her to the hospital to see Dad.

Bev rushed to the top of the road – about 80 metres away – where she could see a parked police car. Suddenly she saw Rocky. He had something in his mouth and was chewing it. To her horror she realized that it was Dad's shoe. But worse was to come: nearing the police car, she saw a large pool of blood in the road. The shoe, the blood . . . she felt sure that our dad was dead.

She managed to put Rocky on his lead and went back home. Rocky seemed unsettled as if he also sensed something wasn't right. Bev waited and waited. The minutes crawled by.

The door knocker went. It was our older cousin Terry, come to sit with her until Mum got back. Mum must have phoned him from the hospital. Hours passed. Then the door knocker sounded again at about 3 a.m. It was Terry's mum and dad, Aunty Do and Uncle Jim. Bev opened the door to them and the look on their faces immediately told her what had happened. 'He's gone, Bev,' they said.

She stared back at them. 'I knew it.'

I don't know what happened between then and 7 a.m., when Mum and Bev came to get me from Andrew's house, but I don't think anyone got any sleep.

People came and went throughout the following day. Then the day turned into night and the next day arrived in a blur and more visitors came to offer their support. The house was constantly full of friends and relatives in the week leading up to Dad's funeral. Bev slept in my mum's bed to be near her and comfort her. I didn't go into school.

One day Uncle Jimmy took me aside. Everyone was scared of Jimmy because he was a really big man. 'Now, Craig,' he said, a dead serious expression on his face. 'You're the only man in the family now, the man of the house. That means that you've got to look after your mum and you've got to look after your sister. They're *your* responsibility now. It's up to *you* to protect them. That's what your dad would want. You have to take his place and be the man in the family.'

His words could not have been more intimidating, because I was four foot nothing. It was true that I was a bit of a scrapper at school, but Jimmy was talking man's stuff now. The area we lived in was quite rough in those days. Things are different now – Seaforth has changed a lot, as has Liverpool – and on the whole the city is a much nicer and safer place than it used to be when I was growing up in the 1970s and 1980s. There's less crime these days, but back then there was a fair number of drug users on the streets and people's houses were constantly getting burgled. In fact that was why we had bought Rocky: to provide more security around the house.

How could I be expected to keep my mum and Bev out of harm's way? Jesus Christ! I thought, frightened out of my wits. I mustn't cry, I can't show weakness and I've got to seem strong. But I felt really weak and unsafe.

About a week later, Rocky bolted again when I let him off the lead as I was walking him across a school playing field. I lost him for about half an hour, and during that time I became terrified that he had gone for good. Oh my God, I thought, what will we do without a dog to defend us? Everyone knows my dad has died and when they find out we've lost the dog as well, we could be broken into! Jimmy's warning kept coming back to me. I was so afraid that, at only thirteen, I wouldn't be able to protect us.

Then I saw Rocky in the distance. I was so relieved I almost collapsed.

'Here, boy!' I shouted desperately. Tears pricked my eyes as he bounded over to me. I needed all the help I could get.

4

Butcher's Boy

Brett listened sympathetically as I told him about my dad's accident.

'Tell me a little bit more about your background,' he said, gently steering me back to my early life and upbringing. 'What sort of boy were you? What were your likes and dislikes? Did you have any hobbies?'

I cast my mind back to the years before Dad's accident. In those days, as I've said, the Seaforth and Bootle area of Liverpool was definitely not the best of areas. Situated near the docks, it was quite run down in places and there was a lot of unemployment. But it was home and it was all I knew. Despite everything, I still have fond memories of growing up there. Now, of course, the whole area has been regenerated.

Like my mum, dad and sister, I am Liverpool born and bred, entering the world at a tiny hospital in Walton on 16 October 1971.

When I was little we lived above a fruit shop called the Apple Barrel at 51 Seaforth Road. Coincidentally, this was the same flat where my pal Andrew's family was living when Dad died, so my mum and Bev broke the news to me outside our old home, which made a sad situation that much sadder. What's more, Dad was killed just ten doors along, outside of number 70. Geographically speaking, our universe was quite small.

When I was about eight, we moved to Hawarden Grove, a small close leading straight off the Seaforth Road. There were only twenty-one houses in the street, so it was an intimate little community within a larger but still close-knit community.

My sister Bev was well behaved, but I was a little rascal, climbing up the back walls behind the houses, running around where I shouldn't and getting told off by the neighbours. 'Don't go climbing those walls! It's dangerous,' my mum would warn me. 'Get off them effing walls!' the neighbours shouted.

My pals and I weren't allowed to go along the canal in Litherland, but we went all the same. Sometimes we used to go with my cousins; they were a bit older, but even they weren't supposed to go there. We were really keen on wildlife, especially birdwatching. So on Saturdays and Sundays we risked all and walked or cycled down to the canal banks, where the best wildlife could be found. It felt like miles from home at the time, but when I drive past there now, it's only two minutes in the car. Everything seems so much bigger and further when you're a kid.

I used to collect garter and grass snakes, tiny snakes that feed on worms. I bought them from the pet shop and searched for worms on the waste ground at the back of our house. I would get up early each morning and dig holes there until one day someone taught me a smarter trick. Add washing-up liquid to a bucket of water, pour it on the grass to soak in and wait. The worms hate the taste of the soap and so they race to the surface! Sometimes I'd sneak my snakes into school in a glass container and scare all the girls with them. Funnily enough, that got me into quite a lot of trouble. I was always getting into trouble back then.

I tried to persuade my parents to let me have a pet bird, but they wouldn't hear of it. Then, when I was twelve, I was walking Rocky in Seaforth Park when something fell out of a tree right in front of me and started fluttering around. At first I thought it was a pigeon, because of its white and grey feathers, but then I wasn't so sure because I could see it had a hooked beak, like a bird of prey. All of a sudden Rocky grabbed it by the wing, held it between his jaws and began to shake it around.

'Stop!' I screamed at the top of my voice. Instantly, he dropped it.

As I went over to Rocky and put him back on the lead, I looked closer at the ball of fluff on the ground. I was amazed to see it was a baby tawny owl! It was absolutely beautiful, with big black eyes. I guessed that it had jumped or fallen out of the tree before it had learned to fly properly. Now its wing appeared to be damaged.

I was aware that once you handle a bird, its mother won't go near it again. She can smell you on her offspring and either she will kill it or some other bird will. What shall I do with it? I wondered. I didn't want to leave it to die.

In the end I decided to take it to the local pet shop, which was owned by my pal Bobby's mum and dad. 'Look what I've found!' I said, reaching forward to show off what I had tucked in my coat.

'You can't keep that!' Bobby's parents said. 'Your mother will go mad.' They knew my mum and dad quite well.

But I was in love with that baby tawny owl. I couldn't bear to let it go. So I found a shoebox, made a little nest for it and hid it in my bedroom at the back of the wardrobe, out of sight.

I knew that owls naturally feed on little birds. So, wanting to give my owl the right food, I set about catching some sparrows. My pals and I managed to get hold of some mousetraps, which we set under the trees in Seaforth Park, with little bits of bread as bait. The bait soon attracted a sparrow or two and *wham*, the trap sprang, and there was supper for my little pet!

I shouldn't have done it. But the owlet seemed very appreciative and ravenously ate every sparrow I offered it, so I thought I was doing the right thing. (At least the traps killed the sparrows instantly, so I hope that they didn't feel any pain.)

Within two weeks my little ball of fluff had doubled in size. It now had a wingspan of 75 centimetres – that's 2.5 feet! I estimated that it was about six to eight weeks old by then and growing bigger by the day.

Meanwhile, my mum had lost patience with the state of my bedroom. She was always nagging me about the mess. 'It's a tip!' she'd say. 'It stinks!' So one morning while I was at school, she started vacuuming around my bed.

All of a sudden, out of the corner of her eye, she sensed movement on the top of the wardrobe. By now, the owl was so big that I couldn't really contain it in a box. It wasn't fair to shut it in the cupboard either, so it had got into the habit of perching on top of the wardrobe. When it slept, its whole head disappeared into its fluffy body of feathers, but I'm guessing it must have woken up when Mum turned the Hoover on. Oh dear.

Now, my mum doesn't really like animals. She especially doesn't like to touch them. Anything to do with animals was left to Bev, Dad and me, because we all loved them.

So it was unfortunate that, just as Mum turned to see what on earth could be moving on top of the wardrobe, the owl popped its head out from its neck, with one eye open and one eye closed, and swivelled its head from front to back. Then it gave her 'a look' and calmly began to fluff its feathers up. Mum promptly screamed the house down.

Her face was like thunder when I got home from school and I knew immediately that I'd been found out. I begged and pleaded with her and Dad, as if my life depended on it.

'Please, Mum, please, Dad, I can't let it go! We've got to keep it! Please, please!'

In the end they relented, but on one condition: it had to be kept outside the house.

And so began my first-ever building project: an aviary for my owl. The next day I put in an order for *Cage and Aviary* magazine at the newsagent's and soon I was reading up on how much space an owl needed, bearing in mind that fully grown tawny owls can have a 1.4-metre wingspan. I also did my homework on perches and feeding systems.

Next I went to the local builders' yard and bought four large pieces of reclaimed wood with my pocket money. I carried them on my shoulders all the way across Seaforth, a journey that felt like 10 miles under all that weight. By the time I'd finished building it, the aviary had four posts holding up a little roof with a chicken-wire surround. I was dead proud, as I did it all by myself.

At this point my owl was eating far too many sparrows – around six a day – so I got in touch with *Cage and Aviary* and started sending off for frozen day-old chicks from a farm they recommended. I paid for them with my pocket money and by doing odd jobs for neighbours in the road, like cleaning cars and washing windows.

My schoolteachers at Manor High School would probably have been amazed to see how intensely I studied the bird's requirements, because I certainly didn't do any studying in the classroom. It didn't help that I was dyslexic, or that teachers weren't trained to recognize and adapt to dyslexia as they are nowadays. I had no idea either. It wasn't until I was twenty-two that a teacher finally picked up on it, during an evening book-keeping class.

As a result I was perceived to be a bit stupid at school. My teachers talked down to me and the other kids took the mickey out of me because I was put in a class with slow learners. Ironically, the school motto was 'Achievements for All'.

Consequently, I didn't have any interest in learning. Schoolwork was the last thing on my mind. In fact, from the age of eleven to fifteen, while I was at senior school, all I was interested in was chasing girls, having fun with the lads, getting into trouble and keeping birds.

Numerous teachers warned me that I was heading down the wrong road. 'If you go on like this,' they said, 'you'll end up on the dole, or in jail.'

I barely listened. What did they know? 'Yeah, whatever.'

I stopped listening altogether after my dad's accident. I just didn't want to know any more. One of my teachers tried to counsel me about my grief, but I found it incredibly hard to express or discuss my feelings in the school environment. It's hard to talk about anything when you're thirteen.

It was difficult for my friends as well. They just didn't know what to say. They didn't want to upset me by talking about what had happened, but they didn't realize that nothing could upset me more than losing my dad. In fact, it would probably have helped to talk. But it wasn't their fault. They were only young, and so was I. You just don't know how to handle it when you're a kid.

There were some really awkward moments, especially in the painful weeks and months just after Dad's accident. I'd be sitting on the school bus and someone would look over and say, 'Hey, Craig, are your mum and dad going to the . . .' Then there would be a pause as they realized what they'd just said and their words tailed off, followed by a deadly silence as people shrank back into their seats and cringed.

It would have been so much easier if they'd just said, 'Hey, I'm really sorry. I made a slip.' It was the silence that did me in. In the minutes that followed, I'd wonder whether to say something or just ignore it and wait for it to go away. Those minutes when everyone went quiet dragged like hours.

Andrew Laird and his brother Gordon, whose house I'd

been staying at the night of Dad's accident, were a lot more understanding, because they had lost their sister Sharon just four months before. So at least I had them and we became a great deal closer during this time.

In the midst of her grief, Mum took on three jobs to try and support the family, working in two pubs in the evenings and by day at the Apple Barrel fruit shop, and Bev threw herself into her school studies. Although I had plenty of pals, I felt alone in my grief a lot of the time.

So it was with real relief that I went to see my mate Lee McCarthey in Shropshire that summer. I desperately needed a change of scene, and some carefree fun with my pal, away from the sorrow at home. Lee's parents were as kind and welcoming as ever and invited me on holiday to Cyprus with them. Never having been abroad, or on a plane, I jumped at the chance. It was an incredibly exciting opportunity. The beauty of the island and the laid-back way of life there enchanted me. It felt like paradise compared to Liverpool and provided a much-needed break from everyday life.

Back home at the end of the summer, my owl became a cause for worry. By now its wingspan stretched so far that I was beginning to think it had outgrown the aviary I had built for it. I confided my fears to an older boy and he suggested swapping it for his kestrel, which was smaller.

I liked the idea of keeping a bird of prey, but I wasn't sure it was entirely legal. 'Don't you have to be licensed to own a kestrel?' I asked him.

'This kestrel is fully licensed,' he assured me.

Soon afterwards, he came to pick up my owl. I really loved that bird, but it was just too big and hungry, so I reluctantly said goodbye and took over his kestrel, which was much more manageable and had ample space in the aviary.

I enjoyed playing the falconer. I made jesses – little leather bands – to strap around its claws and taught it to fly along fields. I also learned how to feed it by swinging its meat around, just as you see on films like *Kes*. In fact, I called the bird Kes and people used to say that I was just like the lad in the film.

Every day after school, I used to buy fifty pence worth of cheap meat from the local butcher's shop at 39 Seaforth Road. One afternoon I emptied my pockets when I got home and found I had £1.20, which was a lot of money for me – and far more than I expected. 'I don't understand it,' I told my mum as I stared at the coins in my hand.

Mum frowned. 'Retrace your steps,' she suggested. 'Think back to what you've done and where you've been.'

'I went to the butcher's, that's all,' I said.

'Did they give you change?'

I thought back to the few minutes that I had spent talking to Mr Watson, the butcher, about my kestrel. I remembered him giving me change from a pound and . . .

'He must have given me back the pound as well, by mistake!' I told Mum.

'Well, you'd better go and explain, then,' she said.

So off I went back to John Watson's family butcher's shop. 'I think you've given me too much change,' I told Mr Watson. 'It looks like you gave me a pound back by mistake.'

'I'm not sure now. I can't remember,' he said, scratching his head. 'And I can't check until the end of the day, when we cash up the till rolls. Can you wait until tomorrow?'

'OK.'

The next day, when I went in to get meat for Kes, Mr Watson gave me a big smile. He was a stereotypical butcher: grey-haired and jolly, with a red face from working in cold conditions all his life. He was always friendly to customers and forever chatting up old ladies. 'We checked the tills last night, son, and you were right, we were down a pound or so,' he said. 'But you can keep the extra money, for being so honest.'

'That's brilliant, thanks!' I said, chuffed to bits.

I ran back home and told my mum. She was really pleased for me. 'You see?' she said happily. 'You may have wanted to keep the money, but you've got to be honest in this life. And if you do a good thing, then good things will come of it.'

Little did I realize then that her words were about to be proved right. It was only a small act of honesty, but it was to change my life for ever.

The following week, Mum happened to drop into the butcher's shop to buy some chops. The shop was owned and run by John Watson senior and his son, John junior, who was also a jolly fella, with brown wavy hair, brown eyes and a brown moustache. Mum had been buying her meat there for years.

'Very impressed with that lad of yours,' John senior told her as he dealt with her order. 'He's a good genuine kid and honest with it.'

Mum beamed with pride. 'He's a good lad, is our Craig,' she

said, 'although he can be a little bugger at times, believe me.'

'That's boys for you,' laughed John. 'But you don't see honesty like that very often these days, especially not in the young ones. Very impressed, I was. There'll be a job here for him if he wants it, when he gets older.'

Mum didn't mention the conversation to me, but over the next couple of weeks, John and I had a little chat every time I went to buy meat for Kes. 'How's school going?' he'd ask.

'I like the sport and seeing my friends,' I'd say, 'but I don't really enjoy the learning. I can't see the point of it half the time, especially when the teachers look as bored as the kids are!'

John laughed at that. 'So what do you want to do when you leave school, son?' he asked.

'I'd like to work with animals,' I told him thoughtfully, 'in a zoo, or a wildlife park, or a vet's surgery. Or I could train birds of prey, or work in an animal sanctuary. That's my dream, I think.'

I enjoyed talking to John. Little did I know that the interest he was showing and the questions he was asking me were actually serving another purpose: he was informally interviewing me for a job as butcher's boy.

A couple of weeks later, he made me an offer. He would pay me ten pounds a week if, at the end of every weekday, I would spend an hour and a half cleaning up the shop, scrubbing the butcher's blocks and the floors. Plus, on Saturdays I had to help out in the shop from 12 to 5 p.m. I was thrilled beyond belief. A job! Wages! I couldn't wait to start.

I owe it to the two Johns for giving me a head start in life when I was only thirteen and a half. They taught me so, so much, from the abattoir side of being a butcher to the buying and selling and the banking. As time went on, I began to learn bookkeeping, too. It was basic stuff – handwritten spreadsheets of each day's takings; what we'd spent each week at the abattoirs; what we'd banked and what we'd paid out in wages – but it was a brilliant learning curve for me. I learned a huge amount; even my teachers at school approved. The two Johns were great mentors, very patient and caring, and I wanted to spend every spare hour in the shop. If it had been open on a Sunday, I would have been there.

What's more, I was rich! I had far more money than any of my pals, who were doing paper rounds and other odd jobs that earned them no more than a couple of quid. After four months, I started doing full days on Saturdays and my wages went up to fifteen pounds a week. I was really on big bucks then! Everyone at school was jealous.

Every day, as soon as school finished, I'd run for the bus home. I'd get off outside the butcher's shop and rush inside to the back of the shop, where I got changed out of my uniform into my white coat and apron before getting down to work.

I absolutely loved my work. I was always dead on time, even when I was kept on late at school to do detention for being naughty. When that happened I'd wait until the moment the teacher's head was turned, then I'd climb out of the classroom window. Gone in seconds!

By now, I was completely losing sight of schoolwork. I just did not want to know. On the other hand, I lapped up everything the two Johns taught me. So when things went from bad to worse at school and I started sagging off for days on end, it was fortunate that I had John senior to pull me up on my behaviour.

The problem was that whenever I was caught playing truant, I'd be excluded for a week or two. So I was like, 'Yeah, thanks very much! I'll do that again!' The punishments weren't working because they didn't feel like punishments. In fact, they were making me worse.

Eventually my case was referred to the school board and the authorities began to put pressure on my mum. At that point, I should have made more of an effort for her sake. She was suffering so much after Dad's accident and struggling to make ends meet, but I went on being blind and stupid and childish. It was really unfair on her.

It was only when John senior stepped in that I finally listened to sense. 'Hang on a minute!' he said. 'Think of your mother here. She could get into real trouble.' Until that point, I hadn't thought of it from her point of view.

John senior was roughly the same age as my dad had been when he died and young John was twenty-four; they became the closest thing I had to a father and a brother. They had a way of keeping me in line when I was going off the rails and they looked after me and pulled me through the hardest, most frightening times of my life. I was very lucky to have them. I was just a boy, struggling to cope with the loss of my dad, trying my hardest to be a man. But every time I thought I was getting older and stronger, something would happen to remind me just how young and vulnerable I was.

At about seven o'clock one winter night, I had the fright of my life. I was in my bedroom, playing on my Commodore 64 with my pal Bobby, whose mum and dad owned the pet shop. Bobby was a couple of years older than me, but we had made friends working together in the butcher's shop and we really got on well.

The phone rang. I went to answer it and a fella on the other end said, 'Is your mum there?'

Mum was out having a driving lesson, so I said, 'No, she's not here. What do you want? Can I give her a message?'

'No problem, I'll give her a call later,' the fella said. 'You're on your own in the house, are you?'

'No, my mate Bob's here,' I replied innocently. 'We're playing on the computer.'

'OK,' he said. 'I'll phone later. Goodbye.' He put the phone down.

Naively, I thought nothing more about it. I went back to Bobby and the Commodore 64. Five minutes later there was a knock on the front door. 'Not again!' I said. 'Hang on, Bob, I'll be back in sec.'

I opened the front door to see a big, unshaven fella standing halfway up the steps leading to our doorway. He was wearing a woolly hat pulled down over his forehead. It virtually covered his eyes.

'You OK?' I asked him.

'Go and tell your mum to come out here now,' he said. His tone of voice was quite aggressive.

'What for?' I asked.

'Go and tell her to come out here!' he said, even more aggressively. He kept his head down and didn't look me in the eye. It was all a bit strange.

'She isn't here. She's gone for a driving lesson,' I said. I still wasn't scared. Although physically I wasn't an adult, I felt as though I could look after myself. After all, I did a lot of my own cooking, washing and everything.

'I'm telling you to go and get your mum,' he said again. He took a step up towards the door.

It was then that I felt he was getting too close for comfort. I took a step backwards, pulling the door shut slightly. Suddenly he rolled his hat down over his face, turning it into a balaclava. As he leaped towards me, his eyes shone menacingly through the slits of his mask. They were all I could see of his face now.

Fear gave me the strength to push the door against him. I started screaming at the top of my voice. His huge hand dwarfed my hand as we pressed against either side of the same glass panel on the top of the front door, his hand on the outside and mine on the inside. It was like a scene from a horror film. Just then, I managed to get extra leverage by jamming one of my feet against the frame of the vestibule door behind me. I pushed the door with every ounce of energy I could muster.

In reality, this man probably wasn't as big as I remember him, but I was still four foot nothing and he looked like a dinosaur. After a few incredibly tense moments of high-pitched screaming and pushing back and forth, I just about managed to close the door. As I ran up the hallway, shouting about calling the police, I noticed Bobby stock still at the top of the stairs, frozen with shock. Suddenly he came racing down the stairs.

I ran to the phone and dialled one of the neighbours. 'Margaret, get Charlie!' I yelled. 'Someone's trying to break in to the house!'

'Oh my God, Craig, he's on his way over right now!' Margaret said. 'Is the back door closed? Are all the windows shut?'

Good point. We lived in the kind of community that kept our front and back doors open half the time. I put the phone down and ran to the back of the house. Rocky was barking ferociously, but there was no way that man would have been scared of our dog. Rocky sounded aggressive and always barked when anyone knocked, but most people in the area knew that he wasn't in the least bit dangerous. As I locked the back door, I shouted out that I had pals in the house. But my attacker obviously didn't care about that; I'd already told him I was with a mate.

There was more banging on the front door. I ran to the window and saw it was Margaret's husband Charlie, so I let him in. Charlie crashed into the hall, yelling madly. He started running around the house and out the back. I was hysterical with fear as he opened the back door. 'He's out there, Charlie. Be careful!' I screamed.

But there was no one there. The man had gone. We came back into the house and locked the back door, then went to bolt up the front door.

Meanwhile, Margaret had called the police. God knows to this day what she actually said to them, but it was something along the lines of how a maniac had broken into a house where some little kids were alone. So all of a sudden I was opening the front door to about ten policemen, who came piling into the hall and began thundering up and down the stairs as if it was a massive raid. When they opened the back door I could see there were even police coming over the back wall! They were definitely under the impression that there was an intruder in the house, which of course there wasn't.

They were very sympathetic when I told them how I had managed to hold him at bay and lock him out. After I'd described the man, they said, 'Ah yes, we know just who you mean. He's done this before.' Apparently, he came from a family of hardened criminals who were in and out of jail all the time. Still shaking from shock and tension, this information filled me with even more trepidation. Was it only a matter of time before he came back? What if he managed to get in next time? The image of his eyes staring out through the holes in his balaclava kept flashing into my mind. Would I ever be able to forget it? I doubted it. Even now, twenty-five years later, I can still picture his eyes.

John Watson junior from the butcher's shop was an amazing support. Although he lived up in Crosby, four or five miles away, he came straight over as soon as he heard what had happened and stayed at our house every night for the next couple of weeks, sleeping next to a baseball bat. 'If they try to come back again, I'll have them!' he kept assuring me, knowing how scared I still was.

It was a huge relief to have him there, but I still couldn't get any sleep. Every night I lay in bed feeling absolutely terrified. I couldn't stop reliving what had happened. Every noise I heard outside the house made me stiffen with fear; I was convinced that someone was going to break in at any minute. I just couldn't relax.

*

A few months later, I was alone in the house again when there was a loud knock at the front door. I looked through the window to see who it was. I never opened the door without looking out first.

There were two men on the doorstep. On their jackets were the letters RSPB. 'Can I help you? What do you want?' I asked them through the door.

'We're from the Royal Society for the Protection of Birds,' they said. 'Someone has informed us that there is a bird of prey being kept at this address. Is that right?'

My heart sank. This could not be good. I opened the door. 'That's right,' I said. 'I keep a kestrel.'

'I'm sure you know that you need a licence to keep a bird of prey,' one of the men said gently, 'so would you mind showing us your documentation?'

I was stymied. As I'm sure they suspected, I didn't have a licence or any documentation. 'A pal gave me the bird,' I explained as I showed them to the aviary. 'He said it was licensed and everything was all above board.'

The men from the RSPB shook their heads in disagreement. The boy who sold me the kestrel had misled me: it was I who needed the licence, not the bird.

They inspected the aviary and asked lots of questions about what I was feeding the kestrel, how I was handling it, and where and when I was flying it. A year beforehand, I had built a second, much bigger aviary on the flat bathroom roof of the house, just outside my bedroom window.

'Son, this aviary is very well made and you're doing everything right,' they said. 'But there are two very big problems here. The first is that you are too young to be a falconer. The second is that you don't have a licence. Now, since you can't get a licence because you're too young to be issued with one, we'll have to confiscate this bird.'

It was a real blow, but they let me off lightly. They could have prosecuted me and my mum as well, because she was responsible for me. However, because I'd looked after the kestrel so well and wasn't mistreating it in any way, they brought no charges at all; I got off with a caution. But they took the bird away and put me on record as an illegal falconer, so I didn't get off scot free, and I was devastated to lose my beloved Kes.

Meanwhile, I still wasn't sleeping and my waking hours were haunted with fear. I talked to John junior about how I was feeling. He was a young, fit, strong man who loved his boxing. 'Why don't you start training with me at the end of the day?' he said.

So I began training with John three or four times a week. It got so that if we weren't at the gym, boxing or weight training, or developing our martial arts, we were on Crosby beach running up and down in the sand. We took it very seriously. In fact, I took it a bit too seriously and hurt my back trying to keep up with the older guys and lift the same weights they were lifting.

John and I became very close friends and I became a black belt in full contact Muay Thai boxing. I was determined that nobody was ever going to break into the house or push me around. My survival instincts were on high alert, twenty-four hours a day.

I don't know how I would have got through those times without the guidance and support of the two Johns. Without a doubt, they taught me a great deal and helped me grow up. I'm sure my confidence today dates back to those early days of working in the butcher's shop, even when it comes to girls. I used to listen in on the older boys chatting up girls and they encouraged me to chat them up, too.

Things started to improve at school when a couple of the teachers acknowledged that I'd changed for the better since getting the job at the butcher's. Mr Woods, my woodwork teacher, and Mr MacDougall, my PE teacher, reported that I was a lot more respectful towards them now. They both recognized that I would rather be working than going to lessons. Now I knew what I wanted, I was focused on my career.

This was 1986, a time of mass unemployment in Liverpool. The tail end of the collapse of the mining and docking industries had affected families all over the north of England, as well as parts of the south, and it was really tough to find a job. It was a terrible time to be leaving school. Even the kids who did well in their exams weren't getting jobs, and no one thought for a minute that I was going to pass any exams.

However, there just wasn't much point in keeping me at school against my will. Mr Woods understood this and worked hard to make special arrangements for me. The school board listened reluctantly at first, but then my mum got involved and John junior went along to vouch for me.

'Craig has a full-time job at the butcher's for as long as he wants it,' he assured them. 'He's learned a lot and he's come on so well. He's good at serving customers, he's great at handling money and he's honest. As far as we're concerned, the sooner he can leave school, the sooner we'll give him full-time employment.'

Mr Woods's plan was that I would spend two days a week at school and the other three days working at the butcher's shop. I was over the moon at the idea. I was very nearly fifteen, so I still had over twelve months left in school and the only way I could see of getting through that year was to be working as well as going to class. Finally it was agreed officially that I could attend school part time and work part time. Fantastic.

All went well for the next four months. I felt well supported by the two Johns and also by a couple of my teachers, who always asked how things were going in the shop and were really pleased to hear how well I was doing. Of course, some of the other teachers were glad to see the back of me!

Then one of my co-workers left the butcher's shop and the two Johns started asking me to put in more time. I was already doing masses of overtime, though. It seemed only sensible to start working full time.

I decided that the moment had come to leave school for good. I sought both my mum's and John's blessing to confront my teachers. 'This is my last day in school,' I announced. 'I'm not coming back.' This might have been going against school regulations, but it was working out better for all parties concerned and I presume the authorities turned a blind eye.

Finally I was on my way. Without a GCSE to my name, I said my last goodbye to school and stepped into the big wide world of full-time employment.

5

Growing Up

I wanted my mum to be happy, but I wasn't keen on her having a boyfriend. It was three years since my dad had been killed, but I still missed him constantly and hated the thought of anyone replacing him.

It was silly to look at it like that, though. Of course there was no replacing my dad, but since there was no way of bringing him back to life either, it was time for Mum to try to move on and start living again. I knew that perfectly well, but all the same, I couldn't help feeling upset when Mum introduced me to Robbie, the new man in her life, whom she had met at the club she worked in. I tried to be accepting, but I did feel pretty bad about it at first, and so did Bev. What did this man want from my mum? Was he going to treat her right? I hadn't forgotten Uncle Jimmy's exhortation to look after her. I felt fiercely protective of her.

It was around this time that the case against the driver who had caused my dad's death came up in court for the final time. There had already been a number of hearings, but I was never allowed to go to them. At sixteen, I was still a bit of a scrapper, a bit insecure; I couldn't predict how I would react if I came face to face with my dad's murderer, which is the way I saw him then. I would probably have wanted to kill him for what he had done. Again, Mum told me to stay away from the court.

Even though he was four times over the legal alcohol limit and driving far in excess of the speeding limit, the driver wasn't charged with manslaughter. This was apparently because my dad was already in the road when he hit him. So he walked away with a hundred-pound fine and a year's driving ban. We felt insulted. It seemed totally unfair. Was that going to be his only punishment for causing Dad's death with his drunken, reckless driving? The law then was nowhere near as harsh as it is today, and I feel there are still some areas within the law regarding convictions of drink-drivers that need to be tightened.

I felt very angry when the court case was over. Dad had lost his life – and we had lost a father – but the driver responsible had lost only a small amount of money and the temporary use of his licence. He'd got off really lightly.

The court proceedings brought back the almost unbearable pain of losing Dad all over again, the sorrow and the emptiness. I still missed Dad so much. A boy needs his father as he's growing up. I felt as if I'd missed out – and still do, especially when I see some of my friends hanging out with their dads now.

Eventually, however, I came round to Mum's boyfriend Robbie. Five or six years older than my mum, he had a little fruit and veg shop with a flat above it. He was like my dad in one way, in that he was a very hard worker, but he also seemed very stubborn and set in his ways.

Deep down I only wanted what was best for my mum, even if Bev and I found it hard to see her with someone who wasn't our dad. It just wasn't fair to expect her to be alone for the rest of her life. She was entitled to love and happiness like the rest of us, and she seemed a lot more contented after they got together. The relationship rapidly became serious and they were married a couple of years later.

When I was seventeen Mum and Robbie decided that they wanted to run a pub, as they both had pub backgrounds, and a country pub seemed the nicer option. Lee McCarthey's parents already had a lovely pub in Shropshire, so they introduced my mum and Robbie to the brewery area manager. Several months later, Mum and Robbie were awarded the licence to run a gorgeous pub in Newport, Shropshire: the Shakespeare Inn. They fell in love with it the moment they saw it.

Bev and I stayed on in our little house. All our friends were in Liverpool, so we didn't want to leave, and we both had good jobs – me at the butcher's and Bev at the gym on the Seaforth Road. Mum didn't need to sell the house to finance the move: Robbie sold his little business and the flat and Mum had some compensation from Dad's accident, which they put together to buy the leasehold of the Shakespeare Inn.

It was brilliant to have the house to ourselves. Bev and I felt really independent and grown up! I had everything that a seventeen-year-old lad could wish for – my own house, my own money and my own vehicle. (Well, when I say I had my own vehicle, it was actually a van and it belonged to the butcher's shop! However, it got me around and none of my girlfriends complained.) I stocked up my aviary with four quails, thirty finches and a couple of cockatiels. Life was good. What's more, I loved my job, which isn't something most teenagers can say. I look back on those days as being some of the best of my life.

As well as my full-time job, I had a nice little sideline. It had all begun a year earlier, when Mum came home from work and said that the girls were clubbing together to get a strip-o-gram for one of her friends' birthdays at the club.

'Why don't you get our Craig to do it and save yourselves thirty quid?' Bev said jokily.

I laughed. 'OK, you're on!'

'Go away!' she said. 'I didn't think you'd take me seriously!'

But after mulling it over with the lads at the gym and the butcher's shop, we thought it would be good fun and easy money.

I just did it for a laugh the first time. I turned up at the club during the disco and gave the manager a wink. The DJ stopped the music and made an announcement; then the lights came on to reveal me standing on the dance floor wearing a long mac. I did a bit of a dance, cheekily stripping down to nothing but a thong and my dicky-bow. My act went down really well and I wasn't embarrassed in the slightest. Any excuse to get my kit off! I was pretty vain at that age and looked after myself well, so it seemed a good way of showing off – sixteen years of age and into my boxing, I was in really good shape! I was also training for bodybuilder shows and constantly holding poses in front of the mirror. (I never made it into competition because I could never get my weight up enough.)

Within two weeks, I'd been asked to do the act again three times by people who were all offering to pay! So I thought, Hang on, I could make a few quid here. 'OK, but I'll have to charge you thirty or forty quid,' I said. Every one of them said yes! So I developed a kiss-o-strip-o-gram-type act, involving silly games with balloons and spray cans of cream. As time went by, I became more confident and started using more props. I even had women kneeling to bite into various things that looked like sausages, or nibble my balloons. I went on getting bookings for a couple of years, about once or twice a month. It was just a bit of fun, really, but the money was good, too.

Life continued much the same at the butcher's: John senior didn't feel the need to expand the business; he was happy to plod along. Young John, however, was more ambitious, and decided to open a second shop in Allerton Road, just off Penny Lane. (Yes, *the* Penny Lane.) I helped him paint and decorate it, launch it and get it up and running. I worked overtime to get everything done by opening day.

John senior went off to manage the new shop and I returned to Seaforth to work alongside Bobby and young John. The three of us got on really well. We worked hard, trained hard and played hard. We had a right good laugh with it.

We'd always had competitors: there was another butcher's

shop across the road and yet another a bit further along. But we all did well and were very friendly with each other, supporting one another if need be. If, for instance, one shop sold out of something, we could rely on one of the other shops to help out, and vice versa. There was enough business to go around.

But then things started to change. The supermarkets were rearing their own livestock on their own farms and producing meat that was much cheaper than the meat our suppliers sent us. We were still OK, but the future wasn't looking all that bright for local butcher's shops.

Meanwhile, young John had expanded his horizons in another direction and begun to do some consultancy work for some sort of finance company in Warrington called Liberty Life. When he told me about an endowment plan that was great for saving money, I was happy to be his first customer. I was now working Monday to Saturday and earning seventy pounds a week, which was a great wage for someone my age in the mid-1980s.

I was easily persuaded to put ten pounds a week away into the plan. It was a fair portion of my wage, but John said that within ten years when the policy matured, the money would have earned a huge amount of interest. I trusted him 100 per cent and I never missed a payment.

I think John had already seen the writing on the wall when it came to the butcher's business. He and his wife had just had a baby and the last thing he needed was money troubles, so he soon joined Liberty Life full time.

'I've got to look at other ways of bringing in more money,'

he told me. 'I'm going to leave you and Bob in charge. I know you'll do a good job.'

I had no doubt that I could manage and handle the shop easily enough. I was pretty much doing everything anyway. I was going to miss working with John, but of course I wished him well. Within no time, it seemed, he was driving a Jaguar and living in a big new house in Litherland, which was quite a posh area. He was on his way to becoming a high-flyer and I admired him for it. Everybody did. In our little world of Bootle and Seaforth, he was seen to be doing really well.

When I turned eighteen, I decided to take out another endowment policy with him.

'You're a sensible man, Craig,' he told me.

Meat kept dropping in price and we started to feel the crunch in the shop. It didn't take us long to realize that we had a big problem on our hands, especially when the supermarket across the road doubled the size of its meat counter. Small butcher's shops began to struggle nationwide.

I still loved my work, but I had started to feel restless. I wasn't sure that there was anything else I could achieve in the industry. Perhaps it was watching John's example, but I had begun to feel more ambitious for myself. I had done well, but I wanted to do more. There was nowhere to go next unless I bought my own shop, but it had become glaringly obvious that the supermarkets were going to wipe out the small shops. It was unavoidable. There was no way of surviving against the big boys – and if I couldn't beat them, I certainly didn't want to join them. I wasn't going to work in a supermarket. The time had also come for me to change direction.

I spoke to John about it. 'This shop isn't going to survive more than a couple of years,' I said. 'I don't think any of the small butchers will. So I'm going to have to start looking around for another pathway, I'm afraid.'

Neither of the Johns could disagree that things were looking bleak. But what was I going to do? What could I do? I could still hardly read or write; I couldn't use computers. Yet I was strong and fit, I was quick, and I learned fast, so perhaps it would be wise to follow in my dad's footsteps and go for some form of manual labour. I thought long and hard, but I couldn't see any other alternative. I began to consider my options for physical work.

The turning point came in the spring of 1990, when I went on holiday to Cyprus with my pal Lee. The McCarthey family had acquired a little villa out there and Lee and I were allowed to go and stay there on our own, now that we were older. I had visited the island regularly with them over the years and I absolutely loved it. Cyprus was beautiful in every way; there was very little crime and the local people had a lovely way of life.

The locals made a big fuss of Lee and his family because they had a place there. They were always really friendly and welcoming to me, too. When I mentioned how much I loved the island, I was suddenly inundated with offers. 'Why don't you come and work here? We'll give you a job on the beach!' 'You can work in my bar.' 'Why not wait tables at my brother's restaurant?'

Hang on a minute! I started thinking. This is interesting.

Let's get this right – I could either work on the beach in beautiful, sunny, peaceful Cyprus or I could hunt for a new job in Liverpool, where there's loads of unemployment and wide-spread crime. Hmm . . .

Next, I met a beautiful Cypriot girl called Katrina. I fell in love with her within about an hour, as you do when you're eighteen. 'I'm thinking of coming to work in Cyprus,' I told her.

Her eyes lit up. 'If you do, you can come and stay with me!' she said.

This is the life, I thought. Everything was coming together.

By the time Lee and I boarded our flight home, there were opportunities lined up for me in at least two local bars and restaurants, along with an offer to work on the beach renting out jet skis and boats. How could I resist? I was determined to return.

Back at the butcher's shop, I explained the situation to John. 'I've met a girl!' I told him excitedly, 'and there are loads of job opportunities. I've got to go back in the near future; I can't miss this chance. Could you start looking to find someone to replace me?' Obviously I wasn't going to leave him in the lurch. I knew that it might take time to find the right person. 'It doesn't matter if it takes a week, a month or more,' I added.

John smiled wistfully. 'I totally support your decision, Craig,' he said. 'If it wasn't for Sue and baby Scott, I'd be coming with you.'

Within a few weeks, he had found someone to take over from me. I said my goodbyes to everybody in Liverpool and went to spend a couple of weeks at the Shakespeare Inn. It was great to spend a bit of time with my mum, but I was also angling for an intensive course in bar work and catering. 'Please, Mum, I need you to teach me everything you know,' I said.

I spent the next few days working flat out behind the bar. Luckily, I'm a quick learner and know how to use my own initiative, so I picked a lot of information up in a short space of time. Serving and dealing with customers was no problem; it was just like serving in the butcher's shop. Soon I had learned the mechanics of running a pub as well, from mixing cocktails to changing barrels and stocking the cellar.

I rang Katrina in Cyprus. 'I'll be there in a week,' I said, excitedly. I couldn't wait to see her again.

That same day I received a phone call out of the blue. 'Craig?' said the voice on the other end. 'Is it true you're going to live in Cyprus?'

'Steve?' I said. 'How are you doing, mate?'

Stephen Horrocks was one of my best pals. We had gone through school together, from infants and juniors right up to seniors, and over the years we'd had a million fights and made up a million times. When we left school, though, we began to lose touch. Steve started a job at the other end of Liverpool while I was wrapped up in the butcher's shop, morning, noon and night. I began hanging around with new mates and lost contact with a lot of my school friends. It felt as if I hadn't seen Steve in ages.

'So is it true?' he asked again. 'Are you really going to live in Cyprus?'

Apparently, the news had shot around Seaforth via the butcher's shop; loads of people who went to our families' school bought their meat there. Don't forget that barely anyone we knew back then had even been out of Liverpool, let alone gone to live abroad. So it was a very big thing. Now it's different. Everyone travels all over the world all the time.

'Yes, it's true, yeah,' I said happily.

'Can I come with you?' he asked, without further ado.

My heart sank ever so slightly. Steve couldn't live at Katrina's house as well! I'd have to rejig my plans. 'Why do you need to come with us?'

He had been having a really hard time, he said. There had been problems at home; he'd done a succession of crap jobs; his love life was non-existent. Now it seemed as if he was halfway to being lured into the murky world of Liverpool's underside. It didn't sound good.

'I need to get out fast,' he said.

I had been hearing on the grapevine about old schoolmates going the wrong route. They were getting involved in drugs or crime, or they were working on nightclub doors as bouncers, which was a nasty business to get into twenty years ago. A few of them were ending up in jail.

I didn't like to think of Steve getting into any kind of trouble. He was a good lad and worth more than that. He was also one of my best pals from school, I reminded myself. So I felt obliged to help him, even though I was also slightly reluctant to take him with me. On the upside, though, he'd had a couple of years' experience doing bar and restaurant work, so perhaps we would make a good team out in Cyprus.

'OK,' I said. 'Come down to the Shakespeare Inn and we'll take it from here.'

I rang Katrina in Cyprus. 'I'm bringing my mate,' I said without further ado – as you do when you're eighteen. 'We'll be leaving in a couple of days!'

There was a pause. 'OK,' she said, 'but I don't think you can both stay with me and my parents. You may have to look for alternative accommodation.'

Steve came to the pub and we started trying to organize our trip. Booking flights on the phone was the first problem. It was the height of the season and, at £600 return, they seemed very expensive. Paying that much would almost have wiped us out, and it was already a beg, borrow or steal scenario when it came to our funds. I'd cadged a bit off my mum and a bit off Robbie and taken out all of my savings. Steve had also cobbled together what he could.

Finally, someone in the pub offered us a lift down to Heathrow. Rather than spend precious days phoning low-price shops, it seemed more sensible to go down there and put ourselves on the standby list for a one-way ticket.

But at every airline desk at Heathrow the answer was always the same: no, no, no.

That night we slept inside the airport building, next to our bags, like tramps. The next morning, it was the same story: no, no, no. This obviously wasn't going to be as easy as we'd thought it would be. Another day went by and we realized we had a serious problem.

An airline worker suggested that we try another London airport. 'Hey, why didn't we think of that?' I said. We caught a bus from Heathrow to Gatwick, where we spent another disheartening day.

'Any spare seats to Cyprus?'

'No, no, no.'

By now, we felt very deflated. After all the excitement of our preparations, we were stuck in another airport eating the cheapest rubbish we could find to fill us up, and even the cheap, rubbish food at Gatwick was expensive. 'What are we going to do, Craig?' Steve asked for the hundredth time.

Just then I had a brilliant idea. There was no way this master plan could fail. 'Let's hitchhike through Europe and take a ferry across to Cyprus!' I said. 'Why didn't I think of it before?'

We were on our way again! We removed a few essentials from our bags – shorts, hair gel, toothbrush: the absolute basics – and stuffed them into a cheap backpack we bought in one of the airport shops. Then we posted our suitcases home.

'This way we'll be there in two or three days,' I told Steve excitedly.

Three months later, we were still wandering around Europe.

Cyprus remained our target destination . . . but we kept getting sidetracked. Our route was circuitous; it zigzagged randomly. We started by catching a ferry across the Channel and so our mission began in France. Our first mistake was forgetting to ring our families to keep them in the picture. Needless to say, Mum wasn't too happy with me when I called her from a phone box in Holland ten days later. In fact, I couldn't get a word in edgeways.

The unexpected arrival of my baggage had really thrown her. What did it mean? She had opened it up wondering what the hell was going on. In no time she was on the phone to Stephen's mum and they had both started to panic. Soon they were calling all the major London airports to see if we'd been listed on any flights to Cyprus. 'No, no, no,' came the answer. Any flights at all? 'No, no, no.'

We weren't registered at passport control either, so where had we disappeared to? It wasn't until four anxious days later that they discovered we had left the country by ferry. Nowadays you can find that sort of thing out within minutes, but information transfer was a lot slower back in the days before the internet.

'What the hell are you doing in Holland?' my mum screamed angrily. 'You're supposed to be in Cyprus!'

'I'm OK, really I am,' I said, trying to reassure her. 'Look, the money's running out. I'd better go!'

I turned to Steve. 'I wouldn't phone your mum, mate,' I warned him. 'I've just had a right earful!'

Over in Cyprus, Katrina was also feeling confused. 'Where are you, Craig?' she asked when I phoned, reversing the charges.

'I'm not sure exactly but I'll be there in a week, I promise!' I said.

But we were young lads, having the time of our lives, so nothing went according to plan. We bunked on trains not knowing where we were going; we did odd jobs to earn our food and shelter; and we chatted up girls in the hope of sharing their hotel beds. Finding somewhere safe and warm to spend the night was our daily mission. Several times we sneaked into train sleeper compartments and crashed out on the empty bunks.

Many a time we were kicked off trains for not having bought

the right ticket. Sometimes we'd get on and pay a basic fare in order to get a seat. Then we'd hide somewhere to avoid the ticket inspector, staying on for as long as we could, asleep in some dusty corner. If we were busted on an express train, it was often a couple of hours before the guard could chuck us off. 'Sorry, we didn't know!' we'd say, playing the innocent. 'We can't understand. We can't speak the language.' Half the time, we didn't even know where we were.

We felt totally carefree. Normal rules didn't apply, because we were abroad. It was huge fun, a good experience, and we met some great pals as well. We even kept in touch with them – but only for a short while, as you do when you're eighteen.

As I said, we'd fall in love with girls in the street and sweet-talk our way into their hotel rooms for the night. Of course, the next morning their friends would kick us out, but at least we'd had a safe night. That was the crucial thing.

Whatever we could do, we did it. Constantly short of money, we begged people to let us do ridiculously small jobs from picking grapes in France to chopping down trees for an old lady in Switzerland. In return for stocking up her winter firewood supply, she fed us casseroles in bowls and let us stay in an outhouse. Steve didn't enjoy it because he wasn't as physical as I was, but it was a workout for me and I loved it. It was the only real exercise we were getting.

Meanwhile, I kept calling Katrina and reversing the charges. 'It's me, it's me!' I'd shout when she tried to refuse the call. 'Where are you now?' she'd say.

'I don't know for sure, but I think I'm in Italy!'

My mum's first and favourite snap of me, aged 4–6 months.

Me aged eleven, starting Manor High School in Crosby, Liverpool.

Top: Mum and Dad on a night out courting in the swinging sixties.

Above: Dad, like myself, liked to get his top off in the sun.

Right: Dad, me and my sister Bev in Seaforth Park in the summer of 1974.

Top: Me and Bev having fun on holiday at Butlins in the seventies. I'm about two or three here.

Middle: Bev giving me a sisterly hug for an early Christmas photo.

Bottom: This is the last picture me and Bev had taken with our dad before the accident in 1984.

Top: Me and cousin Stephen, aged twelve, eating ice cream on a family holiday. Fifteen odd years later he was the only member of my family I was able to celebrate with on the night I won *Big Brother*.

Middle: Me and Lee McCarthey (Joanne Harris's uncle) have been friends for over thirty years, since infant school. Here we are aged sixteen, ready to board a cruise liner in Cyprus on holiday with his mum and dad, Viv and Sam.

Bottom: Me and my first love Shelley, dressed up for a Christmas night out in the early nineties. We're still the best of friends today.

Right: Me aged nineteen as a trainee, mixing cement. What was I thinking with that haircut?

Below: It's a good job this was about twenty years ago, as Health and Safety would lock me away now! Hard hats and high-vis vests are a must these days.

Top: I started boxing and bodybuilding in 1985 after losing my dad.

Middle: The good old days. Me at fifteen with John Watson Junior at the butcher's shop on Seaforth Road.

Bottom: I've always been a keen falconer and animal lover. Here's me aged twenty-three with one of my kestrels.

Top: The Shakespeare Inn, Newport, where I lived with my mum and stepdad Rob; I also started running my building company from there. This snap looks like I'm halfway through renovating the pub back in 1995.

Middle: Rob, Bev, me and Mum enjoying a drink at the Shakespeare Inn in about 1992. Bev never lived there but used to visit on a regular basis.

Bottom: Me taking my nieces, Lauren and Kelly, out for a boat ride in the Lake District in 2002.

Top: The Phillips family in 2009. Left to right: my niece Kelly, mum Brenda, sister Beverley, me, niece Lauren and stepdad Robbie.

Middle: I was Lee's best man at his wedding back in 2002 and am also godfather to his children Macy Erin and Samuel.

Bottom: Enjoying a holiday in Ibiza in 2005 with my good pals Pete Casey, Tommy Doyle and Frankie Dettori. If only Frankie could dance as well as he rides horses!

'You don't know where you are? Why Italy? Aren't you coming to Cyprus any more?'

'Of course I'm coming. I'll be there next week!'

But the next week, we'd find ourselves in Spain, Germany, Poland or who knows where!

Along the way we met lots of hitchhikers and they all had stories to tell. 'You've got to go to such-and-such place,' they'd say. 'You've got to see this or that!' Everywhere sounded good and we were easily influenced, so we often headed off to check out their recommendations.

On our way through Germany, someone told us about Baden-Baden, a town located on the western foothills of the Black Forest. We had train maps by now, so we knew how to get there along the German network. Or so we thought. We did our usual trick of buying a ticket to go just one stop and boarded an overnight express. We weren't exactly sure where we'd end up, but that was all part of the fun.

A couple of hours into the journey, the ticket inspector arrived in our carriage. 'Tickets please!' he announced. When he realized that we didn't have valid tickets, he started shouting at us, quite aggressively, clearly wanting more money.

We did have some money, but it wasn't the right currency and he wouldn't accept it. Next, he demanded to see our passports. All the while he was yelling. We couldn't understand him, but we got the gist: he wasn't happy. He jabbed his finger at various passport stamps and continued to thunder at us. By now he was being really intimidating. He started to walk off with our passports.

Hang on, I thought. This train is about a mile long and there are hundreds of people on it. We may never see our passports again!

I grabbed his arm and pulled him back. 'Mate, you're not going anywhere with those,' I said. At that, he bawled even louder. I tried to grab the passports out of his hand, but he wouldn't let them go. We were coming close to having a scrap over it. Steve darted round him and blocked his exit.

The passengers around us began to get agitated. A couple of English lads stepped up. They had been sitting across the way from us for about two hours. 'Are you OK there?' they asked.

'No, I'm not!' I fumed. 'I want my passport back.'

'What's the problem?' they said. It turned out that the guard only wanted ten pounds or so; there'd been a misunderstanding with the currency. 'Don't worry, we'll help you out,' the lads said. They paid the guard, he gave us back our passports and we paid them in English money. The guard stomped off, still shouting abuse at us, and the atmosphere in the carriage calmed down.

We went to sit with the English lads, who were a bit older than us. There were four of them in all and they came from London. They had loads of beer, which they generously shared, and we played cards through the night. It was great. What could be better than to get drunk, have a laugh, fall asleep and wake up in a new place?

It was lovely and sunny the next morning. Fantastic, we thought, despite our headaches, Baden-Baden, here we come! We made for the nearest WC, where we washed and brushed our teeth, changed into shorts and gelled our hair. As we walked through the station, it became clear that we were at a border crossing. The train wasn't going any further; we'd have to go through customs first. Along with the lads from London, we lined up in the passport-control queue.

Everything seemed absolutely fine until the official opened my passport and frowned.

'Who are you with?' he asked me. I gestured to Steve and the English lads. 'Stand here!' he said, once I'd gone through the gate. One by one he lined us up and made us wait while he talked on his radio. We had no idea what he was saying.

Another official arrived, and then another one. They walked up and down the line, scrutinizing us and inspecting our passports. This isn't good, we thought. Everyone else was being allowed to go through, no problem. We started to feel nervous.

Another official began firing questions at us. 'Where are you going? Who are you with? Why are you here?'

'We're tourists. We're travelling and seeing the sights,' we said, over and over again. 'We must have got on the wrong train, though. This isn't where we wanted to go.'

Although we didn't know it, we had gone over a border into what was then Czechoslovakia, without having the correct visa. For this, we were arrested, which was terrifying, because no one told us why we were being arrested. The lads from London were in the same position as we were. They'd been drunk when they boarded the train and also thought it was heading in the general direction of Baden-Baden. They didn't have visas either.

Being surrounded by a handful of gruff, rough, armed police in a strange country was intimidating enough. Not being able to understand what they were saying made it worse. Not knowing where the hell they were taking us was worst of all. Our luggage went one way and we were taken another, to a holding area that looked very much like a police cell. Oh my God, I thought. This isn't good. This is a big problem.

We tried to decipher the signs on the walls and work out which country we'd landed up in. But it was hopeless; we hadn't a clue. I was really worried. I was sure I'd heard a story about someone who had been arrested at a border and locked up for fifty years, never to be seen again. We shared our fears and got more and more wound up as the hours passed. It wasn't pretty.

After about four hours, a small fella arrived. With his bald head and glasses, he reminded me of Penfold from the *Dangermouse* cartoon. At last, someone who spoke English! He politely explained that we were in Czechoslovakia illegally because we didn't have the correct visa in our passports. Then he got out a map and asked us to explain where we had meant to end up. We pointed to Baden-Baden.

'Can we continue travelling through Czechoslovakia?' I asked.

A shadow passed over his face. 'Definitely not,' he said. 'That would be impossible.'

Instead, we were issued with a deportation order and fined the equivalent of twenty-five pounds, which was a big blow to Steve and me, a real downer! It was a lot of money to us at the time.

A big police escort took us back to the train station and saw us on to a train back to Germany. Someone stayed with us for a couple of stops until we got past the border point, and then they left us to it.

The whole experience was all a bit of a wake-up call. We weren't invincible after all, and now we were practically broke. Steve and I debated what to do. Should we phone home and get money sent over, then try moving on? Or should we give up? We carried on travelling for about another month, much more cautiously. Things had been getting slightly out of control and needed to be reined in.

I rang Katrina. 'You're not coming now, are you?' she said. 'Sometimes I wonder if you're still in England.'

'Katrina, I still want to come, but you won't believe what happened to us in Czechoslovakia,' I began.

'Where are you now?' she said wearily after I'd told her the sorry story.

'I'm on my way,' I said, ever hopeful. 'We'll be travelling through Italy to Turkey . . . '

The next time I phoned her, she refused to accept the charges.

Then on 2 August, Saddam Hussein invaded Kuwait. Steve and I didn't pay much attention at first. We were only interested in what we were going to eat, where we were staying that night and the girls we were going to pull.

But when we phoned home, our families sounded worried. Like everyone else in the UK, Mum had been watching the news avidly. Things weren't looking good.

'Come home, love,' she said. 'Get a flight and get yourself back here as soon as you can. All hell is breaking loose in Kuwait. Things aren't looking good in that whole region. It's probably not safe to carry on travelling now.'

Loads of other tourists had heard the same and it took ages to get a flight home, but in the end we managed it. And so it was that, about a week later, we trooped into Mum's pub looking like a pair of tramps.

'What's happened to the both of you?' she exclaimed, looking totally appalled. I had been big and muscular before we left; but now, after three months of interrupted sleep and living on scraps, I was properly skinny and dishevelled.

I might not have made it to see Katrina, but I'd had some brilliant adventures. I didn't regret a thing.

6

A Job for Life

Steve went back to Liverpool, but I didn't want to go with him. With no job and no money, who knows what might have happened? Would I have turned to crime like some of my friends had? I like to think that I was strong-minded enough not to. I like to think that I had enough respect for myself and my family. But I would have been surrounded by crime. Who's to say I wouldn't have been lured in?

I had heard quite a few stories about people being in the wrong place at the wrong time with the wrong people. That alone could be enough to pull you into the criminal world, if you were unlucky. I was scared of getting entangled like that; I wanted to avoid it at all costs.

I had been thinking things over while Steve and I were travelling. Newport in Shropshire seemed nice. There wasn't much crime or unemployment in the area, so maybe I could make a fresh start there instead of going back to Liverpool full time. I told my mum I'd like to stay with her during the week and go back to Liverpool at weekends.

To begin with, I helped Mum and Robbie out in the pub; I also ended up getting a weekend job, in a little place called Ozzy's just down the road. It was a nice funky wine bar, the place to be in Newport, and I had a lot of fun there. Ozzy Osborne had once owned it and it was packed with Ozzy and Sharon memorabilia.

I needed a permanent job during the week, so I started asking around. Colin Hanley, a local in our pub, said he might be able to fix me up with something, but I didn't hold my breath. Colin liked a drink and he was in the pub most nights of the week so I didn't know how reliable he'd be. His nickname was Pig and he was teased that he looked and grunted like a pig.

However, he turned out to be as good as his word. Colin was a foreman at Wrekin Construction, a company that worked for Wrekin Council, and he got me a start there as a labourer. Being a bricklayer's mate was heavy physical work – mixing sand and cement, carrying bricks and stacking them all day long – but I loved it. It was a real hard workout. What's more, my first week's wage packet contained £153, which compared very favourably with the £120 I'd been getting at the butcher's at the end. It was a good salary to walk into and I was pleased.

Unfortunately, I didn't get on with a few of the local guys on site. The older ones were the worst. For some reason, they hated and despised Scousers and clung to the stereotypical image of us all being robbers and crooks. This annoyed me, because I'd never stolen a thing in my life. In fact, I'd been offered my job at the butcher's because I was so honest! Over the years I had served thousands of people in the shop, some of whom could barely see. Often I had to help them with their money, but never once was I even slightly tempted to steal from any of them. So the jokes and innuendoes really wound me up. There was one fella in his mid-forties who made constant jibes. He rubbed me up the wrong way, morning, noon and night, always putting Scousers down and making me look stupid. It was bullying, plain and simple. He was a big, old builder, arrogant as you like, who thought he knew it all. Everybody had heard of him around Newport, and he was known to be trouble throughout the area.

He was the kind of bloke who made everyone else do all the work while he spent his time ordering us around. He gave me jobs that a machine could do in a fraction of the time. More than once he made me dig a trench while the digger operator was having a break. Working for him felt like hard labour and it got me down.

Eventually, I decided I'd had enough. I wouldn't take it any more. I was young and still into my boxing training and martial arts, so I could stand up for myself. I didn't have to roll over and let people look down on and humiliate me.

One night after work, I went round to his house, banged on his door and told him to come outside. I know it was wrong. It's not something I would advise others to do. But for me it was the right thing at the time. He had wound me up that much.

'You're making my life a misery!' I told him when he opened his front door. 'You won't give me any help when I need it; you criticize Liverpool and my work. I know exactly what you're implying when you say all that stuff. So come outside and say what you really think to my face!' I didn't really want conflict, but I had been pushed so far that I felt I needed to protect myself from further bullying.

'I didn't mean anything by it,' he protested as he tried to pull the door shut. To be honest, I was half hoping he was going to push me around or hit me, so I could flatten him. But he wouldn't fight me and he kept apologizing, so thankfully nothing came of it. And he gave me much more respect after that.

I became less headstrong as time went on. I carried on doing Muay Thai boxing; it's a very disciplined martial art that teaches you restraint. I still like fighting, but only in the ring, when you're both wearing protective gear. Then it's a sporting challenge, a great way of releasing the tension of life's stresses. Back then, too, the more training, sparring and long-distance running I did, the calmer I felt.

However, I used to take it personally when there was trouble in our pub. After all, it was my mum's house as well as being a pub. If a fight broke out, the bar staff, Mum or Rob would always call me down to break it up and chase the aggressors out of the bar. Much of the time it wasn't serious and the most I'd have to do was to restrain and hold, which is the basis of a lot of martial arts training. Sometimes it would just be a case of good buddies having an alcohol-fuelled argument and, in those cases, all I needed to do was get them outside. If the fight carried on in the car park, we called the police.

At Wrekin Construction, I started labouring with a guy named Phil, whose nickname was Jumbo. Jumbo also drank in our pub and, like Pig, he liked a drink. But he was a great bricklayer when you could keep him off the booze.

I found Jumbo hard to work with initially, because he seemed short of patience with beginners. A brickie needs his cement to be mixed properly and precisely. It has to have a certain consistency to be workable and Jumbo used to get annoyed if I didn't get it right. However, it's very hard to tell the difference between a good and bad cement mixture when you're an inexperienced trainee.

It was Jumbo who told me that I was too good to be a labourer. I needed to learn a trade, he said. It was the only way to get anywhere.

'You could teach me bricklaying!' I suggested eagerly, forgetting how impatient he was. He would have been a terrible teacher.

'No, you should go to college,' he said.

'What, me? Go to college?' I said incredulously. At first I dismissed the idea out of hand. How could I go to college when I had hated school so much? I loathed reading and writing (in fact I still wasn't that good at either); I couldn't stand the whole teacher–pupil set-up. On the other hand, I didn't want to be a labourer all my life, did I? And on the upside, I had always been good at maths: I'd helped my mum out when she worked at the Apple Barrel fruit shop and I had learned to be an efficient bookkeeper at the butcher's shop. But I wasn't the type to go to college, was I? No one in my family had done so. We just weren't that way inclined.

I kept mulling it over, changing my mind every day. Should I go for it or would I hate it? Would I get there, only to be made to look stupid? It took me two months to decide that Jumbo was right and college was the answer. Then, once I'd made my mind up, it didn't take long to sort it out. I applied to Wrekin Construction for day release, which they granted, and then I applied to the local education authority for funding.

'I'm going to college!' I announced to Mum. 'I've been accepted on a bricklayer's course at Telford College of Arts and Technology in Wellington.'

'That's great, love,' Mum said, her eyes wide with surprise. 'But are you sure that's really what you want to do?'

No, I wasn't sure. I wasn't sure at all. As the start of term approached, I began to get nervous. I still felt very resistant to the idea of 'education'. I was terrified at the thought of going into a classroom again. The morning of my first day was a nightmare. What am I doing? I thought, wondering whether to sack it off. Was this my only option? Wasn't there something else I could do as a career?

I forced myself to go in. When I arrived, I was directed to some sheds at the back of the grounds. They were a bit like bunkers and I found this reassuring somehow; I felt more comfortable in an old prefab shed than a conventional classroom. I was also pleasantly surprised to find that there were only around twelve of us on the course, a small group of people of different ages and from different walks of life. All in all, the class environment was a lot less intimidating than I had envisaged. I breathed a sigh of relief. I felt even more at home when the bricklaying tools were handed out. Calming down, I remembered that I was there because I actually wanted to learn something – and I wanted to learn it fast.

I ended up enjoying my first day on the course. I was no longer the dunce in the slow class, struggling to write a couple of sentences. Quite the opposite, in fact: I was so eager to learn that I raced ahead at every stage of the class. I felt really happy when I went home that night. This is definitely for me, I thought, confident that I had made the right move. I was learning a proper trade at last.

It was the most important turning point in my life. I had got over my fear of education! After a month, I was so into my course that I signed up for a couple of night-school classes in advanced brickwork. They were harder than the day course, where I was still learning the basics – straight lines, corners and getting everything plumb. The evening course was all about how to make much more complex structures, like brickwork circles, bull's eyes and arches.

I probably jumped into it too soon. It would maybe have been more sensible to sign up to night school about six months into my course. Still, I wasn't fazed. I had a few difficulties at first, but I quickly caught up.

When my supervisor at Wrekin Construction realized how quickly I was coming along, he started letting me do some brickwork underground, which was brilliant practice. Soon I was bricking the manholes on the slip road at Junction 9 of the M6 motorway, working with a blue class A engineering brick, which is one of the strongest, densest bricks around.

It was great experience and it really built up my confidence. It was also the perfect on-the-job learning environment because, since the work was underground, the results didn't have to look perfect. Obviously Wrekin Construction had a clerk of works who came and inspected what I'd done, though. The brickwork still had to be level and the manholes fit for purpose. In fact, the clerk said I was making a good job of it.

I started having a lot more fun at work. When the other guys on site saw that I was willing to learn and get stuck in the trenches, they treated me with more respect. Of course, I could never lay bricks as quickly or as well as they did, but I certainly had a bloody good go at it.

As I often say to the students I meet on vocational building courses, life is not all that enjoyable being a labourer or training to be a tradesman. With a trade, you get more respect, more money and more enjoyment out of your work – and once you've built one thing, you just want to build more. But when you're mixing cement and stacking bricks for somebody else to do the building, there's far less satisfaction in it for you.

On our site, the bricklayers would get there in the morning and have themselves a cup of tea and a bacon sandwich. Meanwhile, the labourers had to run around like maniacs, mixing the cement up. 'Get it over here quickly!' the bricklayers would yell in between gulps of hot tea. 'Make sure you get that mortar mix right!' Sadly the young people on site will always get stick from older builders. That's the way the industry works, unfortunately.

So, life improved immeasurably once I had started my brickwork course. And there was another reason why going to TCAT proved to be crucial: I was getting to know a fella who would turn out to be almost as influential on my life as the two Johns had been back at the butcher's.

As it happened, everyone else on the course, bar one, was

from the Telford area. Now, Telford can be quite a cliquey place and, as a Scouser, I was struggling slightly to be accepted by my classmates. The same old prejudices prevailed: they basically thought that people from Liverpool were untrustworthy.

Tony Chan was different, though. Born in Hong Kong, Tony came to England in his teens. He was the only other non-local on the course and also a bit of an outsider. Tony enrolled the same day I did and we instantly clicked. Although he was more than ten years older than me and from a totally different back-ground, it turned out we had quite a lot in common. Like me, he was really into his martial arts. He was only about my size but he had a great physique – like Bruce Lee.

Tony taught me many things and I'm tremendously grateful to him. His energy and unquenchable thirst for work, edu-cation and knowledge were a huge inspiration for me. More than anything else, he taught me the value of working hard. In fact, I hold him responsible for making me addicted to work!

Also a fantastic chef, renowned throughout the Telford and Birmingham areas, Tony owned a small takeaway where he, his wife and relatives all worked. As the chef, he worked from 4.30 p.m. to midnight, which left his days free. So his daytime project was his house, which he was slowly doing up by him-self. When I met him he had already taught himself basic building skills. Now he was building a big extension and refurbishing his whole house, he wanted to get more experience in the brickwork, so that he didn't have to employ anyone to do it.

Our bricklaying course lasted a year and at the end of it I continued attending night classes. Unfortunately, Tony couldn't join me there, because he was cooking every evening, but he asked me if I'd help him with some work on his house. It was a good way for me to earn extra money and I was happy to oblige. We soon found that we worked really well together.

We got into a routine: I'd go round to his house at about 8 a.m. on a Saturday or Sunday, let myself in, make some break- fast and start preparing the materials for whatever we were going to do that day. Tony didn't get out of bed until about 10.30 a.m., because he got home very late from the takeaway.

Since it was Tony's house and we weren't answering to clients, we had room to be experimental. We tried out all sorts of things, from plastering and woodwork to skirting boards and tiling. Tony had an idea of how to do some things, but we also studied books and magazines for guidance. Gradually we began to teach ourselves a range of building skills. It was a massive learning curve, because you can learn a huge amount from books if you study them properly.

Plastering was one of the hardest things to master, because it's not just about how you apply the materials on the wall. In fact, it's really all down to timing and so many things can make a difference, from the temperature of the room to a light draught under a door. It's a hard thing to learn from a leaflet or a book, because what you actually need is the experience to judge how quickly the plaster will dry in your particular circumstances. It frustrated us half to death.

When we got stressed or were struggling to make something work, Tony would go and lie down in the back garden and meditate, somehow finding a way to be completely still and blank everything out of his mind. Fifteen minutes later, he would come back and say, 'I feel completely refreshed now, like I've had a full night's sleep.'

It intrigued me, because he really did seem renewed and re-energized. I must learn to do that, I thought! It was obviously the secret behind his ability to work seven days and nights a week, without ever taking a break. I used to tell him, 'Take some time off! Go on holiday!' Eventually he took my advice and in the mid-1990s I accompanied his family to China, which was a truly eye-opening experience.

I worked hard, but I'd go and enjoy myself as well. I always saved up for two or three good holidays a year and whenever I wasn't working I went to Liverpool for the weekend. By now I was going out with Shelley Wilson, a tall, elegant, beautiful-looking girl.

Shelley was my first serious girlfriend and about five inches taller than I was. A dance-college student who supplemented her grant by doing promotional work, she was a couple of years younger than me, but very independent. I would either stay with her or at the house Mum had left for Bev and me. We were great friends and stayed together for five years. I'm still very close to Shelley and her family. In fact, Shelley shared some of the very first weeks with me when I came out of the *Big Brother* house.

Meanwhile, Tony and I became really good pals. The more we learned, the more confident we felt in our work. We thought we could take on the world: build anything, do anything. By now Tony's contacts in the Chinese community were offering him all kinds of building work. Plus, I had a whole list of building and maintenance work to do on the

Shakespeare Inn. It was four hundred-odd years old, after all.

I started thinking about leaving Wrekin. I was getting good money, but I would only ever get a set wage working for a construction company. If I want more, I thought, I've got to branch out. Then Tony offered me the chance to work with him, which seemed like a great opportunity. I gave in my notice at Wrekin.

Tony lined up several jobs for us to do when I left Wrekin, through people he knew in the Chinese community. I couldn't wait to get started on them. The idea of working for ourselves was incredibly exciting. But a couple of weekends before I was due to leave my job, I had a motorbike accident.

I hurt my back quite badly and couldn't move around as much as usual, so I did the next best thing to working: I studied. I borrowed some books from Tony and read up on loads of aspects of building.

The accident slowed me down for around eight weeks, but finally I was able to join Tony at work. I helped him refurbish many restaurants and takeaways in both Telford and Birmingham, which was brilliant experience for me. Often I found myself working alongside fifteen or twenty Chinese fellas, all speaking Chinese to one another. It was quite strange at times but everyone was very polite to me and if I was standing right next to them, they always made an effort to speak English. In fact some of them said that I'd really helped them improve their English, because they wouldn't have bothered speaking it if I hadn't been around. So we were all learning!

In 1992, at the age of twenty-one, I set myself up as a sole trader. We were just getting over quite a harsh recession then, so it wasn't a great time to give up a waged job and start out alone. Still, I didn't know any different. Times had been hard as long as I could remember. All I knew for sure was that I had a lot of drive and determination. I was single-minded about the future: I would stick at it and succeed.

Once again, though, I encountered discrimination against my Liverpool roots. It was the big battle of my first three years of running a building company, because I always had to sell myself before I sold my building services.

I started off small, advertising in the Yellow Pages and local magazines. But there would be times when I'd turn up at a family house to measure up for a quote – for anything from tiling a floor to replacing a kitchen – and the prospective clients would say, 'Ah, you're not a local lad, are you? Are you from Liverpool?'

'That's right,' I'd reply. The expression on their faces would change. They'd look at each other and frown. Often I never heard from them again.

It just didn't seem fair, because in the eight years I ran my building company, I never ripped anyone off or overcharged them. I always broke down my quotes so that they were completely transparent and I always honoured them. I was even prepared to make a loss if I'd underestimated on time or materials. I never cut corners as a result, nor let it affect my workmanship.

In the end, this meant that I established a reputation as a good and honest builder, which led to many word-of-mouth recommendations. One job led to another. The size and scale of my work kept growing. I'd proved that people wanted a builder who would do a good job, in good time, whether he was a Scouser or not.

Sadly, it's still common to encounter the stereotypical view of Scousers as untrustworthy. Comedians in particular seem to love perpetuating it. I was at an awards ceremony in Liverpool recently and a brilliant stand-up comic entertained us with a really good set, but not before he had cracked five or six jokes about Scousers nicking your car. A few weeks before that, I was on a cruise where four out of the five comedians on the ship echoed his sentiments. It was so boring, so disappointing! It's not as if we haven't all heard those jokes a million times before. There really isn't a new way to tell them.

Still, as I say to the building students I meet today, don't be put off, whether you're starting out in a recession, or people prejudge you, or you're just finding it hard to keep going. Of course, it is always going to be difficult when you start out, but if you do the job properly, stick to the right price, don't rip people off and honour your quotes, you'll build yourself a good reputation along with a great client base by word of mouth. You'll win some and you'll lose some, but you'll get there in the end. If I managed to do it, with barely any education, then other people can definitely manage it too. You just have to believe in yourself and work hard.

Through Tony Chan I was lucky enough to meet Stan Yam, which led to another big break for me. Stan is a very clever plumber and electrician, and he became another great friend of mine. He often did electrics and plumbing on Tony's jobs and we clicked from the moment we met.

In 1993, Stan employed me to build a two-storey extension

on the side of a house, with two bedrooms and a bathroom at the top, a kitchen at the back and a double garage at the front. It was a huge leap for me, as the jobs I'd been getting until then had been a lot, lot smaller: things like building walls, refitting kitchens and the odd single-storey extension.

I learned a huge amount working on an extension that size with Stan – and it's still standing perfectly today. After the architect had drawn up his plans, I did all the quantity surveying – measuring up all the materials we needed – and drew up a building schedule of what to do and who would be doing what. By then I had two other builders working for me: another bricklayer, Ben Martin, and an all-rounder, Simon Lane, who went on to work with me for seven years. I was even employing Jumbo, the bricklayer from Wrekin who had advised me to go to college. We completed the job on time and on budget.

I vaguely remember that it cost about £40,000 to build; I vividly remember that it instantly added £80,000 of value to the house. It was an unforgettable lesson for me and I stored up everything I learned for my future ventures. Later on down the line, when I began to buy and do up properties of my own, my rule of thumb was always this: whatever you spend doing up a property, make sure that it will add double the cost of the refurb to the value of your purchase.

Once I'd built Stan's extension, I felt confident enough to build anything. I was ready to expand my business. I was ready to take on the world.

7

Bombshells

Life was looking pretty sorted by the time I was twenty-three. Business was going well and the company was thriving. Some good contracts were coming my way and I had taken on seven or eight employees.

After years of hard work and careful saving, my finances were beginning to look quite healthy. My outgoings were still reasonably low. I had no dependants, no mortgage and no children, and I was still living at the Shakespeare Inn with my mum and Robbie, paying basic keep, so I had quite a bit of spare cash. I felt I could afford to splash out, so I bought my very first brand-new car, a Vauxhall Tigra. I was the first person in Newport to get one the week they came out.

One day my mum mentioned that she and Robbie were planning to retire in a few years' time. That got me thinking about the future. By my calculations their retirement would coincide with the maturation of the ten-year savings plans I had taken out with John at Liberty Life. Perhaps I could buy the pub with the money I'd made? It was a beautiful pub and I loved living there. I often ran it while they were on holiday.

I began tallying up dates and figures. I had two policies with Liberty Life, which John had predicted would both yield a couple of hundred thousand pounds when they came good. As the pub was worth around £350,000 in the mid-1990s, that meant I would easily be able to buy it without a mortgage. It was a really exciting thought. I talked it over with Mum and Robbie and they seemed thrilled at the thought of handing on the business to me.

Hang on a minute, I thought. I can afford to put a little more money away each month in my savings plan at Liberty Life, can't I? With all that cash floating around, it seemed a good moment to do something sensible with it.

By now John had left Liberty Life. I'd lost touch with him in the past couple of years, but I'd heard that things had gone a bit upside down for him. He'd had his house and car re-possessed, apparently, and there had been some problems with Liberty Life. But I only heard half-stories, little snippets and rumours. I had no real idea what had actually gone on.

I phoned up Liberty Life and explained that I would like to send more business their way, but couldn't do it through John because he was no longer with them.

'Do you want to increase your policies?' I was asked.

'That's the idea, yes,' I said.

'We'll send a representative round to see you, then!'

A few days later, a man from Liberty Life arrived at the pub and we sat down for a chat.

'My dream is to buy this pub when my policies mature,' I told him, explaining that I felt I could afford to put a little more into the pot now. I told him what I was earning, how much I planned to save and what I thought that would mean in terms of dividends when the policies matured. 'Is that about right?' I asked.

To my dismay, the blood was draining from his face before my eyes. He glanced down at the documents in front of him and up at me again, his expression pained.

There was a long silence. 'I don't quite know how to put this, Mr Phillips, because I've never been in this position before . . .' he said in a faltering tone.

'Why, what's the problem?' I asked, my heart sinking.

'Well,' he went on, 'the only way I can describe it is to say that you haven't bought into the kind of scheme that you think you've bought into.'

I didn't follow. 'Really? Why's that?'

'Basically, you've been sold two insurance policies. Not one penny of your monthly payments has been going towards any form of savings plan.'

'Insurance policies?' My mind went blank. I still didn't understand.

'Yes,' he said. 'If you died, your mortgage would be taken care of, along with your debts. There would be a lump sum payment made to your dependants, as well. But you get nothing as long as you're alive.'

At last I began to grasp what he was saying. I was insured up to the hilt. Things would be taken care of if I died. Great. With no mortgage, no debts and no children, I clearly did not need this level of life insurance.

'There must be some mistake. It just can't be true,' I said, shaking my head. 'I was sold these policies by a really good friend. There's no way he would have ripped me off.'

I thought back to my conversations with John, trying to remember exactly what he had said about the financial rewards I could expect from the policies. I had trusted him so much that it didn't even occur to me to read through the paperwork and check the small print. Of course, I probably wouldn't have understood it, anyway, bearing in mind that I wasn't particularly literate and had only been a teenager when I took out the policies. But that's not the point. John had been like a brother to me. His father had been a surrogate dad. I couldn't believe that he'd mislead me deliberately. My mind reeled. Images of his big house and posh car kept flashing through my head. I felt completely stunned.

'Why would someone do this?' I asked the man from Liberty Life.

He hesitated again. 'I hate to say it, but I can't rule out a financial motive. I don't know the figures but your friend might have earned a big fat commission from selling you these policies, whereas an endowment scheme might have had a much smaller commission.'

I drew in a sharp breath. Greed? I couldn't believe that John could have been motivated by greed. But . . . I couldn't get the image of his house and flash Jag out of my head. 'This is un-believable,' I said, putting my head in my hands. Could John have betrayed me? The pain was overwhelming. It felt like something tearing at my insides.

Bewilderment turned to disappointment and then anger as the seriousness of the situation began to sink in.

'What can I do?' I asked the Liberty Life man. 'Is there any way of getting compensation?'

He was full of sympathy. 'I can't be seen to help because I work for the company,' he said. 'However, something has gone wrong and I want to help.'

He went on to sketch out my options. In short, I did have a right of redress: I could take the case to the financial services ombudsman and there was a chance I might be awarded compensation.

I felt totally shattered after he left, in pieces, as if a giant steel fist had smashed me into the ground. I felt so let down by John. All my 'savings' had vanished into thin air. I wouldn't be able to afford to take on the business that Mum and Robbie had worked so hard to build up over the years. How would I ever be able to trust anyone again? I was absolutely gutted.

I knew I would have to confront John about what had happened. There was no getting round it. I needed answers. I was busy on site all that week in Shropshire, but I called and told him I was going to be coming to see him while I was in Liverpool at the weekend.

He was no longer living in the nice big house in Litherland. He, his wife and their three children were crammed into a little council flat. I was shocked when he opened the front door. He had aged and put on weight, a hell of a lot of it, and it didn't suit him at all.

'Why did you do it?' I asked him as soon as we were inside.

He looked at me with sad eyes. 'To be completely honest, Craig, I was misled myself,' he said.

Liberty Life hadn't trained him correctly, he explained. He

hadn't known the true nature of the packages he was selling. Now he was suing them, or they were suing him and he was counter-suing them. Either way, it sounded messy.

I listened to what he was saying. With all those years of friendship behind us, I really wanted to believe him. But I only half trusted his words. I'd always thought John was smart. He could read and write extremely well; I thought he was excellent at deciphering small print. So how could he have been under the impression that the insurance policies he sold me were actually a savings plan? He was not a stupid man. How could he have got something so fundamentally wrong? And yet, of the two of us, he was the one really suffering now – at least in financial terms. So who was the stupid one? It was all very confusing.

'I'm so sorry, Craig,' he kept saying. He was close to tears at one point. I actually started to feel sorry for him.

I'll probably never get to the bottom of what actually happened. Whether John was misled or brainwashed, whether he was naïve or greedy, or a bit of everything, I'll never really know. All I do know is that it backfired on him and he was left with nothing. His life was totally ruined.

Of the five hours I spent at his house, we only argued for the first hour. After that, we talked about good times and it turned into a nice reunion. I'm quite a forgiving person, generally. Of course, I won't ever give anyone the chance to do something like that to me again, but I don't hold grudges. Life's too short. I had been naïve but we all make mistakes and there's no point in moping around and moaning about things. If it's done it's done. Just forget it and move on. Much worse things happen, like my dad's accident.

I left John's house feeling sorrier for him than I did for myself. A few days previously, I had wanted to punch him, but instead I gave him a hug. Later, when I saw his mum and John senior, I explained what had happened and they were desperately sorry for me. It was all very sad for everybody.

At least my business was going in the right direction. I was my own boss and I was working hard. I didn't see John again for a long time. Our friendship was badly dented by what had happened. But when I heard on the grapevine that he had got himself back on track and fit again, working as a full-time fireman, I was extremely pleased for him. After all, he had been through a lot. Plus, I will always be grateful to him and his dad for their support when I was younger.

I took my case to the financial ombudsman service, which supported my claim for compensation. Eventually I was awarded £15,000, which wasn't even as much as I had paid into the policies, but it was definitely better than nothing.

In the years that followed, I worked hard and saved hard, until I had enough to buy my first house, a little place in Newport. It was a wreck when I bought it, with no electricity or running water. I lived outside it in my mum's caravan for months, slowly doing it up in my spare time.

Every morning at 7 a.m., I went to the supermarket for a cooked breakfast in the café there. Then I'd brush my teeth and have a shave before going to work on site. After work I'd go to the gym, where I'd shower after training. I was still really into my Muay Thai boxing.

My Muay Thai teacher, Nick Hewitson, was a world title-holder and the most placid guy in the world. He taught me an amazing visualization technique that has been very useful over the years. He used it to help me prepare mentally before I went in the ring during a boxing competition; I've since used it in many different situations.

First I would lie on the floor. Sitting very close to me, Nick would tell me to imagine that I was on a beach. 'All you can hear is the water lapping on the shore,' he'd say. 'Now you can feel your body getting warmer from the sun.' As his description unfolded, the sun would come closer and get bigger and warmer. Slowly it would start to melt my body, which was a wonderful sensation. In my imagination, all the definition in my muscles melted away and turned into sand.

Next Nick described a bright light travelling through my toes and up through my body, until it came out of my fingertips and through my hair. This left me with an all-over relaxing, tingling feeling. By the end of the session, he had reversed the process in my mind. The light would come down my body, returning it to material form, strengthening it into steel, tightening the definition in my muscles and making them stronger and bigger. Feeling calm and confident and strong, I'd stand up and think I could walk through a wall.

In early 1998, Keele University approached Nick and asked him to put together a team of people to keep the peace at a series of big dance nights at the Student Union. After a couple of bad experiences using heavy-handed bullies as security, they were looking for people who would restrain and control any troublemakers, before escorting them off the premises.

Nick was asked to pick people at our gym who would be unlikely to start a fight, but were tough enough to do the job. I was one of the team and I enjoyed the work; it was a change from building and had a sociable aspect to it, because I was working alongside guys I was also training with. Student life definitely looked like a lot of fun. There was the odd fight or two, but nothing that required much more than firm restraint.

From there I went on to work with the security team at a wine bar in the Shrewsbury area, where I saw a load more trouble than I had at Keele. I was then offered a job doing security at a nightclub around the corner from the wine bar. So when the wine bar closed at 11.30 p.m., I'd go on to the club. I collected a hundred pounds for each shift, but it wasn't long before I decided to get out. There were huge amounts of drugs in those days and people used to go ballistic because they were so high, at which point the big doormen would sometimes clout them, which I didn't like to see and didn't want to be a part of. So I stopped doing night work and concentrated purely on building work. The business continued to grow and, within a couple of years, I was employing about thirty people.

I felt lucky that it was up to me when and where I worked. It was nice to have the choice. Funnily enough, this was a subject that came up when I was being vetted during the *Big Brother* selection process, the same day I saw the psychiatrist at the head office of Bazal Productions in London.

One of the questions I was asked was: 'How successful are you generally when you go to job interviews?'

I was being bombarded with questions by a group of people

that included Peter Bazalgette, who owned the company, Channel 4's press officer, Matt Baker, the series producer, the executive producer and a couple of other producers.

'I've never been to a job interview in my life. I've never had to!' I said. 'If you read my application form, you'll see that I was a butcher, a brickie and then I ran my own company. So I've never even written a CV. This is probably the nearest I've been to a job interview, in fact.'

I don't think they were expecting to hear this. They all looked a bit alarmed. Oh God, I thought, as I looked at their perplexed expressions, I've probably said the wrong thing here! But all I could do was tell them the truth.

They moved quickly on. 'Have you ever considered working on television? Would you like to?'

'No,' I replied. 'I've never even once thought that I would want to work on television.'

'OK, well, have you ever thought you might want to be famous in any way?'

'Nope,' I said. 'I've got no ambitions in that area, either. I'm going on this show solely for one reason: to win the money. That's it, really – although I'm sure it'll be a great experience and I'll get on with everybody else in the house and have fun with them.'

They asked how it would affect my business if I spent time away from my company. I explained that it was quite usual for me to go on holiday for a fortnight, even three weeks. There were people I could put in charge in my absence. But I did need time to plan.

At this point, it was about six weeks before the show was

due to start. Six weeks previously, I had been told that I was down to the final fifty, so I could only assume that I was getting close to being among the final ten. Just in case, I had to make it clear that I would need time to organize cover while I was away.

'If you want me in the show, I need to know as quickly as possible,' I said. 'You can't just tell me the night before. I've got to plan for my thirty staff. For instance, I'll need to appoint someone to give them their wages and order materials.' At this point I was halfway through three very large jobs.

Everyone nodded, but nothing was confirmed, so I went back to Newport none the wiser. The following week, one of the producers arranged a night out with my mates and me.

'I'd like you to get about ten of your good friends together and I'll take you all for a drink and a meal,' she said. Her plan was obviously to check out my friends, watch how I socialized with them and see if my personality changed or my behaviour deteriorated when I had a drink. I assume I passed. About fifteen or twenty of us went out. The programme makers told me to tell everyone invited as little as possible: just to say that they were making a show and they were interested in putting me in it.

Two weeks before the show was due to start, I still hadn't been told whether I was going to be a housemate. I rang Bazal Productions again. 'You've got to tell me what's happening!' I said.

'Craig, you're down to the last fifteen now. Please, please, just hang in there with us.'

Months before I had signed a confidentiality agreement

stating that I wouldn't discuss *Big Brother* with anyone. But that was a problem now, because how could I plan for being away from my company – potentially for nine weeks – without giving any of my staff a reason why? I signed, of course, but as the days passed, I felt compelled to confide in some of my main core of staff, the ones who would manage things for me while I was gone. I also told close members of the family, who would be looking after the financial arrangements.

Ten days before *Big Brother* was due to air, I rang Bazal Productions once again. 'Please don't leave me hanging on like this!' I said. 'I really need to know what's going on. This is my business. I can't just walk away from it at the last minute.'

The producer on the other end of the phone kept saying, 'I know, Craig, I know. As soon as we're sure, we'll tell you.'

Then, eight days before the transmission date, the same producer called up at 8 p.m. 'Craig, I've got some news for you,' she said very quietly.

My heart began to race. 'Am I in or am I out?'

'What do you think?'

'I don't know.'

'You're in the house,' she whispered. 'We want you to be a housemate.'

'Oh!' I said. My mind went blank.

'How do you feel?' she asked.

'I feel calm now, but without a doubt I'm going to be panicking in a minute!' I said. 'I've got to make lots of phone calls right now. I've got to get the ball rolling and sort out who's going to take over the business while I'm away.'

'OK, but remember, you're not supposed to be telling anybody.'

This wasn't fair. I had to be firm. 'I need to ring them as soon as I put this phone down so that they're prepared for what they've got to do. Don't worry; they're trustworthy. They're not going to go to discuss it with anyone but me.'

'OK,' she said. 'And, Craig, I'll be talking to you every second of the day and night from now on!'

'No problem,' I said.

I later learned that in the final week before I went into the *Big Brother* house, private investigators were sent out to watch all the housemates. I don't know why exactly, but I suppose it was just to see what we were up to, where we were going and what we were doing. One friend, Simon Edwards, who lived in a farming area, remembers seeing a posh car waiting at the end of his drive. There were two people inside, obviously doing some kind of surveillance. When he went down to ask them what they wanted, they drove off. It was such strange behaviour that he actually wondered whether to call the police or not, but in the end he decide to ignore it.

Unaware that I was being spied on, I spent every waking hour of the following week trying to get my business organized. I didn't feel at all excited: I just kept thinking, Oh God! Will I get everything done in time? My company still had three jobs going at the time, all at different sites. Among them was a two-storey extension in Newport, a huge job that was set to go on for a few months. The other two projects were due to wind up within a month.

I went to see all my clients to explain that I was going away for anything from two to nine weeks. 'I just can't predict when I'll be back,' I said. 'Your guess is as good as mine.'

I left my good friend Barry Tongue in charge of all three projects. Normally Barry would manage one of the sites and I would float between all three, but now he took on my role and I designated a manager for each individual site. With the management side of things sorted, I began to feel a bit more relaxed. I knew I could rely on Barry 100 per cent.

Then, two days before I went into the house, Telford and Wrekin Council dropped a bombshell. It came in the form of a letter serving a 28-day demolition order on a large outside garage I had built. If it went ahead, as threatened, I was set to lose at least £50,000 and the fruit of many long months of hard work.

By now, I had been at loggerheads with the council for eighteen months. A year before, I had built a huge external garage at my house in Newport. Initially, the plan was to run my building company out of the garage, which was twice the size of the house. I had vans, trailers and all sorts of materials and tools that I wanted to store in there.

When you build an external garage, the rules at that time stated that as long as it's more than 5 metres away from the house and below 4 metres in height, you can use up to 50 per cent of your garden for the site (as long as it's not interfering with any driveway). I did a lot of research into it, so I knew exactly what was what. I didn't need planning permission if I stuck to these rules, so I dug out the garage foundations with a big JCB one morning, in the process shifting about ten lorry-loads of earth.

I might not have needed planning permission, but I did need building-regulation control approval on the specification and materials. I knew that, technically, if you faxed over the information before 10 a.m., you were allowed to start work that day. Doing this really annoys the council, though, because they like to take two months to look at everything. However, I sent my fax at 9.50 a.m. It was all perfectly legal.

Part of the building-control department's remit is to come out and inspect the depth of the foundations and the subsoil below, to see if it can take the weight of whatever you're building. So the next day, a building inspector came out to check my foundations. I called a halt to work while he carried out his inspections. I had ten guys working there that day, so I was hoping he would get it over quickly.

'Jesus Christ, Craig! What are you building here? A block of flats?' he yelled.

'No, no,' I assured him, unfolding the architect's plans. 'These are my plans.'

He pursed his lips. 'Yes, we got your fax through this morning and we're not happy about it. How big is this building going to be?'

I talked him through the dimensions of the floor and ceiling, and where the doors and windows would go.

'You definitely need planning permission for this,' he said, shaking his head.

'Well, my architect says that I don't.'

We began to discuss the regulations. After about fifteen minutes, the discussion turned into a heated debate. He was threatening to cause a serious delay.

'I've got ten lads here working for me on a day rate,' I told him. 'You can't just come here and tell me to stop work, not unless you're one hundred per cent sure that I'm breaking the rules. You've got doubts about things, but I haven't got doubts, I've done my research and I'm sure I'm allowed to do what I'm doing.'

We went into the house, where he phoned the planning department and asked a couple of staff there to look into the regulations. The phone call took about an hour. While we stood around waiting for an answer, all I could think about was the ten lads sitting outside doing nothing. Every minute wasted was costing me money.

It turns out I was right on all counts, which can't have pleased him. He seemed so annoyed that when he went outside it looked like he was scouring the landscape for something else to find fault with. 'You'll have to make those foundations deeper because of those trees,' he said finally, pointing to a nearby cluster of conifers.

It was nonsense. The house had not moved in the hundred years it had been standing, despite being built on very shallow foundations. So why would the garage be any different?

'Look, I'll cut the trees down,' I said, 'and I'll plant some more over there.'

There wasn't much he could say to that, so he left.

I couldn't afford to build the garage in one go, so I built it in stages over six months. And during those six months, the council picked up on every little thing it could possibly think of and persuaded me to make amendments here and there, which I agreed to do simply because I thought it would keep them happy. I didn't want to argue over every tiny thing.

Unbeknown to me, the amendments were turning the

property into commercial premises, which meant I would have to apply for commercial use. Knowing that I could easily be turned down, that was the last thing I wanted. All along my plan had been to keep it as a personal garage to store my van and building equipment.

When I applied for a final-completion certificate, the official said, 'You've put a fire door here and you've made an adjustment there and now these are commercial premises!' I thought his tone sounded triumphant. He obviously thought he had me beaten.

I applied for commercial use and was rejected. I appealed against the ruling and was rejected again. Then articles started appearing in the newspaper asking why Craig Phillips was building such a big garage. One was by the mayor; another suggested that I was storing flammable fluids in the garage. As if! The implication was that there was a risk to the public, and in particular to a nearby school.

I wrote a letter to the newspaper announcing an open day at the garage; any interested party could come and check out the premises and voice their questions or anxieties. The debate was still raging in the week before *Big Brother*, and then the demolition order arrived. If I didn't take down the garage within twenty-eight days, the council would take it down and charge me for doing so. It was a complete disaster.

Barry Tongue and a few other senior staff were really supportive when they heard about the letter. 'Don't worry, Craig. We'll chain ourselves to the garage if they try to take it down,' they promised.

I didn't sleep a wink that night, and not just because I was worrying about my garage and going into the *Big Brother* house. There was one last thing that I had to do before I left for London – and I couldn't leave without doing it.

In my van there was a wooden bench that Chris, a good friend and customer, had given me a week or so prior to this. Chris's 21-year-old daughter Michelle had recently been killed in a tragic car accident; the bench was to go beside her grave in the cemetery where she was buried, so that Chris and his wife Pauline could sit there peacefully on their frequent visits.

I had a personal connection with Michelle because she had worked in my mum and Robbie's pub. She was a lovely girl; she and her parents were good friends and customers. I'd done quite a lot of work at their house, too. They were the nicest people you could ever meet.

A few weeks before this, I had laid down some slabs next to Michelle's grave and left them to set, in readiness for the bench. But I was so hectically busy with my three sites and all my preparations before going to London that I had struggled to find time to take it to the cemetery and screw it down. Now, on the eve of my trip to London, I found myself with this essential job still not done. There was nothing for it but to sneak into the cemetery in the middle of the night.

The cemetery was locked when I arrived. So, in the dead of night, I had to heave the bench up on to the railings, balance it and carefully climb over myself, taking care not to let it tip over. It was made of mahogany, so it wasn't exactly light! Somehow I managed to put it in place single-handedly and screw down the brackets so that it was firmly fixed, before I scurried back over the fence and drove home to pack.

I hadn't been able to tell people about *Big Brother*, but particularly not Chris, because he worked for the *Shropshire Star*. He has since said that when he saw me on the front of the paper two days later, he thought, Oh no, he'll have never had a chance to do the bench! So he was pleasantly surprised to find everything in place when he went to visit Michelle's grave the following day. How's he done that, then? he wondered. It wasn't until many months later that I told him about my night-time escapade.

8

Big Brother Is Watching

I left for London the next day. Each housemate was allowed to bring someone with them, so Bev accompanied me. We stayed in a two-thousand-room Hilton hotel somewhere in London. All the housemates were staying in the same hotel, in rooms as far apart from each other as could possibly be arranged. It was important that none of us met before we entered the *Big Brother* house.

Our mobile phones were taken away from us the moment we arrived and we weren't allowed to tell our friends or families where we were. Since I couldn't do any work without my phone, I could relax at last. It was a huge relief. After a hectic, stressful week of trying to organize my business, this was my chance to start enjoying myself. Hey, this could be fun, I thought. But almost immediately I started to feel really nervous. What the hell had I actually got myself into?

Chaperones accompanied us whenever we left our room. Bev

and I bombarded them with questions, but they didn't give anything away. Their presence was solely to ensure that we didn't communicate with the press or anyone else, including the other housemates. The chances of us bumping into one another in that enormous hotel were low, and of starting a conversation even lower. But I suppose it was a possibility, one night in the bar:

'Do you come here often?'

'As it happens, I'm only here because I'm about to appear in a new TV series called *Big Brother*.'

'Really? What a coincidence, so am I!'

The new suitcases I had bought for the occasion were taken off me and checked over for pens, logos, libellous material and anything else that I might be trying to smuggle into the house. I was left with the outfit I would wear going in and a small case that was just for show. This was checked again before I entered the house, so how Nick Bateman managed to sneak a pen inside, I still don't know to this day. I always ask him about it when we meet up, but he just laughs.

I hardly slept the night before I was due to go in. The chaperones had taken Bev and me out for a meal and we'd had a few drinks, but nothing could stop the whirring thoughts in my mind. Was I doing the right thing? What would it be like in the house? Would my business be OK?

The week before, I'd had another chat with Brett, the psychiatrist.

'How do you think you'll cope without having your own space?' he had asked.

As it turned out, none of us really had an answer for that,

because none of us had experienced living in a sealed environment. Unless you'd spent time in jail, how would you know what it felt like?

'I couldn't really say,' I replied. 'I've never shared a dormitory. Mind you, living in my mum's tiny caravan was a bit like living without my own space. It was so basic that I couldn't do anything more than sleep in it.'

The one thing I was quite confident about was being able to mix with people from different walks of life. Living in a pub helps develop your social skills and I had lived at the Shakespeare Inn for nearly ten years. But it's one thing to be sociable when you choose to – and something else altogether to be unable to get away from people.

Then there's the added pressure of having TV cameras watching you night and day. There were going to be nearly thirty visible cameras in the house, plus a further ten that were hidden behind the mirrors. That left nowhere, absolutely nowhere, to hide. Added to that, there would be a radio microphone picking up everything you said and every noise you made, voluntary or involuntary . . .

A couple of producers came to my room the following morning with a camera. They went through all the regulations on film; there were only a small number of things you couldn't do, such as tamper with recording equipment, talk about nominations and leave the house without warning. There was also a lot of legal stuff that I had to agree to.

'Yes,' I said solemnly, looking straight at the lens, 'I am going into the house of my own accord.'

The producers showed me to how to wear the radio mic and

instructed me to change the batteries at least twice a day. 'This will be recording everything you say, every hour of the day and night,' they said, going on to warn me against slandering people. They also told me not to sing any songs, because Channel 4 would have to pay out royalties if the songs were still protected by copyright.

By now I just wanted to get into the house. The selection process had been incredibly long-winded; the build-up had gone on for long enough. I was nervous, but I was also excited and I wanted to get on with it. Enough chat – the anticipation was driving me mad.

At last it was time to go. We drove to the house in East London and I said goodbye to Bev. 'Good luck, Craig,' she said, giving me a hug. 'You can win, I know you can.'

'I'll do my best!' I said as I set off across the bridge.

Lee and Barry were at the bridge crossing to say goodbye. 'Last one in, last one out, mate!' one of them shouted. I gave them a final wave.

I wanted to win, that's for sure. First and foremost, I was determined to get the money for Joanne's operation. What's more, I wouldn't have jeopardized my business or gone through all those auditions if I wasn't in it to win it. I think it's a load of rubbish when people say that they don't care about winning; all that matters is the taking part. You don't enter a competition if you don't want to win it. Having said that, I already felt like a winner when I went through those doors on 14 July 2000. Over forty-five thousand people had applied to be where I was – and I had made it down to the final ten. That felt like an amazing achievement in itself.

When I went into the *Big Brother* house, I barely knew a thing about the concept behind it. I didn't know that Big Brother was the name of a fictional character in the novel *Nineteen Eighty-Four* by George Orwell – a dictator in a police state who is 'always watching you'.

I've since heard that the idea for the TV programme came out of a brainstorming session in 1997 at John de Mol Produkties, a production company that was part of Endemol. Apparently the producers were inspired partly by the 1991 Biosphere 2 experiment in the Arizona desert, in which eight men and women lived alone inside an airtight dome that replicated the Earth's environment.

MTV's *The Real World* was perhaps another influence – this first aired in 1992 and showed some of the drama that can go down when strangers spend time together in a house. There were also elements in common with the Swedish TV programme *Expedition: Robinson*, which went on to be called *Survivor* in other countries. I hadn't seen either programme before I applied to be in *Big Brother*, though.

A lot of people have said to me that *Big Brother* reminded them of the 1998 film *The Truman Show*, in which Jim Carrey plays an insurance salesman who discovers that his whole life is a TV show. I keep meaning to watch it, but I haven't got round to it yet!

I've also heard that *Big Brother* has been compared to the Stanford Prison Experiment, which took place in 1971 at Stanford University in California. In a mock prison in the basement of the psychology department, volunteer students apparently revealed the darker side of human nature when they agreed to play the roles of guards and prisoners. Some of the 'guards' relished the power they'd been given, so I'm told; they took things too far and became seriously sadistic, emotionally traumatizing some of the 'prisoners', who were just their fellow students in everyday life. After six days, the experiment had to be halted because of the psychological dangers it posed to the participants.

But I knew none of this when I went into the house, which looked bright and shiny and new at first glance. There were rows and rows of powerful lights along the ceiling of every room, and cameras mounted on all the walls. The sight of them spooked me a bit. It was weird to think that I was already being filmed. This was it. I was lit up and live on air.

The contestants had entered the house one by one; I was the last to go in. The first few minutes passed in a blur of people jumping around and introducing themselves. One of the girls looked familiar. Then it clicked. 'I saw you in the hotel yesterday!' I said.

'That must have been why my chaperone suddenly stopped me and told me to go in another direction!' she said. 'He made me wait around a corner for a couple of minutes – while you went past, I expect.'

This was Caroline O'Shea, or 'Caggy' as she was also known, a 36-year-old from Birmingham. Caroline was unemployed at the time she entered the house, but had done all kinds of jobs in the past, including special constable, cleaner and sex-toy saleswoman, as she was only too keen to tell us. Loud and boisterous from the outset, she got even louder as the days passed, so she wasn't my favourite housemate. Her voice and personality grated on me. She annoyed some of the others, too. When I first met Jade Goody some years later, she reminded me of Caroline.

The blokes in the house all seemed fine at first. Tom McDermott came across as a nice fella. He had grown up on a farm in County Tyrone in Northern Ireland and was a computer engineer; he was also a qualified bricklayer and joiner.

Darren Ramsey seemed a good, solid guy, a chef who had also worked as a greeter at the Millennium Dome. Darren was the only one in the house with children. He missed his kids more and more as the weeks went by and he had a tough time coping with being in the house for so long without them.

I immediately tipped Andy Davidson to win. A fun, sociable guy from Hemel Hempstead, Andy was a really nice person. Mel Hill obviously thought so too. There was an instant attraction between them. Mel, who was from North London and had a degree in Psychology, was the best-looking and most attractive girl in the house, in my opinion.

In the beginning, I got on quite well with Nichola Holt, who was an art teacher from Bolton. Like me, she shaved her head in the first week, as did Darren, Andy and Tom. It was a spontaneous chain reaction that started off as a joke and ended up with half of the house becoming baldy, for no apparent reason. It was slightly childish perhaps, yet great fun at the time. It's the best feeling, putting your newly shaved head on the pillow for the first time, and it reminded me of the time Lee and I had shaved our heads in the Shakespeare Inn, when we were trying to raise money for Joanne's campaign.

But back to Nichola. She could be a good laugh, but the problem was, she could just turn with the wind and I find people like that difficult, because you never know where you stand with them. When she was in a good mood, I enjoyed her company. But then she would flip and become loud and argumentative, like Caroline, and I wanted to get away from her. She could have a foul mouth on her if she wanted to.

I warmed to Anna Nolan straight away; she was from Dublin. Like many of the other housemates, Anna had done various different jobs, the most surprising of them being novice nun. She had a pleasant, easygoing personality.

Then there was Sada Wilkington, who was really into her yoga. Sada and I didn't have much in common and she was the first to leave, so I don't remember all that much about her.

Finally, there was Nick Bateman. Nick struck me as a bit of a div at times, but a lot of the things he said and did were entertaining, in a clownish way. He thought he was dead clever, but sometimes acted rather stupid. Nick was a city broker and an ex-public schoolboy – he claimed that he had been to school with royalty. He seemed to think he was above everyone else: he looked down on people like me, who were from Up North and not as well educated as he was. All the same, I liked him. He was funny and interesting; I enjoyed his company – which will probably come as a surprise to millions!

Full of outlandish tales about his life, Nick claimed to have once been a male escort. He also said that he'd been in the Territorial Army for three years and made himself out to be some kind of élite ninja fighter. Somehow I couldn't quite picture it. His anecdotes puzzled me: at the time I had no idea what a storyteller he was.

Our first day in the house was fun. Everyone was on a high because they'd made it this far. I immediately started sizing people up, trying to work out who had the most potential to win. Over the previous few days, I had worked out a plan of campaign, which was to try and nominate anyone I saw as a threat. I wasn't going in there to make friends. Remember, I was in there to win.

But after a week in the house, I realized that I'd be much better off with housemates whose company I enjoyed, people who were fun. The days and weeks were going to drag if I managed to stay until the end: nine weeks was a hell of a long time to spend without friends, family, phones, work, TV, news-papers, money, responsibilities or even my car keys. So my strategy totally changed. I wanted the nicest people to stay.

I often say that I learned a lot about myself in the *Big Brother* house. I certainly found it surprising how easy it was to adapt to being in the palm of Big Brother's hand. When Big Brother said jump, you said, 'How high?' without asking why. It was bizarre, really. I didn't think I could be controlled and bribed so easily.

The control was achieved by stripping everything away, as they do to young cadets when they join the army. Big Brother would deprive us of items such as food, alcohol or cigarettes and the atmosphere in the house would become very tense. Then we'd be given a feast or some wine and our moods would completely change. By the end, we would do whatever Big Brother wanted for a couple of bottles of cheap cider.

Years later I was at Vanessa Feltz's house and I spoke to her about how it felt to be manipulated in this way. Vanessa took part in the first *Celebrity Big Brother* and found life in the house very challenging. She told me that she just could not handle the fact that Big Brother had so much control over her.

Now, I think I'm a very self-motivated person. I'm used to doing what I want and I don't wait to be told to do things; I just get up and do them. Yet, unlike Vanessa, obeying Big Brother didn't bother me; I didn't mind that it wasn't my choice when we did a task, which surprised me. Perhaps that's because I knew it was only for a limited amount of time.

I found Big Brother's whims easier to cope with than being cut off from the outside world. In everyday life, you know what's going on in the world and among your friends and family, but in the Big Brother house we had absolutely no communication with anyone who wasn't connected with the programme – and no news updates at all. I didn't realize how much I took television for granted until it was taken away from me. I found myself really missing the chance to watch the news or listen to the radio in the car. It was even worse not being able to speak to people on the phone or send texts, which most of us do on a daily basis.

It must be like going to jail, people say, but it's not. I know, because I actually spent two days and two nights in Altcourse Prison in Fazakerley, Liverpool, for charity, a few years after I was in *Big Brother*. I was locked up along with the fundraising manager of a local hospice for the terminally ill. The aim was to raise money for the hospice by asking the public to bail us out; before we could be released, we had to hit a target of

£5,000. I found being in jail very different to being in the *Big Brother* house, because I was able to watch television every night, make phone calls and play pool. We even had our meals cooked for us. Prisoners aren't cut off in the same way as *Big Brother* housemates. On the other hand, I was free to walk out of the *Big Brother* house at any time, which you obviously can't do in prison.

The nights weren't easy at first. I didn't get much kip during the first week. We were in a new, unnatural environment and everyone was very excited, so not a lot of sleeping went on. I did sleep OK some nights, but if any of the others were still up drinking and having a laugh, I could hear them from the bedroom because the walls were very thin. I could also hear things going on behind the walls as the cameramen walked past, dragging cables, plugging in wires and dropping things. There was always a bit of a disturbance when they swapped over shifts. They only did four-hour stints in the camera room because it was so hot and uncomfortable in there. The noises were a constant reminder that there was somebody watching us behind the walls and mirrors.

Frustratingly, it always seemed as though when I did finally get into a nice deep sleep, the blazing bright lights used for day-time filming would suddenly flood the bedroom, and I'd be rudely awoken. The bedrooms were never fully dark either; there always had to be some infra-red lighting for night-time filming.

Months later, long after I'd left the house, I met more than one cameraman who said, 'Hi, Craig, you don't know me, but I used to do the twelve to four a.m., or the four to eight a.m.

shift in the *Big Brother* house. Whether you were asleep or not, I had camera five on your eyeline all the time, for the whole sixty-four days.'

I have to say that it was a weird feeling, and not a very nice one, to meet the person who has spent nine weeks' worth of night shifts watching my face. It was even more unnerving when he recalled how I occasionally got up and began sleepwalking, bumping into things on my way to the toilet. 'That was the highlight of my night shift!' one cameraman said.

I met production staff who said similarly strange things: 'Craig, I was responsible for collecting data on how many cups of tea and coffee you drank and how many showers you had . . .' These people were each assigned to watch one camera for six hours at a time. What a job! I'd think, as they chirpily told me all about it.

I've been asked a million times why I think I won *Big Brother*. It's a hard question to answer. I've never actually watched the whole programme back in all these years, so I don't know exactly how the cameras presented me or how the public saw me. I can really only go by what my friends say, which was that I came across as a genuine person, a little bit mischievous and lots of fun.

I was the first person in the house to strip off, I know that much! It all began with our first weekly task. As anyone who has ever watched *Big Brother* will know, every week the house-mates had to complete a particular group challenge. Our first task was each to make a clay bowl and a mug using a potter's wheel. If more than three objects cracked when they were cooked in the kiln, we would fail the task. If we succeeded, we would be rewarded.

Unfortunately, there weren't many natural potters among us. The wheel was quite old-fashioned and you had to power it with a foot pump, which was hard work. It was frustrating, too, because just at the moment you thought you were about to finish moulding a masterpiece, the sides of your mug or bowl would collapse back on to the wheel. After a couple of days of not getting very far, it began to get boring. So we decided to stop trying and just have our own fun.

First Nichola smeared her hands with clay and started painting on the wall. I think she was just writing her name, but as soon as the producers saw letters, they thought it might be a way of trying to communicate with the outside world.

Suddenly a voice came over the loudspeaker.

'This is Big Brother. Will Nichola please stop writing on the wall right now!' That was our first telling-off, I think.

At that point, I decided to strip off, cover my naked body in clay and make a body print on the wall. We were just innocently mucking about, but the executive producers told me later that they watched in horror, thinking, Oh God! What are these people going to do next? Where is it all going to lead? The entire show was an experiment; they were terrified that things might go wrong and transmission would have to be halted.

Next, I encouraged the other housemates to take off their clothes and soon there were lots of us making body prints on the wall. It turned out to be nothing but harmless fun, so, later that day, Channel 4 took stills from the video footage, printed them up and sent them out to the press. Apparently, this helped to generate loads of interest in the programme.

The weekly tasks helped to break the monotony of the days, but as the novelty of being in the house wore off, time started to crawl. We were bored a lot of the time. I'm normally so active that I found it difficult to stop the enforced idleness getting me down. One of the only things that kept me sane was doing exercises. Luckily, I'd learned from an early age that if you can keep your body nice and strong, then your mind will follow. So each morning I ran around the small garden, sometimes fifty or a hundred times. That would take up a good hour of the day, helping to relieve the tedium. If I wanted to do any weightlifting, I had to improvise: I filled pillowcases with tins of beans or bottles of water to use for weights and did press-ups upside down.

Generally, we didn't have any set time to do anything, so it didn't matter if you had an afternoon nap. This was a whole new concept for me, because I'd never been able to slip away and have an hour's sleep in the afternoon at work. Now I could do it two or three times a day if I wanted to. However, when you are having a little doze of an afternoon, it's obviously harder to get to sleep at night. My sleep patterns became quite severely disrupted. In the early stages of the programme, the producers decided to edit in clips of me sleeping more than any other housemate, even though we all had naps. So, initially, the public perceived me as the lazy one. This really upset my family and they started to wonder if there was something wrong with me and rang up the producers to make sure I was OK.

We were all allowed to take one book into the house and I took Richard Branson's autobiography. It was fascinating to read about how he overcame his problems with dyslexia and struggled to set up his businesses, the chances he had and the risks he took. I identified with him in many ways. There were loads of things in the book that I could relate to, just on a smaller scale. When he talked about bluffing his way into getting a big contract despite not having the necessary experience, I thought, I've done that! It was a really motivating read. I vowed that when I came out of the house and got my hands on a pen I would highlight all the passages that I found most inspiring.

When there was a lull in activities – when people were mooching off in the corners, not doing very much at all – Big Brother would think up something for us to do. After all, mooching doesn't make very good TV. Often alcohol would appear and we'd be given a topic to discuss.

One particular night, Big Brother started off a conversation about first love. 'What happened? Where are they now?'

This got me thinking about Shelley, the lovely girl I went out with for the five years after I moved away from Liverpool. Ten years previously, Shelley and I had made a pact to get married on 25 July 2000. Like many lovers who can't quite bear to split up but want to go in different directions for the time being, our plan had been to do our own thing in the interim, before coming back together for good. She wanted to travel the world; I had my business; but we still loved each other and wanted to be together one day.

By this point, I had lost track of the exact date inside the house. Without appointments to remind you, a diary, the news or sell-by dates, the calendar loses its relevance. But I did know that we were having this conversation in the house around 25 July, ten years to the day since Shelley and I had made our promise to one another. Since everyone else was sharing their stories, I didn't have a chance to go into a lot of detail, but I did recall how crazily in love I had been with Shelley all those years ago.

The next day, I asked Big Brother what the date was, but of course, Big Brother refused to tell me. However, I later found out that it had actually been 25 July! It was quite a coincidence. The footage was transmitted the following day.

None of the housemates thought anybody would be interested in watching *Big Brother*. We wondered how on earth the producers could make a TV show out of ten people sitting around, quietly bored. OK, there was the odd fun moment, but most of our conversations were arguments over petty, pathetic things. The rest was silence and fidgeting. This is going to be an absolutely rubbish programme, I thought to myself. Just try and stick at it for the money.

Getting drunk was obviously one of the best ways to make time pass quickly, but alcohol changed people: it seemed to bring out the best in some of us, but, unfortunately, the worst in others. It often changed the mood in the house for the better and we'd all gather round for a good chat, but sometimes it led to arguments. I tended to let other people's disagreements wash over me. Caroline and Nichola, especially, could be very confrontational. They always seemed to have a problem with something and wanted to shout about it. Perhaps they thought that this was what people wanted to watch on television, or maybe that was how they really were. Some people just seem to enjoy arguing about petty things.

People got up to all sorts of things to try and relieve their boredom. There was quite a bit of mischief-making, some of it upsetting. But the things I did were never intended to make serious trouble or distress people. For instance, I didn't much like people smoking inside, so one day I hid everyone's cigarettes. As I found a hiding place for each packet, I gave the nearest camera a little wink. Then I sat back to watch all the smokers crack up when they couldn't find their ciggies.

Hiding cigarettes became a theme for me and the smokers thanked me for it in the end. Often I just took one or two ciggies out of their packets so that they didn't notice any were missing. If anything, they thought they must have smoked them all the night before, while they were drunk. Inevitably, they ran out of cigarettes and started climbing the walls, begging Big Brother for a smoke. At that point, I showed them the hidden supply of cigarettes and they were all made up!

Meanwhile, Nick was making mischief on another level altogether. He had developed a particular strategy for winning, which was to manipulate the other housemates and influence their votes, thereby getting rid of his rivals and making sure he remained in the house. It was very successful, too, up to a point.

One of the first things he did to help his case was to win people's sympathy and get them on his side. It was evening time; we were sitting around having a drink and we started playing the truth game. When it came to Nick's turn, he told us a really heartbreaking story about something that had happened ten years before. Tears sprang to his eyes as he recounted how he had emigrated to Australia to start a new life with his fiancée, how the two of them had married out there, but then she was tragically killed in a car accident. The housemates were stunned to hear this. Poor Nick! we thought. What a terrible thing to happen; what a deeply sad, painful story. Everyone felt so sorry for him.

After a while, the house began to divide along certain lines. Caroline, Nichola and Sada were often to be found together in the house, sometimes with Anna, but personally, I preferred hanging around with people like Tom, Andy and Mel, Nick and Darren.

There were no nominations or evictions the first week, but everyone got nervous a couple of days before the nominations in the second week. Naturally, you started thinking about who might nominate you. Did I upset her last week? Did he misinterpret what I said yesterday? People started being much nicer to each other. Quite a few apologies were made.

Caroline and Sada were nominated first, which didn't surprise me. A lot of us had nominated them, myself included. Out of the two of them, the public chose to evict Sada; again, no great surprise, although I would rather have seen Caroline go, I think.

But the next eviction, in the third week, was a real shocker. Caroline was nominated again, but this time she was up against Andy, and Andy was voted out. I was amazed. Couldn't the public see what a cool guy he was? Never bitchy, loud or argumentative like some of the girls, he didn't get involved in any of the fights. Instead, he was good company. I'd been convinced he was winner material. It was then that I began to realize that there was a big gap between what was actually happening in the house and the public's perception of it.

I also had to really wonder why Andy had been nominated by the other housemates. He was a good person to have around. Why would anyone want him to leave the house instead of, say, Nichola? It didn't take a genius to realize that some people were voting tactically, as I had planned to do when I first entered the house. They saw Andy as a likely winner: they were prepared to put up with Nichola as long as he no longer posed a threat.

Caroline was the third housemate to be kicked out of the house. When Davina explained that she would be coming to get her in an hour's time I saw panic set in. Mixed emotions were racing through her, she told me: she was happy to be leaving, but she was nervous as hell. It got to the point where her whole body began to shake. The same thing happened to Nichola the following week. Both times I watched as they necked a load of wine and chain-smoked to try and control their nerves, worried that their legs would go when they walked out of the door.

None of us knew what was waiting for us outside the house. Often Big Brother locked the back door to the garden on eviction nights, but sometimes we managed to get out. In the garden we could hear the crowds from across the water. Big Brother would play loud music to drown out the sound of what was going on, but we still managed to get a sense of a live audience out there. It was nerve-racking and made everybody really scared about leaving.

'Listen, I think I can help you feel OK and get focused for this,' I said to Caroline.

I wasn't sure I could reproduce my Muay Thai teacher's relaxation technique, but it was worth a try, even if I couldn't deliver it as well as he could. I wasn't all that keen on Caroline, but she was in such a state that I felt I had to do something for her.

I took her into one of the bedrooms and she lay on the floor. Then I told her the story about the sun warming your body and your body melting in the sand and the light going through your toes and out through your hair. It took a good ten minutes before I described the process in reverse, when the light comes down your body and makes you feel strong and relaxed.

Amazingly, it seemed to work: she stopped shaking and no longer felt the urge to smoke and drink. I went on talking until it was time for her to leave, trying to help her feel calm and focused; to look forward to what would happen, rather than being afraid.

'It's just a small audience out there,' I said. 'It sounds louder than it is. There's nothing to worry about. Your friends and family will be there and you'll only be filmed for a bit, that's all.'

Little did I know the mayhem that would greet her when she walked out of the door! Or, indeed, the trouble that was about to erupt inside the house before the next eviction.

9

Confrontation

People who knew me said afterwards that I was uncharacteristically quiet during my first month in the house. It's true that I was tired and slept a fair amount. My problems at work were still on my mind, nagging at me in quiet moments. Would everything run smoothly without me? I couldn't help worrying about the demolition order that had been served on me for my garage. What would I do if the council went ahead and knocked it down? It was unthinkable, but I kept on brooding about it. I was very conscious of the fact that, if I were evicted from the house after a fortnight, or three weeks, I would still have a chance to fight it.

'I know it's against all the rules, but will you tell me what has happened?' I asked Big Brother, once the twenty-eight days of the demolition order had passed.

The answer was no, of course. 'You know the rules, Craig. We can't tell you what's going on outside.' I stopped fretting after that. Well, I'm still here, I thought, so there's nothing I can do about the garage. Either it's still standing or it's been demolished, so it's time to let go, move on and enjoy myself in the madhouse.

The days stretched ahead, with not much to do in them, so I tried to treat this time as a holiday, a time to rest. But actually time became my biggest problem. Normally my whole week is mapped out. I know where I'm going to be and what I'm going to do. However, now there was very little purpose to anything.

Before I went into the house, I was constantly chasing my tail, because things were so hectic with my company. I was late for everything but trying to get places as quickly as I could, because every last thing was as important as the next. Stopping all of a sudden – and doing nothing – opened up another part of my mind, and not necessarily in a good way. I became lethargic because there were no challenges or choices and I didn't have to worry about people, money, work, time, planning . . .

What happens in that situation is that you mull over every aspect of your business a hundred times, until you're totally sick of thinking about it. Then you blank work out of your mind and start thinking about your family, over and over again, until you get to a point where you need to try and blank that out, too. That's when you find that the tiniest things start to wind you up. I could see it happening to everyone.

I tried hard not to be like the others, but we were all crumbling. Really petty things affected us all: someone would put a cup of coffee right on the edge of the table and you'd think, Why have you put it there, where it's obviously going to fall and break?

'Put that in the middle of the table,' you'd say. 'It's going to get knocked over.'

At that, they would give you a funny look, as if to say, What's it got to do with you?

Then you think to yourself, Well, it's not my cup of coffee, it's not my cup if it breaks, it's not my floor. Does it really matter? Should I actually care? You give yourself a mental slap and think, I shouldn't be bothered . . . but I am! And now he's just done it again and it's winding me up again! What's happening?

The situation would rumble on: 'I've told you once!' you'd say. 'Don't put that on the edge; it's going to get knocked off.'

It was another side to me altogether, and one I didn't know was there. Normally, if I'm on site and a lad knocks over a cup of tea and it breaks on the floor, it doesn't bother me, as long as he cleans up the mess. I've got too many more important things to be dealing with. But when you've nothing else to think about, nothing to do and no responsibilities to consider, your mind just gets sucked into minute little problems. It's a product of boredom, something I've never experienced before and don't want to again.

Slowly I learned more about emotions and how to control them. I began to think about myself and my family differently. I didn't think I'd done anything to hurt my family in recent times, because I'd been pretty sensible for ten years, trying to run a business. But Bev was a single parent now and still living in Liverpool: had I spent enough time with my nieces? Had I missed out on parts of their childhood? Should I have been more of a father figure to them?

Within no time I found myself feeling guilty and worrying about how I could do things better. Since there was nothing else to distract me, the same thoughts kept coming back round again to torture me.

I tried to think positively about the future. I had to keep strong in the house so that I could win the money for little Joanne's operation. (I still called her little Jo, even though she was well into her teens by this point.) Poor Jo had experienced ups and downs in her health in recent years. Sometimes she would get so poorly that she had to be taken into hospital and then there would be a bit of a panic.

Yet, so far, she had always somehow managed to come back stronger than ever, which amazed the specialists. Nevertheless, it was still crucial to get the money together for her operation in case she suddenly became very ill and needed her transplant urgently. We knew it could happen out of the blue, without warning.

I thought back to the last time I'd seen little Jo, at Lee's parents' pub. Viv and Sam absolutely adored her and often had her to stay with them. Bubblier than ever, she had kept us all entertained with her lively chatter. She really was the star of the family, the central focus, whether she was in the room or not. Whenever you were with any part of the family, someone or other would be telling a Joanne story. The conversation always seemed to come back to her.

What about me? Do I want children? I asked myself. I'm twenty-eight now; at some point I've got to start thinking about settling down. So how old do I want to be when I have children?

I've heard that when people have been very ill or are diagnosed as being terminally ill, they often start living their lives differently or seeing things from another perspective. Having all that time in the *Big Brother* house had a similar effect on me, I think. Although I wasn't ill, in a way I was paralysed. I learned a lot about myself and realized more than ever how important my family is to me.

What do they think of me? I wondered. Are they going to be pleased with how I'm behaving myself in here, or have I said something that might have offended or upset them? I began to over-analyse my behaviour. I was desperately in need of something to distract me. Well, something was about to . . .

Trouble was brewing in the house. We had by now come to realize that Nick was a bit of a fraud and most of what he had told us was a load of rubbish. He had been playing us off against one another for quite some time, but now people were starting to wake up to it. Mel confided to Big Brother that he had been saying things about me to her behind my back. She felt he was definitely trying to influence her nominations.

Everything began to unravel for Nick in the fifth week in the house. First he admitted to Mel and Tom that he had lied about the death of his wife in a car crash in Australia. Next it came to light that his career as a ruthless ninja was a figment of his imagination.

This was the week when our group challenge was to complete an assault course in the garden in less than eight minutes.

I flew round it in the fastest time, with no errors, but Nick fell at every obstacle. Bearing in mind that he had told us he had been in the Territorial Army for three years, it was hard not to laugh out loud. It was hilarious; even the girls beat him. Tom, Mel and I stood there thinking, If that's what the army has taken on, let's hope Nick doesn't get called up to defend his country!

At first I had no idea that Nick had smuggled a pen into the house, or that he was writing people's names on tiny pieces of paper and flashing them at selected housemates. Big Brother was aware that he was up to something, but the producers let it be. They didn't interfere because they couldn't work out what exactly he was doing and how he was doing it. I can only imagine that he must have found the one place in the house where no one could see him writing things down.

With all that time on my hands, I had studied the entire house to see where you could hide from the camera if you wanted to. I worked out that there was one place in the far corner of the main living room, where the door to the girls' bedroom was. If you opened the door all the way out into the room and pulled it against the corner of the wall, you'd make a small triangular cavity that could fit one person. It was only as wide as my shoulders. Was that where he went to write names on pieces of paper? Since then, I've asked him more than once, but he's never given me an answer.

As I've said, I liked Nick and had felt that we were becoming friends. We had even talked about how we would go and visit Tom in Ireland after we left the house. But then he did something very odd just before the week-five nominations. I was sitting under a camera, in full view of Big Brother, writing out a shopping list for food on a chalkboard. We only had £1.50 a day and we were allowed just an hour a week to work out how to spend it, so I was adding up all the items as quickly as I could.

Just then, Nick walked up. Without saying a word, he took the chalk out of my hand and quickly wrote a name in the top corner of the board, shielding it from the camera with his other hand. It's been so long that I can't remember whose name it was, but I think it was Darren or Anna. Then, just as quickly as he had written it, he wiped it off and walked away.

Hang on a minute, I thought. Something's going on here! I had already noticed that Nick was extra nice to certain people a couple of days before nominations. What's more, the previous week, he had pointed at Tom and Mel and said, 'If you, you, me and Craig voted for Anna, it wouldn't matter.' I was careful not to react, because it was against the rules to discuss nominations. Funny, Big Brother did have a unique hold on you.

I had put it out of my mind, but now the incident with the chalkboard had me thinking again. Was Nick trying to influence the way everyone voted, even though this was forbidden? Had he been behind Andy's surprise nomination and eviction? Was he attempting to outsmart us all, including Big Brother?

Little did I know that the whole country was now transfixed by Nick's dirty tricks. In fact, in the eyes of the nation, he was a complete baddie. I had no idea either that the *Sun* newspaper had sent a helicopter flying over the garden to drop a thousand leaflets saying, 'Kick Out Nick!'

I suspected nothing, because the moment this happened, Big Brother called us all into the house and locked the doors, then ordered us into a windowless room for an hour, while someone cleared the garden of leaflets. Later, more helicopters flew over, including remote-control helicopters, but we were totally cut off from the world.

Nick's attempt to influence my vote got nowhere. He didn't sway my nomination: I made my own decisions and justified them reasonably. But, going by what members of the public have told me, he did have an impact on the nominations and I'm pretty sure he influenced some of the other housemates. It's interesting that he was never once nominated for eviction himself then.

On the other hand, my turn had finally come: that week I was nominated along with Nichola. I shouldn't have taken it to heart, but I couldn't help feeling rejected when Davina said: 'The housemates have now spoken. Today two people are up for eviction. They are . . . Craig and Nichola.'

Oh God! I thought. I looked around at the housemates. I'd opened up to these people, I'd thought we'd started to become friends over the previous month, but somewhere down the line they had decided that they liked me the least out of all the contestants, or they saw me as a threat and wanted me out. It was galling, not to mention humiliating.

Within fifteen minutes, though, I had reminded myself that I was on a game show. This is exactly what we've come on here for, I told myself. We all know the rules. We have to nominate someone. I've nominated people too and it's not because I hate them. It's simply part of the deal, part of the show. Don't take it personally!

In fact, people gave some really stupid, trivial reasons for nominating housemates, such as, 'He doesn't wash up enough,' or, 'She eats too much.'

Fortunately for me, things don't generally get me down for long. I'm good at moving on. But I didn't feel so accepting the next day, when Tom took me aside and confided that Nick had shown him a name earlier in the week – my name. 'What?' I said, incredulous. So Nick was plotting to get me out as well! I could hardly believe it and I felt horribly let down, because he and I were mates – or so I thought. I had certainly talked to him like a friend. Why, then, had he flashed my name at Tom? It seemed incredibly shallow and two-faced.

My gut instinct was to go in guns blazing – to find him immediately and confront him. Then I realized that I needed to get my facts clear first, so I had a chat with each individual housemate in the bedroom.

'Has Nick shown you a note with my name on it, to encourage you to nominate me?' I asked each one of them, in turn. 'I'm not going to be mad at you for not telling me before, and I won't mention any names to Nick. I just want a simple yes or no before I confront him. I've got reason to believe he's been going behind all our backs.'

Some people said, 'No, he's done nothing.' Others admitted, 'Well, yes, he has.'

By now, it was about 2 a.m. We'd all had a drink and I thought, You know what? Everybody's starting to get wound up. This could easily kick off. Darren was in an angry mood and I was worried about what he might do.

I decided that it would be much better to sit around the table and thrash it out properly the next day, when people had slept off the drink. Some housemates had already gone to bed and I didn't want to leave them out of the proceedings. This was something that needed dealing with properly, since it affected us all.

Meanwhile, Big Brother had seen what was going on and was calling me into the diary room every few minutes. 'What do you think is happening here?' Big Brother asked. 'Are you going to approach Nick? If so, when and how?'

'I don't think it's appropriate to confront him tonight when everyone's had a drink, because people are going to get angry and there's going to be fighting,' I said.

I could feel the tension building up fast. This worried me. Darren and Nick were both big lads and they'd be quite a handful to control. If they started fighting, someone could get hurt.

Having done security work, I had often seen how people turn stupid when they've been drinking. So my first thought was to eliminate any potential dangers. I made sure all the bottles were out of harm's way and moved the kitchen knives from the drawer to the cupboard.

Neil Higgins later told me he'd had to put extra security staff on all the fire doors and outside the bedroom doors all night long that night, just in case things kicked off. Everyone was aware that the situation could get nasty. Fortunately, it didn't.

I didn't sleep very well that night. Thoughts kept whirring

around my head as I tried to work out to what extent Nick had managed to influence the other housemates' votes and attitudes. I hated the fact that I was so wound up about it, but I just couldn't help myself. Normally, I couldn't care less what people say about me, or what they get up to. But when you've got nothing else to focus on, these things do bother you. They really, *really* bother you!

The next morning, a house meeting was called. As soon as Mel, Tom, Anna, Nichola, Darren, Nick and I were all sitting around the kitchen table, I confronted Nick about his behaviour. Of course, none of us was aware that 8.5 million people were watching this scene online; we were totally oblivious to the fact that we were making internet history. At the time, Intel said that it was the most traffic it had ever seen on a website.

For many people in the media, this marked the moment where streamed web content became a mass-market medium. There was so much traffic to the site, in fact, that the service provider couldn't handle the volume of hits and the site crashed. The following evening, 46 per cent of the viewing audience watched the highlights show on Channel 4. Nearly half of the country was watching television that night. This was the day that the future of the *Big Brother* format was secured, once and for all.

17 August 2000, 12.28 p.m.

'There's something very important I want to bring up and I think everybody should be aware of it, because it's everybody's concern,' I said, looking directly at Nick. 'Basically, I'm sorry I have to say it, Nick, but I'm very disappointed in you . . . I not only feel, but I'm quite positive – and I've got evidence to show – that you're plotting a very dirty plan to make everybody here vote against each other.'

'That's absurd, Craig,' Nick said, dismissively. But the blood had drained from his face.

I swallowed hard. I wasn't enjoying this. 'You may think it's absurd, Nick, but I'm going to offer you facts here,' I said. 'There are a number of people sitting around this table who have come to me over the weekend and said that you have shown them a piece of paper with various names on it, includ-ing my name on a number of occasions . . . How could you be so two-faced?'

'If this is true!' Nick said, as if it might not be. And yet there were tears welling up in his eyes.

'I know it's true. You know it's true,' I said, feeling really cut up.

I went on to explain that this wasn't about me being nominated. It wasn't about the possibility of being evicted. For me, it was about being betrayed by a guy I thought was my friend. It was also about breaking the rules of the game, which was unfair to all of us.

Nick blustered for a bit and said that I was always making wild accusations about people.

Darren interrupted. 'Is it true what he's saying about you showing people names?' he asked Nick.

'No,' Nick said. 'It's not.'

'You've shown me names,' mumbled Tom.

'And you've shown me names,' Mel added.

'Nick hasn't shown me any names,' Darren said, loud and clear. 'Have you, Nick?'

'No,' Nick said.

Everyone started talking at once. 'Have you shown Melanie a name?' Anna asked Nick over the hubbub.

Finally he gave in. 'Yeah, I have,' he admitted. 'It was a mistake. I shouldn't have done it.'

At last! I felt relieved that we were finally getting the truth out of him, but at the same time a wave of anger swept over me. How could he have been so hypocritical, smiling to my face while trying to get me evicted behind my back?

I asked to see the bits of paper. 'No, I'll not do that,' he said. 'I'll pack my suitcase, simple as that.'

But I insisted. 'Nick, I'm asking you to show me where they are. If you don't, we'll go to Big Brother and someone will go through your stuff. So it's much better if you just go and get them.' Still he refused.

At this point Darren lost patience with Nick, went into the bedroom and started pulling Nick's suitcases apart. Amazingly, he actually found a couple of scraps of paper with people's names on them.

'How stupid could you have been to think that this wouldn't catch up with you?' I asked Nick.

He shrugged. Later in the diary room, he said, 'You live by the sword, you die by the sword.'

And that's exactly what he did.

I went into the diary room to speak to Big Brother. 'I don't care what strategies people employ in order to win,' I said. 'That's their business. We've all come in here to win. But Nick has blatantly broken the rules and if you don't kick him out, I'm leaving. I'll go tomorrow, and the rest of the housemates will probably go too, so you won't have a programme.'

Nick was called to the diary room and told that he would have to leave the house. His strategy had backfired. The game was over for him now. He was visibly upset for the rest of the day. He pretty much lay on his bed and cried until the time came for him to leave. It was impossible not to feel sorry for him. Every one of us had come into the house to win, just as he had. But he had cheated in a cowardly way. Now he had lost, big time.

We helped him to get his bags together. Then we walked him to the door, hugged him, shook his hand and wished him all the best. I was relieved that we parted on reasonable terms. I thought back to the hidden knives and bottles. Things could have ended up a lot, lot messier.

It was always fairly depressing when someone left the house. Even if you didn't like them that much, you naturally felt close to them because you had been living in such close proximity to them. In Nick's case, most of us had got on with him well and enjoyed his company, so we really missed him when he left. His absence was very noticeable. After his departure, the atmosphere in the house turned almost funeral-like. We all became silent and withdrawn, sitting around on the sofas, saying nothing, doing nothing.

Then something happened that revealed just how much control Big Brother wielded over our moods. All of a sudden, a huge banquet appeared, along with loads of alcohol. Hey presto! We soon forgot our sadness over Nick. Within an hour, we were bouncing off the ceiling.

It was only afterwards that I thought how shallow we were, how easily manipulated. So it was up to Big Brother if and when we had fun, was it? What's more, a few bottles of alcohol made all the difference. It's embarrassing to think how cheaply we were bought off by Big Brother.

However, our high spirits didn't last long. The entire house went into a slump again the following day. Everyone felt bad; we were all grumpy and depressed. I think it was partly because something had gone seriously wrong in the *Big Brother* scheme of things, and partly because we were only halfway through the nine weeks. We had already been in the house for what felt like ages. In our minds the next month stretched ahead like a year.

Nick's departure was a bit of a turning point, actually. The mood in the house became much darker in the days after he left, making life much harder. The time dragged as never before and the housemates became more and more irritable.

One day Big Brother made a surprising suggestion: 'Would any of you like to have a chat with a psychiatrist?'

'No, no, we're fine,' everyone replied.

'Well, there are psychiatrists watching over you all twenty-four hours a day and they can see that you're all experiencing a low,' Big Brother said. 'They feel that it would be advisable to talk things through, so why not give it a go?'

What's the worst that can happen? I thought. 'Will we be on air?' I asked.

'No, this is your chance to talk in confidence about anything that might be bothering you – anything at all – and get it out of your system. We give you our word that what you say will not be broadcast.'

If I were on a reality programme today and the producers told me that I could talk to someone in confidence, I wouldn't believe them. After some of the experiences I've had, I simply would not trust them to keep their word. But I was a lot less cynical back then – and so were reality TV producers.

'Yes, OK, we'll have a go,' a couple of us said, tempted by the idea of talking to someone new. The others soon followed suit.

Again, it was Brett Kahr that I spoke to, the guy who had done all the psychoanalysing before we went into the house. We had a really good chat. At the end of it I felt completely refreshed, as if I had recharged my batteries. How was I feeling? Brett asked. Why did I think I'd started feeling so low? How was I getting on with everybody else in the house? How did I think my family was seeing me over these weeks?

I talked about how I might be coming across to Bev and my mum. Hopefully I hadn't said or done anything offensive. Like many of the others, I had got drunk a few times, but generally I hadn't said anything too stupid. As I talked things over with Brett, I realized that although I may have said a few embarrassing things, there was nothing that had jeopardized my relationship with my family.

There was one moment that made me cringe later, though. About a year afterwards, my mum and I watched a three-hour DVD called *Big Brother Uncut*, which contains highlights from the first series. I never watched the whole ninety hours of footage, but I had a little skim through this. There was a clip of me talking drunkenly to Nichola about a time I'd had sex with somebody: I was describing where I'd been at the time, what I'd said and what I'd done. Aside from the fact that I wasn't overly pleased that this conversation had probably been broadcast to millions of people on Channel 4, it wasn't the kind of thing you wanted to be watching with your mum, believe me!

Every single one of us came away from our talk with Brett with a bounce in our step. We were walking on springs, in fact, totally on a high. It was unbelievable how just a couple of hours could change the mood and energy levels in the house. It seemed to give everyone a new lease of life, which was brilliant. It gave us the lift we needed to carry on.

We had been told that Big Brother didn't mind how much mess we made in the house, as long as we didn't vandalize the cameras. 'If you make a mess, you live with it. That's your problem,' the producers had said.

No one cared about the state of the house, because it was never meant to be a permanent structure. No one was going to get cross if we damaged anything. No one would tell us off. This gave us a wonderful sense of freedom to ransack the place if we wanted to – and boy did we take full advantage of it.

While Darren, Tom and I were fast asleep in the bedroom that night, suddenly in rushed Anna, Nichola and Mel armed with food. Ambush!

The girls had sneaked to the kitchen and opened loads of tins of beans, tomatoes and other canned food. Then they had mixed them with flour, eggs and anything else they could find that was wet, gooey or sticky. The first we boys knew about it was when we were splattered with these weird smelly concoctions. Within seconds, there was egg mixture everywhere – all across the floor and on the walls and the bed covers. 'Aaargh!' we screamed.

The other boys and I immediately jumped out of bed in the dark. We rushed down to the kitchen and grabbed pretty much everything edible that was left in the cupboards and fridge. In an instant we were little kids again. Now it was the girls' turn. They'd started it. We were out to get them.

We bombarded them with every bit of food we could get our hands on. Rice pudding flew across the living room. Baked beans were poured over each other's heads. It was absolutely fantastic, the best fun I'd had in ages. We totally let ourselves go.

OK, the walls of our bedroom smelled of egg for weeks afterwards and the living area never really recovered, but it was definitely worth it. It was such a great feeling to do something you would never normally do, even though it made a right awful mess.

After a couple of days of letting off steam, I began to tense up again. Friday's eviction was fast approaching and, as one of the nominees, I had to prepare myself for the possibility that the public would vote me out of the house.

I tried to look on the positive side. If I left the house, at least it meant I'd be seeing my mum, Rob, Bev and my nieces, because if you were up for eviction, your family would be outside to meet you. Little did I know that, after the confrontation with Nick, the tide of public opinion had begun to flow my way. I thought that there was every chance I might be evicted, but Channel 4 obviously thought not. They hinted to Bev that she needn't bother bringing the entire family down to greet me outside the house.

I was incredibly nervous as the live show began. Nichola and I sat together, holding hands tightly. We were wearing our eviction outfits and our bags were packed and ready.

Davina said, 'Hello, *Big Brother* house, this is Davina. You are live on Channel 4, please do not swear. The next person to leave the *Big Brother* house is . . .' There was a deadly silence for what must have been fifteen seconds.

Will I go or won't I? I wondered. The silence stretched out. Oh God, just get on with it, please! I cuddled Nichola and squeezed her hand.

'. . . Nichola!' Davina cried.

Yes! I thought, exhaling loudly. Relief washed over me. My heartbeat slowed. I had made it through to fight another week.

I was up for eviction every week after that. Although I desperately wanted to win *Big Brother*, sometimes I half hoped that I would be voted out. On the other hand, with every eviction I survived, I felt more and more like a winner. I'd already achieved a lot by getting into the house in the first place, so I felt proud of myself as I came nearer to surviving the whole nine weeks.

On Day 37, a new housemate arrived in Nick's place. This was 25-year-old Claire Stratton, a florist from Gerrards Cross. Claire and I soon became good friends, but sadly she was voted out of the house thirteen days later. Claire was a breath of fresh air and I kind of fancied her, too. She was always smiling and laughing and we had such a great laugh together. I missed her when she went. Tom had gone the week before and after Claire went Mel. I was sad to see them all go. I genuinely liked them all.

The power of editing is such that it can make anyone look really bad if the executive editors want it to, and in Mel's case it apparently did. It's true that she liked to have a little bit of a flirt, but there's nothing wrong with that. She had kissed two of the lads: first Andrew, and then Tom after Andrew had left. But so what? I have no idea why this was frowned upon, but it was, and the editing reflected that. I personally thought Mel was a lovely, respectful person and by far the most sensible girl in the house. She was great company and not at all the slapper they made her out to be.

Mel's departure left Darren, Anna and me: the three finalists. The house suddenly felt empty. The three of us rattled around. It was quite a lonely time and I found it hard to stay level-headed. All we could think about was the end result. I thought Darren would win as I was sure he would come across as a like-able fella, always cooking for the other housemates and talking about his children and what a good dad he was. I wasn't sure whether Anna or I would come second, but it was fantastic to know that I was in the final three and would be in the house for the full duration of the show.

Time limped along even more slowly than ever in that final week. There were hours and hours of silence. At least Big Brother was much easier on us. We were set loads of discussion tasks to keep the three of us together and talking to one another, just so that there would be some footage to put out every night on the highlights show. However, we didn't really want to talk. We'd more or less covered everything that we wanted to cover. Nothing seemed interesting.

It sometimes got to the point where we didn't have the energy to say anything at all. We felt totally lethargic and frequently dozed off. Occasionally I tried to think up something worthwhile to talk about that we hadn't already discussed, but then I'd decide that it wasn't worth the bother of trying to rouse the others. Once again I wondered how on earth anyone could make a TV show out of what was going on. I think the producers must have really struggled in that final week.

Eventually the last day arrived. The final hour, and then I would be free. Or so I thought.

10

Threats and Promises

It had been a long, hot summer. England had been knocked out of Euro 2000 in the group stages. The Olympics in Sydney had come and gone. Audley Harrison had boxed for Britain and won a gold medal and Steve Redgrave had won his fifth. Now the country was in the middle of a fuel strike.

But it was *Big Brother* that had made the biggest impact of all on the British public during the summer of 2000. As well as making television history and breaking viewing records, it was a massive cultural phenomenon. The whole country was talking about it.

This may sound silly, but I felt as if I'd missed out! Unlike everyone else, I hadn't avidly watched *Big Brother*, read about it and discussed it for weeks on end. Until I finally got out of the house, I had no idea that anyone was even watching it.

In the weeks and months that followed, thousands of people stopped me in the street all over the country to tell me how they loved the programme. They were addicted to it, they said. Letters poured in to Channel 4 from people saying how depressed they were that the show had ended, because they'd loved it so much. Now they had nothing to watch!

Despite my involvement in the first series, in the years to come *Big Brother* was never my cup of tea. I only ever watched it if I was getting paid to comment on it so it became a job to watch it. However, all that changed in early 2007, when I was given the opportunity to spend some time behind the scenes of the notorious *Celebrity Big Brother 5*, which included Jade Goody and Shilpa Shetty among the housemates. This was a real turning point for me. I glimpsed a different side to the show altogether and became totally fascinated by it. Now I understood.

It was January 2007 and I had just been interviewed by Dermot O'Leary for *Celebrity Big Brother's Little Brother*. 'Would it be OK to have a little nose around the camera runs surrounding the *Celebrity Big Brother* house?' I asked a producer.

Since it was just a little way across the studios, he agreed to give me a tour. 'But you know what it's like, Craig. You've got to be as quiet as possible!'

It felt very strange to creep along the camera runs behind the walls, spying on people. I mean, you wouldn't dare to go looking through people's living-room windows, would you? You wouldn't eavesdrop on private conversations! No, you wouldn't dream of it, because you've been brought up to think that sort of thing is wrong.

And it did feel as if I was doing something very wrong as I

furtively tiptoed along the narrow hidden corridors of the house, peeping into rooms, spying on the celebrity housemates. It felt especially strange when I found myself behind the mirror in the girls' bedroom, where a load of women were standing around in their underwear, getting ready!

Of course, weird as it felt, I wasn't actually doing anything wrong. The whole world could have been watching online if they had wanted to. There's live streaming pretty much all the time now on these shows.

Then suddenly my heart skipped a beat. It had actually been me in there once! I had been back to my *Big Brother* house and explored behind the scenes in the days after I'd left, but that wasn't the same as seeing the minute-by-minute action in close-up from behind the mirrors. However, it was only then, at the *Celebrity Big Brother* house, that I realized what a huge operation *Big Brother* was. There were cameramen all around me filming, sound engineers recording every noise and lots of producers and editors deciding what to put it in the highlights show for the country to watch.

Listening in to people's conversations was a really guilty pleasure. Chris Moyles from Radio 1 had told me about the times he came down to the house. 'Sometimes the housemates think they're having a secret little whisper and they're not!' he'd said. Now I could see exactly what he meant.

It still felt a bit seedy, but it was fascinating to overhear what the housemates were saying to one another. At one point I came across Dirk Benedict, Face from the *A-Team*, and Jermaine Jackson from the Jackson 5 having a chat about life in America. I stayed behind the window for about an hour, captivated by their views on the way the US media works. They were putting the world to rights. It was particularly interesting when they discussed how they themselves were portrayed in the press, because they've spent their lifetime in the public eye. I was so enthralled that I could have sat there all day. But then things turned weird when Jade Goody started rowing heavily with Shilpa Shetty.

I met Dirk Benedict a year later in 2008 and he gave me his view on the Jade/Shilpa saga, and it was different to the media take on it. I was interested to hear what he had to say, because I'd got to know Jade a couple of years previously and had formed my own (not exactly favourable) opinion after living and working with her in a house for a Channel 5 programme called *Back to Reality* in 2004.

Dirk said that it was clear from the start that the two women would clash because they both wanted to win so much. Of course everyone wanted to win, but Jade and Shilpa were on a mission and saw each other as rivals. According to Dirk, Shilpa could give as good as she got and was perfectly able to wind Jade up if she wanted. He thought that she should have known what was going on. Jade, on the other hand, was foolish enough to react, and she exploded.

Watching from behind the scenes brought back all kinds of memories for me. I thought back to the day after I had won *Big Brother*, when I went back to the house for the press conference. The day before, I had been desperate to leave, never to return, but going back was unexpectedly OK, because I was no longer trapped in there.

The house already looked different by then, even if it still stank of old food. The majority of the cameras had been taken down, the windows had been taken out and the furniture removed. What struck me most of all was that the atmosphere was completely dead. All the tension, anxiety and irritation had disappeared along with the housemates. Weirdly, it felt like a long time since I'd last been there, even though it was less than twenty-four hours.

I did an interview in the garden with Claudia Winkleman and after that I was caught up in a huge whirlwind of press and media events. I barely managed to catch my breath for days, weeks, months even. The moment I left one place, I was instantly rushed to the next.

Life became so hectic that I didn't even get to see my family. I kept saying that I wanted to go to them, but security insisted it wasn't possible. After four days, they'd had so much hassle with the press at their hotel that they decided to go back home without me. I, on the other hand, didn't go home for ninety-seven days.

Some housemates complained that they weren't looked after when they left the house. But for me, the aftercare was fantastic. Peter Bazalgette took care of everything I needed. This included new clothes, because the gear I'd had in the Big Brother house was pretty mangled. Bazal Productions also organized food, hotels, cars, security: you name it, it was covered; I had to move hotels every night to avoid the crowds and press.

I started panicking after a few days, though. The hotel rooms were so swanky that I knew they must be costing thousands of pounds a night; I had bodyguards surrounding me everywhere

I went; we had a lovely Mercedes to transport me around and a people carrier for the security and luggage. I was living the lifestyle of a rock star. Hang on a minute, I thought. Who's paying for this?

I kept on at Neil Higgins, the head of security. 'Don't worry, it's not your problem,' he assured me, again and again.

By now I had been introduced to Keith Woodall, who was proposing to be my agent. Overly friendly from the moment we met, he reminded me of a rep or a pushy salesman. He was the kind of man who stands too close to you when he's speaking to you. 'Offers for work are coming in thick and fast, Craig, my friend,' he said. 'This is a very exciting time for you. There are all kinds of weird and wonderful opportunities coming your way.'

He gave the impression that these opportunities were somehow linked to him. As my agent, he explained, he would sift through all the proposals, negotiate the best deals for me and make all the arrangements. For this he would take a very small percentage of my earnings.

I found it hard to concentrate on what he was saying. There was already so much going through my mind and I was still struggling to take in everything that had happened. I had been out of the house for less than forty-eight hours and had hardly had a wink of sleep. The past two days had been a mad round of interviews, chat-show appearances, awards and photo shoots. It felt as if I hadn't stopped talking since I'd left the house.

Now I was in my hotel room with Keith, supposedly having a break. He took a sheaf of papers out of his briefcase.

'How about you read this and sign it?' he said, smiling warmly.

'Why, what is it?' I asked.

'It's an exclusive three-year agreement to secure me as your agent,' he said. 'And, mate, you'll definitely be needing me if you're interested in all these opportunities I've been telling you about. I can assure you of that.'

I wasn't sure of anything. Sitting down, I picked up the contract and started trying to read it. Long legal-sounding words in bold black type swam in front of my eyes. I looked up at Keith and blinked at him exhaustedly. 'I'm sorry, but to be honest, I just can't take this in,' I said. 'I'm trying to read it, but I don't understand half the terms in here, plus this is an industry I know nothing about.'

'No worries! It's a fairly standard contract,' he said. 'Just sign it. You don't really need to understand it all . . .'

However, after what had happened with John Watson and the policies with Liberty Life, I wasn't taking any chances. Once bitten, twice shy, as they say. These days I had a solicitor. He was one of my customers in Newport and he worked in a local, family-run business.

'Could you forward this to my solicitor?' I said, handing it back to him. 'If you send it on to him and he's happy with it, fine. All I need is a phone call from him to say yes and I'll sign it straight away.'

Keith pushed the contract back into my hands. 'That's not how it goes, I'm afraid,' he said. 'Think of all that work I'm offering you, Craig! You're the one losing out if you don't sign, not me. But perhaps you don't want to be on television any more? Perhaps you don't want to earn hundreds of thousands of pounds? Maybe you just want to go back to your building sites in Shropshire?'

'Well, I'm very happy to go back to building,' I said. 'That's what I thought I'd be doing when I got out of the house. But I'm also very interested in what you're saying and all the offers you've mentioned. Of course I'd like to earn a nice lot of money! However, no matter what you or anyone else says, I won't sign anything before I understand what it is I'm signing. So if you'll just show it to my solicitor, I'm sure this will all be sorted out within a day or two.'

'Trust me here, Craig!' he said. 'This is a once-in-a-lifetime opportunity, mate. Just sign the contract.'

'I will, but only when my solicitor's seen it,' I said again.

'OK, let's talk about this tomorrow,' he said impatiently, stuffing the contract back into his briefcase.

It seemed really strange. Why wouldn't he let me OK it with my solicitor? I thought back to what Tom McDermott had said on stage two nights previously: 'F*** Keith Woodall off!' I wished I could call Tom and ask him what exactly he'd meant by that. But I didn't have his number and I didn't have a phone to call him with.

'I need a phone,' I said. But I wasn't allowed one, or so said Keith. Having a phone would jeopardize my upcoming deals with the press, he said, or something to that effect. It was important that I stayed out of contact, even from my family and friends, in case a story leaked. 'You mustn't speak to anyone!' he said. 'Trust me; it's the only way to get a big-money exclusive with one of the newspapers for your story.'

I didn't understand it, but I accepted it. My life was so mad, so chaotic and surreal at that point that I just went along with what I was being told. It was like living in a dream or a fairytale: perhaps the bubble would burst if I didn't go along with the plan.

My mission in that first week was to capitalize on the publicity I had already generated. I wanted to do everything I possibly could to raise more funds for little Joanne's operation. I had already given my £70,000 prize money to my solicitor in Shropshire to put into a trust fund account, but we needed a hell of a lot more to reach the £250,000 goal.

The *Mirror* got right behind us and ran a very successful front-page campaign. People started sending in donations: the pounds turned into hundreds and then into thousands. The *Mirror* trust fund alone raised more than £17,000. Then there were a few big hitters: Peter Bazalgette even pledged to match my £70,000 with £70,000 of his own. I was astounded by his generosity and couldn't stop thanking him. As the days passed, we got closer and closer to our target.

I was thrilled when Sir Richard Branson presented me with a cheque for £10,000. I thought he was one of the coolest people I'd ever met. 'I read your book while I was in the house!' I told him excitedly. He seemed really pleased that I'd liked it.

'I have to apologize to you, because I didn't manage to see much of *Big Brother*,' Sir Richard said. He explained that he had been run off his feet recently; he was competing against Camelot to run the Lottery at the time. 'But my kids don't stop talking about it,' he added.

'In fairness, I haven't had a chance to see any of it myself!' I said. 'I've hardly slept this last week.'

'Well, maybe one day after this Lottery business has died down and you're less busy, we can sit down over a beer and watch it together!' he said. I would have really liked to take him up on the offer, but I think he was just being polite!

About five days after I came out of the house, I went on Chris Evans's breakfast show on Virgin Radio. For some reason, he had a tray of shots in front of him. We downed a couple during the show. I think there must have been a promotion on or something.

Like everyone else, Chris wanted to know how I'd managed to survive without sex in the *Big Brother* house.

As it turned out, it hadn't been as hard as I'd thought it would be. The first few weeks were the most difficult, but what could I do about it? The only remotely private place in the whole house was in the triangular cavity behind the door to the girls' bedroom.

'In fairness, Chris, it wasn't too bad,' I said. The red light went off in the studio and we went off air while a song played. He gave me a cheeky look, made a hand gesture and asked, 'Did you knock one out?'

'No, I didn't!' I said, laughing. 'There were cameras everywhere! It wouldn't have been possible.'

He gaped at me. 'You're telling me there was nowhere at all, not one place in that house where you could actually masturbate?'

'No,' I insisted. 'There was a camera in the shower and even right above the toilet!' I told him how I had studied the entire building and worked out that only place where the cameras couldn't see you.

We had a little laugh about it off air. When the red light went on and we were back on air, his opening line was, 'So, Craig, you've just been telling me where you could masturbate in the house without being seen by the cameras. Where was it?'

Now it was my turn to gape. 'I can't believe you just said that!' I said. I should have remembered who I was talking to. Chris Evans can get away with murder, can't he?

'Let's make this very clear,' I said. 'I didn't do what you're suggesting I did in the house, but if I had, there is only one place I think I could have actually done it without being seen.'

'Are you coming for a drink with us after the show?' Chris asked, off air. 'We finish at nine a.m.'

But I was due back at the *Big Brother* house to take part in a sponsored bike ride with Davina McCall and the members of Westlife. 'No, no, I can't drink any more!' I laughed, putting down my second jellied vodka shot. 'I've got to do a charity bike ride in a little bit.'

'How much in total do you need to reach your target?' he asked casually.

'A quarter of a million pounds,' I said.

'And how much have you got so far?'

'Well, I was told last night that we had about two hundred and two thousand.'

'So how much more do you need?'

'Fifty-odd thousand pounds,' I said.

He picked up a pen started writing out a cheque. Then he tore it out of his chequebook and slid it across the table to me. 'There you go,' he said.

I looked down at the cheque in astonishment. It was one of

his own personal cheques. The number in the amount box read 50,000. It took my breath away. I was dumbstruck.

'What do you want to say?' he asked.

'I'm speechless! You've just given me fifty thousand pounds!' I said. 'It's incredible. I need to tell Marion, little Jo's mum. I want to leave this studio right now and phone her to tell her that we've got the last fifty grand.'

He pressed a button. 'We've got Marion on the phone for you now, live on air,' he said.

The sound of Marion screaming for joy echoed through the studio. I could hear Jo too, yelling in delight. 'When are you coming home, Craig? We're missing you!' Jo shouted. She didn't really understand the scale of the money or quite what it was for, bless her.

I left the studio reeling. I had done it! Now little Jo could go to America if she needed to. She could have all the specialist care that she required and be treated by the best doctors in the best hospitals in the world. Her family had dreamed of this moment for so long! No more wacky stunts were needed to raise the money; no more collections on rainy days in Shrewsbury town centre; no more auctions. Joanne's health was still a worry, of course. But there was hope now, where before there had been nothing but anxiety.

During this week, the NHS also decided to revise their decision about treating Jo. She could have her operation in Birmingham, if she needed. This was great news for the Down's Syndrome Association, and for families with children with Down's. Jo's family was thrilled, although they still planned to take her to America when the time came, because they believed that was where the top surgeons were. In the event that Joanne for some reason didn't have the operation, it was agreed that the money would be distributed between charities generally connected with her, including children's and adult hospices, Down's syndrome charities and Alder Hey Hospital.

It was definitely time to celebrate and it just so happened that London Fashion Week was in full flow. It was also awards season, I think; there seemed to be some massive event in London every night and everybody wanted me along. But how could I go alone? Wouldn't it look a little lonely and pathetic if I turned up to all these red carpet events without a glamorous girl by my side?

Despite Keith's objections, the security firm made arrangements for my best friend Shelley to visit me the following day and she stayed with me for the next few weeks, accompanying me to a string of extraordinary and glamorous events. We laughed about our ten-year pact to get married and Shelley went on to tell me that the media had been calling on anyone who knew of her or her whereabouts to phone in to the papers and identify her, for a reward. How disappointed they would have been to find that our relationship was purely platonic now!

In the days that followed, we went to the Elle Style Awards and the TV Quick Awards, among others; at Julien MacDonald's catwalk show on 25 September, I was pictured holding up a million-pound dress covered with diamonds. I mixed with the likes of Jodie Kidd and Emma Bunton, Gail Porter, Frank Skinner, David Coulthard, Martine McCutcheon and Barbara Windsor. I also met David and Victoria Beckham.

'David voted for you every week,' Victoria told me. 'And if I wasn't already married, I would have come straight down to the studio on the night you won and asked you to marry me!'

How amazing! I thought. It was a world away from the monotony of the *Big Brother* house – and a million miles from Newport. I kept wanting to pinch myself to see if it was all really happening.

Everywhere I went, people knew my name. Every time I did a personal appearance, there would be a crowd waiting for me outside, waving banners and cheering me on. It was a strange kind of fame – a new kind of fame – because they all knew a lot about me personally. When you think about it, most famous people's profiles are made up of images and footage of them performing or posing for photos; you don't ever get to see them relaxing at home. In my case, however, the public had watched me every night, sitting around, just being myself. They didn't just think they knew me; they *did* know me.

I was constantly being photographed. The papers were full of stories about me. The second Sunday after I came out of the house, one of the security guys came into the bedroom wearing a long face. 'You're not going to like this, Craig,' he said.

I was on the front page of the *News of the World* again, but this time it was because an ex-girlfriend had sold a story about me. 'Britain may be short of fuel but Craig certainly isn't!' said the headline. There was a picture of me at a beach party in Jamaica, where I'd been on holiday some years previously. It wasn't a bad picture, actually, except for the fact that I was naked! But I couldn't really complain, as the article was basically flattering.

Shelley was pretty much the only ex-girlfriend who didn't sell a story about me. She was working for an airline at the time and her salary wasn't great, but she wasn't ever interested in talking about us publicly, even when she was offered £50,000. In her view, it could only ever be a stitch-up. There would probably be a catch or her comments would be twisted to imply something she didn't mean. I admired her for her integrity.

As the days passed and we moved from one top London hotel to the next, I became concerned all over again about the amount of money that was being spent on me. Keith Woodall said it didn't matter: I was going to be earning so much that this was peanuts. Neil Higgins kept repeating that it wasn't my problem. But I felt very strongly that it *was* my problem.

Finally, I told Neil that I urgently needed to see Peter Bazalgette to discuss it with him. So the next time we were in the area, we popped into the Bazal Productions office.

Peter soon calmed me down. 'Don't worry,' he said. 'The hotels and cars are there for your disposal. Use them as much as you want.'

'What about security?' I asked. 'How much does it cost? Do I pay for it and if I do, when do I pay for I?'

'We're paying for your security, Craig, and you can keep Neil and the others for as long as you want,' he said. It was really good of him and I left his offices feeling very relieved.

The situation with Keith Woodall, on the other hand, was becoming more and more difficult. It felt as if he was starting to bully me. He kept showing me all these lists and saying that he could make me X amount of money here and X amount there. 'We can get you eighty thousand to pose once for *Playgirl*!' he said. Apparently this was just one of the offers that had come in. Another proposal had arrived from a company that wanted to pay hundreds of thousands of pounds to put a bare-chested photo of me on the side of all their lorries.

'These ideas really do all sound weird and wonderful,' I said, laughing. 'Should I accept? I just don't know.'

'That's what your agent is for,' said Keith. 'If you just sign the contract, I'll get the ball rolling.'

'Please, Keith, I don't want to sign anything that my solicitor hasn't checked,' I said for the umpteenth time.

'You must, Craig. You must,' he kept insisting.

The next evening, he arrived at my hotel room with a gleam in his eye. 'The newspapers want your story and there's a huge amount of money on the table,' he told me. 'Sixty thousand pounds, maybe more.'

'OK,' I said, swallowing hard. I could hardly believe anyone would want to pay me such a huge amount of money just for an interview.

'All they want is half a day, an interview with you and some photographs.'

I swallowed my doubts. 'Right,' I said, clapping my hands. 'When do we do it?'

'Hang fire,' he said. 'Don't worry, I know what I'm doing.

Tomorrow the offer will go up. They're all bidding against each other now.'

Sure enough, the next day the offer went up to £70,000. 'Hold on,' he said again. 'Just wait.'

'Fine, you're the expert,' I said. Eventually the offer went up to £120,000.

'In the meantime, you must sign this, now. You must!' he insisted. Once again the contract came out.

Slowly he was wearing me down, first by dangling the jobs and the promises of money before me and then by insisting that I sign on the dotted line. 'No, please,' I pleaded. 'I don't understand it. Just send it to my solicitor.'

Things went from bad to worse. 'If you do not sign this by tomorrow morning, everything you see around you will be gone,' he snarled. 'You will be responsible for your own security, your own cars, your own hotels and your own itinerary. Do you understand me?'

I didn't like what I was hearing. When you're getting mobbed wherever you go, you don't want to be on your own. But I wasn't going to tolerate his bullying ways any longer. 'You appear to be threatening me,' I said. 'So I want you out of this room.'

He curled his lip and pointed a finger at me. 'You're stupid, Craig!' he yelled. 'You're going to regret this!'

'Maybe I will, but I won't be threatened,' I said. 'Get out now!'

He turned his back on me and strode out of the hotel suite.

Neil Higgins stepped into the room. 'I couldn't help hearing what you two were saying,' he said. 'Are you OK?'

'No, I'm not,' I said. 'I'm terrified. Keith has just said that you're all going to be gone in the morning and I'll have to go out on the street on my own.'

'No chance,' he said. 'He's got no right to say that. You won't be left on your own at all. I'll guarantee that, Craig. We'll speak to Channel 4 in the morning.'

What was I going to do? Things had seemed to be going so well, but could it all crash around me now? 'There is one thing,' I told Neil. 'When I saw Davina the other night, she told me to ring her straight away if I had any problems. Do you think she meant it?'

'We look after Davina,' he said. 'We can ring her house now if you want.'

It was worth a try. He lent me his phone and I rang Davina, who was outraged when I explained the situation. She immediately offered to introduce me to her agent, John Noel, the very next morning. I breathed a sigh of relief. It was a huge weight off my mind.

Whereas Keith Woodall had been promising me the world, John Noel told a different story altogether. He didn't say, 'I can make you millions!' Instead he simply said, 'What do you want out of it? Do you want it to last a few months and make a fast killing? Or do you want to make it last longer? Because if you can make it last a year or two, you might be able to make an ongoing career out of it.'

'I haven't thought about it. All I know is how to build houses,' I said. 'I'm a good builder. That's all I really know what to do.'

'OK, let's see if we can get you some regular TV slots doing some building work. Would you like that?'

'I'd love that! See what you can do.'

In my first four years with John Noel, he got me on about five hundred TV shows. Keith Woodall, meanwhile, was gradually dropped by many other housemates.

11

Living in a Whirlwind

3 October 2000

I'm back in Liverpool for a *Big Brother* book signing. A police escort has just driven me into the town centre. There are six bodyguards surrounding me and thirty-two stewards from Liverpool football ground have been called in to help get me in and out of the building through the back way. When I enter the shop a huge roar goes up. 'Craig! Craig! Craig!' There are crowds everywhere, jostling to get a look at me. I don't know whether to be excited or terrified.

The line of people wanting books signed seems to go on and on for ever. It's like an endless conveyor belt. It's a real buzz to meet everyone, however briefly. They're all being so complimentary about me! I'm getting a lot of kisses and people keep asking to have their photograph taken with me.

At least five hundred of them have said, 'Craig, did you get the letter I sent you?'

I don't know what to say. My mail is going mostly to Channel 4, where it's being opened and vetted. After that it's going to be forwarded to John Noel and I'll get to see it, but I can't explain all of this to every person who asks me. I'd be here for years if I did that. So I say, 'Yes I did, thanks very much, cheers! I'll be writing back in due course.' Then I sign their book and it's the next person's turn.

A couple of really strange people have come along – they cling on and don't want to let go, and then bombard me with question after question – but it's nothing too scary. There's a nice atmosphere in the store.

Now the signing is finished. There's no easy exit. The streets are jammed with people. Eventually I leave with a ring of security guards around me. A helicopter takes me to the airport and I fly straight over to Belfast, where the whole thing happens all over again.

The next day's headlines say it all: 'IT'S CRAIGMANIA AT *BIG BROTHER* LAUNCH – THOUSANDS CHEER CRAIG – OH BROTHER! It was just like the days of Beatlemania. Thousands of screaming teenagers . . . Liverpool's Church Street packed to bursting . . . All to give TV's *Big Brother* winner Craig Phillips a rousing welcome home.'

The article in the *Liverpool Echo* went on to say that I had caused chaos in the centre of the city as thousands of people tried to catch a glimpse of me. An elderly lady had even been caught up in the mayhem and collapsed, poor thing.

'Crowd-safety stewards struggled to keep control of the hundreds of hysterical youngsters waiting outside the WH Smith's store,' the article reported.

Apparently, the crowds had been gathering since morning and the queue was over 150 metres long. At one point the police were considering calling it off.

10 October 2000

I'm in a dressing room at the Royal Albert Hall getting my make-up done for the National Television Awards. On my left is Sir Cliff Richard. Cliff and I are talking via the dressing-room mirror, because we can't turn our heads while we're being made up.

We're chatting about my experiences in the *Big Brother* house. Cliff is being ever so nice and polite. I can't help admiring how lovely and young the skin on his face looks. While we chat, I think about the rumours that he's had plastic surgery. He's always denied it, hasn't he?

As Cliff asks me how I managed to stay sane in the house, my gaze slips down to his neck. From where I am sitting the contrast between his face and neck looks striking; his neck seemed to be quite lined and a different texture.

I try to tear my eyes away, but they keep returning to Cliff's neck. Suddenly Barbara Windsor comes into the dressing room. Oh my God, she's brought Lulu with her! I've already spoken to Barbara because we're about to present an award together; now I'm bowled over to meet Lulu, who wants to chat about my boxers. Apparently, she's seen clips of them on *Big Brother*.

What a strange life I'm living! I chat away to Lulu, Barbara Windsor and Cliff Richard about my dogs. They seem to know quite a bit about me, which is nice and flattering. But what shall I ask them about? Luckily, they fire questions at me about *Big Brother*, so I don't have to try too hard. None of them are big fans of the programme, but they all admit that after watching it for a while, you do get hooked.

An hour later, I'm standing at the top of a staircase above the Royal Albert Hall stage. Barbara walks across to join me. We've been briefed to pause for two or three seconds, so the cameras get a shot of us while the audience applauds. Then we're to walk slowly down the stairs and across the stage, as Sir Trevor McDonald introduces us.

We've got thirty seconds to go. I'm buzzing. I can't wait to get out there and do my stuff. Suddenly Barbara squeezes my hand and gives me a hug.

'After fifty-one years, I'm still shitting myself before I go out there!' she whispers.

'What?' I say. It's so hard to believe. She's the consummate professional and I'm the rank amateur, but she's the one who is terrified. Later she says to me: 'Television is a lovely industry to be in when you don't need it.'

I remember these words to this day. It's only now that I realize how very true they are.

A few days later

I am still in a complete whirlwind, so it's helpful that the aftercare set up by Bazal Productions includes the chance to check in with Brett Kahr, the psychiatrist. He's been assigned to speak to me every week. Sometimes he comes to my hotel; more often I speak to him on the phone.

'What have you done this week?' he asks.

'Where do I start?' I say, listing some of the highlights.

'How does it make you feel when people are telling you how much they love you?' he says. 'What's it like to share the stage with Barbara Windsor at the Royal Albert Hall?'

I pause to think about it. 'To be honest, it doesn't seem to be affecting me,' I tell him. 'I can see it all, hear it all and taste it all, but for some reason I'm not getting all that excited about any of it, not like I imagine some people might if they were in my position.'

'It's still a case of delayed reactions,' he says. 'All these things will hit you at another time. They'll catch up with you in the end.'

He's right. Everything is on time delay, because it's so rushed. I'll be sitting in the car a week after something has happened and think, Bloody hell, was I really there? Did I say that? Did they do this? Was all that around me? How fantastic! Then, just as I'm starting to have my own little moment about it, I'm hurrying off to do something else totally amazing, something that overrides the memory of the previous experience. And because these things are happening morning, noon and night, I don't have the chance to digest and appreciate them properly. Ideally, I'd like to take my time, to indulge and enjoy some of the experiences I'm having. But there isn't time. It's all about now. This is life in the fast lane.

Looking back, nearly ten years later, I realize that I've never felt as lonely in all my life as I did in the months after *Big Brother*. It's hard to explain, because from the outside it seems impossible. How can you be lonely when you're surrounded by people, you're so popular and everyone loves you? People were nice to me wherever I went; they complimented me left, right and centre on TV and radio shows. Studio audiences of three hundred or four hundred people were giving me standing ovations. Yet I felt lonely. Even with Shelley there, even when I had other friends along with me. It was very strange.

Don't get me wrong; I was having a brilliant time. But you are obviously going to feel alone when something is happening to you and only you. Before *Big Brother*, ordinary people hadn't ever become so famous, so quickly, simply by appearing on television. No one else had experienced it at the time; no one else knew what it felt like. There was no one to share it with, so I was the only one who could absorb it, deal with it, feel it and enjoy it. That came on top of all the mixed emotions that come with suddenly being recognized by everyone, which was exciting and nerve-racking at the same time.

It wasn't necessarily my choice. Yes, I signed up to go on a TV programme, but *Big Brother*'s phenomenal success set a precedent and I wasn't prepared for it. Channel 4 hadn't expected it; neither had Endemol. No one knew it was going to happen.

Having security around me contributed to the feeling of isolation; they wouldn't let anyone near me. As much as I got on with all the security guards – we actually became very good friends and still keep in close contact now – I'm not soft, I knew they were with me because they were being paid to be there. They were just doing their job.

My life and self-image changed in other ways. Before I went on *Big Brother* I was fairly confident in myself. It would be fair to say that I was quite vain, too. I worked out and looked after myself, used creams and gels on my hair, bought nice clothes and tried to make myself look good.

But then a funny thing happened: when I came out of the house, I stopped caring about my looks. I think this was because there were pictures all over the newspapers of me with no clothes on; there was footage of me running around the house in the nude; there were endless clips on TV where I was farting and burping and eating noisily. I quickly realized that the whole of Britain had seen every side of me: dressed and undressed; animated and half asleep – even walking in my sleep; happy and laughing; upset and angry; and so on.

Who cares what you look like? I thought. You'd expect a builder who suddenly became famous to take a lot more care of his hair and skin and body and clothes. But I went the other way. It was really strange.

'I'm turning up to appear on TV shows without bothering about how my hair looks,' I told Brett Kahr. 'But a couple of years ago, I'd go to a nightclub and look in the mirror ten times to check my hair was all right!'

He couldn't work it out. 'That's interesting,' he said. 'Most people would probably react differently and become more vain and self-conscious of their looks – to a point where they would be panicking about whether they looked good or not.'

Maybe it was because everywhere I went there were hundreds of people screaming and shouting my name and saying they loved me. The thousands of compliments gave me confidence, whether they came from radio presenters or people who stopped me in the street. The public seemed to love me and everything about me on *Big Brother*, so perhaps I didn't have to worry about what I looked like any more.

To my amazement, I had beautiful girls throwing themselves at me. It was unbelievable: models, pop stars and TV presenters were giving me their phone numbers and asking me to their parties. I was very flattered. How could anyone not be?

I was so grateful that Shelley stayed close and kept me company during the many weeks of havoc after I left the house, but it kind of became a problem, as Shelley was my best friend. We were sleeping together but we weren't sleeping together, if you know what I mean. Perhaps it was time for me to branch out.

'Shell,' I said to her one day. 'As you know, I haven't had sex since before I went into the *Big Brother* house. I'm getting kind of desperate and all these girls are throwing themselves at me, so do you mind giving me a bit of time alone? A man's got to do what a man's got to do . . .'

She laughed. 'OK, I understand.' She was a good sport about it and to this day we're the best of friends and we laugh about it regularly.

Just before Shelley left to go home, *OK!* magazine got wind of our friendship and contacted John Noel to offer her £50,000 for her story. It was huge sum of money, especially for someone earning a basic salary. Although I knew how much she distrusted the press, I tried to persuade her to do it.

'It won't be tacky like the other stories my ex-girlfriends have sold,' I assured her. 'The press office at John Noel will organize it and we'll have full control over what they write about us.'

But she was adamant. She had seen what had happened when my other ex-girlfriends had sold stories to make a few quid. It had backfired on them. They'd been conned by journalists who had edited their words to distort their meaning.

'I can't trust the press and I don't want people knowing about our time together. It's personal,' she said. I had to respect her decision; I admired her for it.

After she went home, I started dating a bit. Life was so fast-moving that it wasn't really possible to have a steady girlfriend, but I met some lovely women and had loads of fun. I was pictured with quite a lot of different girls. I remember one full centre-page spread that speculated about whom I would be dating next. There were pictures of me chatting to about six different celebrity girls, and there was one photo in which it looked as if I was half kissing Emma Bunton. Newspapers'll do anything to fill space!

One evening at a glitzy awards do, a young Irish guy came up to me, introduced himself as Brian, and said how much he admired me for what I'd done for Joanne. 'Listen, if we can do anything to help raise money, we'd be happy to. We could produce or sing a song to support your campaign, perhaps?' He seemed very polite, well spoken and genuinely keen to help.

'Thanks very much for your offer, it's lovely. What did you say your name was? Do you have a business card? What company are you from?'

'No, I don't!' he said. 'I'm Brian McFadden from Westlife!'

I apologized frantically while the security guys doubled up laughing next to me. We swapped numbers and stayed in touch.

Brian was going out with Kerry Katona at the time, so I hung around with them and the other members of Westlife and Atomic Kitten. When they weren't working, they partied – hard – which was good fun. We went to glamorous clubs and hotels and afterwards it was often back to someone's big hotel suite to continue the party.

Initially I didn't feel at home. Frankly, I was overawed. After all, I wasn't a pop star; I was a Scouser builder. But everyone made me feel really welcome. They accepted me like another celebrity and trusted me not to betray their privacy. It was intimidating at times and a real eye-opener, but I came around to seeing it as just part of the journey of my life.

One night at an awards ceremony we were all joking around quite drunkenly when a paparazzo photographer caught us out. He snapped a picture of me pretending to kiss Kerry, but in the photo it looks as if I really am kissing her. The next picture was of Brian pretending to punch me. Again, we were only joking around. But of course, the photos were splashed across the papers the next day!

Afterwards we went back to Brian's suite for a big old party. Loads of famous people were there, from Ant and Dec to Michael Barrymore. I was made up to meet Michael Barrymore, because I'd always admired him when I was younger, and it was a pleasure to meet those sorts of people in a private environment, as opposed to at an awards ceremony.

Some of the famous people I met fell short of my expectations, some came up to the mark and some exceeded them. Robbie Williams was in the last category. I enjoyed meeting him so much. He's got this charisma about him: when he walks into a room he lights the place up and everybody stops and stares, open-mouthed. He's also a tremendously nice person and we had some good conversations.

It was interesting to compare our situations. At the time we first met we were both household names, but whereas Robbie had spent ten years building up his career until he was as big as he could possibly be, being famous had never been my aim. It just happened by default while I was trying to raise money for Joanne's operation. This made me feel a bit of a fraud, as though I hadn't earned my fame. Still, there was nothing I could do about it.

One evening at an awards ceremony, Robbie introduced me to his mum. Jan Williams was really, really sweet to me. 'How is your mum coping with your fame, Craig?' she asked me.

'Well, she seems all right,' I said, 'but I'm not getting that much time with her. Still, I speak to her on the phone a lot and tell her where I am and what I'm doing.'

'I'd love to have a chat with her, just to see if she's OK,' Jan said.

'Would you?' I said. 'That would be great!'

I was so grateful to her. After all she'd been through with Robert, as she calls him, and with her understanding of the highs and lows of his career, there was no one more experienced from a mother's perspective to advise another mother. We continued to chat over dinner and afterwards she said, 'Give me your mum's number and I'll give her a call.'

I phoned my mum later and told her to expect a call from Robert Williams's mum. She didn't catch on that it was Robbie Williams, the singer, and I thought I'd leave it that way, because

I didn't want her to start panicking because she was talking to a superstar's mother. So she had no idea who Jan was talking about when she rang and said, 'You know, my Robert's been very successful and I know what it's like to have a famous son.' They spoke a number of times after that, which was nice for both of them, I think.

Mum and Bev weren't affected by my fame at all; they were always supportive. But I think they may have been worried for me because it was a big change of lifestyle. You often read in the papers about people going off the rails the moment they get a taste of fame, money or power. All of a sudden they can't control themselves.

I was twenty-eight when I won *Big Brother*. At that age, I was pretty stable and focused. I knew who I was and where I was going, so being in the limelight and earning lots of money was really just a bonus for me. It was relatively easy to keep calm about it.

It must have been harder for someone such as Billie Piper to handle, because money and success came her way when she was so much younger. When I became friends with young Billie, she was more grown up than she had been and admitted that fame is more difficult to handle when you're young. On the other hand, I was fortunate enough to have been running a company for eight years and knew how important every pound was.

Although the media interest in me was never again as fevered as it was in the week after I left the *Big Brother* house, the interview requests were still coming in thick and fast. 'Chris Moyles wants you on his afternoon show,' John Noel told me.

Top: The last in and the last out. Here I am waving goodbye to my family and friends. In front of me are the nine other housemates I am about to meet, July 2000.

Left: Sixty-four days later, I emerge victorious with Davina, as Britain's first *Big Brother* winner.

Inset: Picking up a *TV Quick* award in 2001. This was for Best Live TV Moment of the Year, when I came out of the *BB* house to tell Joanne Harris I'd give her my prize money towards the cost of her operation.

Top: Walking out with Jo to 45,000 cheering Liverpool fans at Anfield was an exhilarating experience that I'll never forget. We were there to raise more money for Jo's appeal but also had a great day meeting all the players.

Middle: Sharing a joke with Sir Richard Branson as he pledged £10,000 towards Joanne's appeal.

Bottom: Chris Evans stunned me live on national radio with his generosity, donating the final £50,000 needed to reach Jo's target amount . . . and filled me with vodka jelly shots at six in the morning in the process!

Above: It's not every day you have dinner with the Beckhams; they were lovely. I still can't believe what Victoria told me – that if she wasn't already married, she'd have come down to the studio the night I won *BB* and asked me to marry her!

Top right: Presenting a style award to Steven Gerrard in 2008 at the Liverpool Fashion Awards. He's a quiet guy off the pitch and I respect him and Jamie Carragher tremendously.

Right: Presenting a Breathing Life award with Barbara Windsor at the Royal Albert Hall in 2000 was great fun.

Below: Bev's proudest moment, with me and Robbie Williams at the after-show party following his swing concert at the Royal Albert Hall in 2001. Robbie and I get on well and so do our mums.

Left: With the lovely Linda Robson on *Renovation Street*, my first TV DIY show, in November 2000.

Below: Anna Nolan and I went head to head again, this time on *Celebrity Ready Steady Cook*. I went on to work with James Martin on hundreds of live BBC *Housecall* shows.

Left: Wearing my trusty toolbelt with Scottish design duo Colin and Justin on *Trading Up*. We've filmed hundreds of shows and performed live exhibitions together over the years throughout Europe.

Below: A promo shot taken in my Shropshire workshop for BBC's *Big Strong Boys*, with co-presenters yachtswoman Debra Veal and ex-footballer Stewart Castledine.

Above left: One of my many TV guest appearances (this one wasn't fun, though) on *The Weakest Link*. Not because of the questions – I did OK – I just didn't like Anne Robinson!

Above right: With Avid Merrion on one of the few occasions he let me out of his cupboard, at the launch of the *Bo' Selecta!* Christmas single 'Proper Crimbo' in London, 2003. I'm frowning as he had me handcuffed the whole time!

Below left: Boy, what a ride! On location with Andy Bennett about to film *Hung, Drawn and Quartered* for the British Forces Broadcasting Service.

Below right: Producing another show for the British Forces Broadcasting Service. Of all the forces challenges I've done across the world, the one with the Royal Marine Commandos was probably the hardest, on an icy winter's day in Faslane, Scotland, 2005. Never again!

Above: One of my first charity
ventures: pre-*Big Brother*,
shaving my hair to raise funds
for Joanne's operation in the
late 1990s. Our appeal was just
beginning . . .

Right: With beautiful
newsreader Kate Silverton,
fashion model Sinta
Soekadarova and weather
girl Andrea McLean as we
take part in a record-breaking
tandem skydive for the Cystic
Fibrosis Trust in Oxfordshire,
2003.

Why would anyone want to
jump out of an aeroplane that's
perfectly capable of landing?
For charity, of course!

Left: Dad's looking on: I launched the 'Think!' drink-drive campaign in 2000 by talking about my dad, and have since championed many drink-drive campaigns across the country. Here I am with panto pal Syd Little as we launch the 2005 Devon and Cornwall campaign in Torquay.

Right: Bev and I completed the gruelling London Marathon in just under 5 hours, raising £15,000 for the Downs Syndrome Association in 2001.

Below right: Comedian John Bishop, me, Kenny Dalglish, Gerry Marsden and my good friend Lord Mayor of Liverpool Steve Rotherham, celebrating the Superlambanana statue auction, which raised over half a million pounds for the Lord Mayor's Charity Appeal in Liverpool, 2008.

Below: Youngsters Ella and Sam Wright (both in need of bone-marrow donors) look on, whilst I try to raise awareness of their plight by diving with Europe's largest collection of sharks near Chester in 2007.

I've also met many members of the Royal Family. Here I am sharing a joke at a charity event at St James's Palace with Sophie, Countess of Wessex.

I've met Tony Blair on many occasions. Here I am voicing my views on construction education in Bolton, 2006.

13 January, 2006 was a very proud day for me as Cherie Blair and I at last formally opened my building skills centre in Aintree, Liverpool.

Some of the many guests who came to support the launch (*left to right*): Mark Moraghan, Dean Sullivan, Ricky Tomlinson, John Aldridge, actor/comedian Tony Barton and my BBC colleague Jake Robinson.

'He's a tough cookie – he rips into everyone – but I think you can handle it. If he gives you any jip, just get him in a headlock and show him who's the boss!'

I agreed to do the show but couldn't help feeling nervous beforehand. I'd been out of the house for six weeks now and I was expecting to get a real slaughtering. But it was great. Chris hardly gave me any stick. There was one bit I was slightly dubious about at first. It was a storyline about a house that contained ten Scousers – and all ten of them were called Craig. Using clips from the show, they had edited together a scenario in which I argued with myself, chatted myself up, and so on. But it was actually really funny, so I wasn't offended at all.

'Are you going to come out for a drink with us later?' Chris asked at the end of the show. I couldn't go that night because I was booked up somewhere else, but he gave me his mobile number and I caught up with him a few nights later.

We got on well and became quite good friends after that, and I went on to do some training with him in the mornings, running on Hampstead Heath. We also had a few nights out, including one time in Leeds with his mum, dad and brother, when we went to a church to see a private Travis concert that was being covered by Radio 1. Another one-off experience!

Before *Big Brother*, it didn't occur to me that one day I would become accustomed to meeting celebrities and pop stars, but I suppose it wasn't beyond the realms of my imagination. However, the idea of becoming a pop star myself was totally inconceivable, because I'm tone deaf and always have been.

So I couldn't help laughing when, a couple of weeks after I

was on *The Chris Moyles Show*, I got a call from John Noel. 'Can you sing?' he asked.

'Not really,' I said. It was an overstatement. Even my mum said I was a bad singer.

'You see, this proposal has come in from a songwriter connected with Liverpool. He's called Chris Anderson and he was one of the musicians on the Cher song "Believe". Now he's written a song for you and taken it to Warner Music, and Warner Music has come to me . . .'

In fairness, I wasn't too keen on the idea. I wasn't a singer and John had started to get some interest in me for DIY programmes, so it seemed a risky moment to go into something I knew nothing about. OK, in this day and age, everyone knows you don't have to be the best singer to record a song. The technology exists to make you sound better than you actually are. But it seemed a stretch for me.

'I'm not sure about this,' I told John.

Then he started going into the finer details. Apparently, they were proposing to sign me up to a £500,000 five-album deal. Well, that sounds appealing, I thought, gobsmacked.

They would pay me £47,000 to record the first single, they said. 'You can complete it in a day and we'll donate fifty per cent of the profits to the Down's Syndrome Association.' Even better. It seemed like a no-lose situation.

'Let's see what you sound like,' said the producer. So I went to a little studio and did a singing test. 'Sing higher, sing lower, lengthen your vowels,' the vocal coach told me. 'Mimic this,' he said, singing a line. I sang the line back to him. 'And this.' He sang another line. I sang it back. It didn't sound great.

'OK,' the producer said. 'We'll see what we can do with this recording and we'll let you know by the end of the day.' I didn't hold my breath. But to my surprise, he came back from the mixing room later and said, 'Yep, your voice is fine. We can get a song out of it.'

'Really? That's amazing!' I said. Bloody hell, I thought. I'm going to be bringing out a Christmas single!

The song was called 'At This Time Of Year'. Chris Anderson had sung a demo to give me an idea of the melody and tempo. It sounded good and the lyrics were OK too: 'At this time of year/Friends and lovers should be near . . .' It was nice and Christmassy. Of course, Chris Moyles and Comedy Dave went on to record their own version, which went: 'At this time of year/Chris and Dave drink lots of beer . . .'

It took a day and a half to record. For hours on end, I stood in a little recording booth with a sound engineer or voice coach as they demonstrated how the words should be enunciated, gently guiding me on the pitch of each individual note. First they sang a line and then I repeated it. Then they sang it again and I repeated it. I sang some of the lines as many as fifty times until they felt they were happy with it. It was exhausting!

It was November now, so we were cutting it very fine for releasing a Christmas single. To my surprise, the final song sounded great and I was very pleased with it. As soon as the single was recorded, mixed and mastered, there was a rush to shoot the accompanying video. The original plan was to shoot it in Lapland, but the record company changed the plan after a very heavy snowfall up in Fort William in Scotland. Instead we set off to Inverlochy Castle, an imposing nineteenth-century castle situated in the foothills of Ben Nevis and surrounded by stunning views. Inverlochy has been a popular shoot location over the years: the Spice Girls also made a video there and I'm sure I recognized it in the 2008 Marks & Spencer/Take That Christmas advert.

We took little Jo with us to appear in the video, so Marion came too. Both Jo and Marion had been having a brilliant time since *Big Brother* had ended. Joanne was now famous in her own right and loving every minute of it. Everyone in Shrewsbury wanted to chat and have their photograph taken with her; taxi drivers were constantly stopping to pick her and Marion up. What's more, she was coming with me to some weird and wonderful events and meeting the stars. She was in her element. Now here we were up in Scotland in the snow!

The idea for the video was to create a family atmosphere, so the director cast a wife for me, and a rainbow family of kids. The first shots show us all playing around in the snow and making a home video. Then we go inside to our lovely warm log fire. Next we're seen wrapping our presents in the evening and looking back at the home-video footage. All of this is interspersed with shots of me at the top of a snow-capped mountain singing my heart out.

It was a big operation. Slightly unnecessarily, they sent a stylist, a make-up artist and a hairdresser to get the look right. The stylist arrived all the way from London with about twenty-five different outfits for me to try on – and not one thing fitted me! She hadn't bothered to find out my measurements and seemed to assume that I'd be six foot four! Ironically, I ended up wearing the Christmas jumper that the director's nan had given him one year. It was a shocking affair, with a terrible black, white and red checked pattern on the arms. But what could I do? I had nothing else to wear, so when the director suggested it, I said, 'Yeah, whatever!' He was a nice guy, a good director; and at that point I was just doing what I was told.

Despite wearing a granny jumper, it was a great day for me. After a hectic two months, it was a real escape to be in a beautiful wintry environment, building snowmen and having snowball fights, all wrapped up lovely and warm, with kids climbing all over me. Unfortunately, it wasn't so much fun for little Joanne. She was fine inside the castle, but she had problems with her breathing outside because of the altitude.

When she started to struggle, Marion decided that Jo couldn't go up in the chairlift to where some of the outside scenes were being filmed at a higher altitude. Unfortunately, this meant that she wasn't going to be in half of the video. She was really upset. There were tears and it was horrible, especially when she had to go back to the castle with Marion and wait for us. No matter how often we reassured her, she was worried that she might not be in the video at all. It must have been so frustrating for her.

The next day, the location manager flew me up in a helicopter around the highland ranges. Our mission was to find a scenic mountaintop where I could stand and mime my song. As we flew along, he pointed out the different mountains and we discussed where would be the best spot to film. Meanwhile, the camera crew had taken away the whole side of another, much bigger, helicopter and built a big swivelling chair into it, so that a cameraman could hang out of it and film me.

It was a challenging shoot. Yes, the sky was lovely and blue above the cloud line and the mountains looked stunning, but it was really difficult for the helicopter to land. We had to hover 5 feet above the jagged peaks while I climbed out through the door on to the rail and then lowered myself down into the snow. What with the wind and the noise and force of the propellers above me, it was terrifying.

Since I didn't know how deep the snow would be when I jumped off the helicopter, I had a radio transmitter on me, just in case I sank without trace. Luckily, the pilot was very skilled. He managed to keep the helicopter nice and level until I let go of the rails. But it was a just small craft and I could feel it tilt a bit when I let go. For a moment, the blades came way too close for comfort. Jesus Christ, I thought. I don't want those hitting me!

Once I'd dropped into the snow, the pilot pulled back and headed off. I had to wait until he'd gone before I could start climbing up out of the powder, because the force of the propellers kept pushing me back down again.

Now I had to stand tall and pretend to sing. I had an earpiece piping the track into my ear and I mimed along while the helicopter containing the camera crew flew past and filmed me from different angles: quickly and slowly; above and below me. They were constantly wheeling around and coming back at another angle.

Once or twice the helicopters flew out of sight and I was totally alone on a mountain peak, in the still, silent air. It was stunning up there. Is this really me? I thought. Making a pop video? Flying around in a helicopter? Staying in a castle?

Standing on a mountaintop? Wow! I felt incredibly privileged.

Then I saw a little dot in the air coming towards me and getting bigger. 'Make it look like you're singing!' came a voice through the earpiece. The next time it was, 'Stand completely still and look away into the distance. Don't look at the helicopter or the camera!'

Believe me, it is very hard to stand still without wobbling while a helicopter bombs towards you, deafening you with its noise, and then shears through the air just above you! Your instinct is to fall to your knees in case it takes your head off.

'No, don't move!' they'd shout. 'Right, we're going to have to shoot that again. Stay standing up this time!'

'You come down here and try it!' I'd yell. It was incredibly scary!

'OK, go over there where there's less snow,' they'd say.

But as I made my way to where they were pointing, I'd sink up to my waist. 'Whoa, I'm not going any further in that direction!'

'OK,' they radioed back. 'We'll pick you up. Just make your way to the highest point and then we can get close to you.'

But then they'd have problems landing, so they would hover about four or five feet above me while I made desperate attempts to jump up to the rail and pull myself on board. It was like something out of a James Bond film! Yet despite the difficulties, it was a great experience and I loved every minute of it.

'At This Time Of Year' went silver on the first day it was released in mid-December, selling more than sixty thousand copies. It was in the charts for three weeks and got to number fourteen. Widely thought to be the best single that anyone from *Big Brother* has brought out, it still gets played around the Christmas period every year. It's even earned me some royalties by being on a Christmas compilation album.

Straight off, we were able to give £40,000 of the profits to the Down's Syndrome Association. We also did a photo shoot at a hotel in London and Damon Hill, whose son Oliver has Down's syndrome, collected the presentation cheque. I was really pleased.

Meanwhile, it was back to the day job for me – well, in a manner of speaking, anyway. A call came through to John Noel requesting me for a new DIY programme for ITV called *Renovation Street*. My TV career was beginning.

12

Fans and Building Plans

In the first few months after *Big Brother*, a lot of very successful people asked me, 'Are you having a good time?'

'Yeah, fantastic, I'm loving it!' I replied.

'Well, make hay while the sun shines, because it won't last for ever,' they all said.

Perhaps they didn't realize that they were bursting my bubble, but constantly hearing those words worried me. I was really enjoying life, so it was a downer to be constantly told it was all temporary. My heart would pound and I'd think, I'd better do something, quick!

Back in my hotel room, I'd give it more thought. Did I want this chaos and mayhem to last for ever anyway? It struck me that I was lucky to be having so many amazing experiences; when my life returned to normal, at least I could say that they had happened to me. Eventually, I decided to just enjoy the present and let the future take care of itself.

I didn't audition for *Renovation Street*. I got the call, turned up and did it. Linda Robson was the main presenter. She had a small team of builders who went into people's houses from Billericay to Watford to do niggling DIY jobs and sort out DIY dilemmas. The jobs were tiny: renewing work surfaces; retiling bathrooms; and building picket fences. I could do them with my eyes shut.

I was a builder-presenter on the show. On the first day, the producer asked, 'Craig, are you all right to mend this wall?'

'Yes, I was doing this sort of stuff ten years ago,' I assured him.

'And are you OK with a camera right in your face?'

'Well, I spent sixty-four days with twenty-eight cameras trained on me, so I think I probably am all right, yes!'

I wasn't intimidated at all. In fact, I felt totally confident and looked straight at the camera as I explained what I was doing.

The producer was really pleased. 'This is great!' he said.

I did about eight days' filming with Linda and her crew, but couldn't give them any more time because I had so many other commitments booked in.

My last day of filming was in London and that same evening I was due to mime 'At This Time Of Year' at the official ceremony to celebrate switching on the Liverpool Christmas lights. It was a huge honour. I thought back to how I had queued up as an excited kid to see the lights go on: it was one of the big Christmas highlights of my childhood.

For some reason, we couldn't get flights up to Liverpool, so Neil Higgins picked me up in a people carrier the moment I came off set and we bombed up the motorway to Liverpool.

This was to be the first time I would mime my song in public. But, hand on heart, I hadn't practised it once, not even in the mirror with a hairbrush! My non-stop schedule had got in the way and I didn't even know the lyrics by heart because I hadn't sung it all the way through. I tried not to think about what it would feel like to sing in front of ten thousand people. I had never sung in front of anyone in my life! As usual, I was going to have to wing it.

I didn't have time to get nervous. I'd been booked in to do fifteen phone interviews in the car during the journey, so I had to focus on speaking to journalists. Most of the interviews kicked off with the same question. 'So, Craig, what was it really like in the *Big Brother* house?'

'I haven't actually watched the show, so all I can do is build up an image of how it went,' I replied, every time I was asked this. Then I'd go on to explain that, from the thousands of interviews that I'd done and all the different accounts I'd been given, I had gleaned that most people saw life in the *Big Brother* house as exciting, with lots of fun and activity. However, my personal feelings were that, yes, we'd enjoyed ourselves and there were small amounts of drama, but for the vast majority of the time I was dead bored in there. I stressed that the public saw only the highlights, half an hour each day, so they didn't get the whole picture.

A couple of interviewers went for the jugular. 'Craig, you're not a singer and you can't sing, so why are you doing this?'

I never tried to kid anybody. At no point did I say, 'Hey, I can sing!' I was totally honest about how the project had come together, how I'd recorded the track and filmed the video.

People usually backed off when I explained that we were donating 50 per cent of the proceeds to charity and had already raised £40,000 for the Down's Syndrome Association.

After the fifteenth interview was done and dusted, I played my single on repeat inside the car and tried to memorize the words, singing into my phone in lieu of a microphone (or hairbrush). Needless to say, the security guards practically had their hands glued over their ears by the time we were getting near to Liverpool!

The security phone rang persistently. 'Where are you?' Liverpool City Council needed to know when I was going to arrive. It was time to switch on the lights, but we were still twenty minutes away from the city on the M62. 'Don't worry,' someone said. 'Atomic Kitten have just agreed to sing another couple of songs.'

Just off the motorway, a police escort was waiting to take us through the city by the fastest route, surrounded by police motorbikes, jumping red lights, blue lights flashing. It was a huge buzz. We went so fast that I became disorientated and couldn't even work out which part of Liverpool we were in!

Finally we arrived down at the docks. A pair of big gates opened up and we sped in to the backstage area. Now it hit me. Oh God, I've got to mime the song now! I jumped out of the people carrier. Instantly, a mass of security people surrounded me. They rushed me up on stage before I had a chance to say hello to any of my friends and family, who were waiting at the side of the stage.

'Hi, how're you doing?' I said to a crowd of ten thousand cheering people.

The reply was deafening.

There was a local radio DJ on the stage. 'You do know that you're late, don't you?' he said genially. 'We held everything up for twenty minutes because we knew you were en route.'

'I'm sorry,' I said sheepishly. 'I got here as quick as I could. Thanks very much for waiting, everybody.'

'You're going to sing your new Christmas song for us, aren't you?'

'That's right,' I said. The crowd roared again.

'But first, it's time to turn on the lights! Ten, nine, eight, seven, six, five, four, three, two . . .

'*One!*'

The Lord Mayor of Liverpool, Paul Gascoigne, the members of Atomic Kitten, Claire Sweeney and I gathered around a big mock-up switch in the middle of the stage and pressed it. Fireworks exploded and the crowd went mad. The Liverpool City Centre Christmas lights were officially on! It was absolutely brilliant.

Next, I sang my song and I think it went OK. No one complained, anyway! The way I see it, when you're thrown in the deep end, you've got a choice: either sink or swim. In such a situation, I always make myself swim.

It's a question of confidence – and I'll always be grateful, yet again, to the two Johns for helping to build my confidence. At the butcher's shop, I learned that if you sell yourself, you can sell whatever else you're selling around you, whether it's a product, a material – or a song.

Fantastic and funny things were happening every day around

this time. But it was also when I discovered a much darker side to fame.

I still hadn't had a chance to read any of the letters that people had been sending in to Channel 4, but I knew they were arriving and I was planning to acknowledge them in writing as soon as I could. One fan was very seriously disappointed by the delay, however. She had met me at the *Big Brother* book signing in Liverpool, asked me if I had received her letter and taken me at my word when I'd said yes, and I would be writing back to everyone eventually. She had been waiting for my letter ever since.

Meanwhile, she had written me another letter asking why I hadn't replied yet: 'You said that you would write!'

Then there was a third letter. 'Why are you ignoring my letters? I know you're getting them, so why are you doing this to me?'

I was unaware of any of this until she had written a fourth and fifth letter and someone from John Noel called and said there was a problem. Her later letters were a little more disturbing. 'When I met you, Craig, you looked me in the eye and you promised me that you would write back to me . . .'

Finally, Channel 4 handed the letters to the police, who wrote to the girl explaining that I was not receiving her letters and not to write any more. I was told that under no circumstances was I to contact her because an unstable person can easily misread any form of communication and she might think I was leading her on. The whole incident made me sad. Several months later, I made sure that a thank-you letter was sent out to everyone who had written to me. Believe me, it cost a few quid! In the first week, I was getting about two thousand letters a day. Mail was even arriving from abroad, addressed only to 'Craig, *Big Brother*'. I was told that only people like the Queen and Michael Jackson actually received mail without their address on, but some of these letters did make it to my house!

I did one last signing before Christmas. This time it was at Hamleys toyshop on Regent Street in London and Claire Strutton from the *Big Brother* house came with me. Claire and I had dated occasionally since we'd come out of the house and we got on very well.

It was a really Christmassy day. Inside the store, a small choir was singing carols and the atmosphere was lovely. Hundreds of kids queued up for hours to get my autograph and I was determined to sign every book and scrap of paper.

All of a sudden, a guy with bright ginger hair appeared in front of the table where I was sitting. He was wearing a prominent neck brace and carrying a bag and a camcorder. 'Hello to you, the Craig,' he said in what sounded like an Eastern European accent. Without further ado, he began to come on very strong, saying, 'I love you, I really love you; let me touch you, let me feel your hand.'

I was very polite to him, but I was thinking, Oh dear, what's going on here?

He walked over to John Noel's press officer, Catherine Wheaver. 'My love, would you please video me while I say something to the Craig?' he asked. 'I love him so much, you see.'

I expected her to say no. There were TV cameras outside and she wasn't letting them anywhere near me, so why would she allow a strange-looking and -sounding guy in a neck brace to film me? But at this point I tended not to ask questions.

To my surprise, Catherine took the video camera off this man and happily began filming us. He kept saying, 'I love you so much! I really enjoyed watching you on the *Big Brother*.'

How strange he looks! I thought. He's a bit of a freak, isn't he?

I kept on smiling and nodding, but I was starting to feel uncomfortable with some of the things he was saying. Then he looked me directly in the eye and said, 'Craig, I know everything about you.'

'Right, good for you,' I said. By now it was also irritating me that this guy was blocking the flow of people coming to get autographs. We'd had a good momentum going and he had interrupted it.

'I really do know everything about you,' he went on. 'How's school for your beautiful nieces, Kelly and Lauren?'

I felt a prickle beneath my skin. 'How do you know my nieces?' I asked.

'Believe me, I know everything about you,' he said. 'What about Barry and Lee, your best friends?'

This was getting too personal for my liking. I looked over at Neil Higgins. Seeing that I was feeling uncomfortable, Neil walked around the table and said, 'Come along, sir, you're blocking the queue. You have to go now.'

'Do not touch me!' the guy shouted. 'I am disabled. You are hurting my neck!' He started making a loud scene.

'No, sir, I'm not touching you, but I'm asking you to continue walking, please,' Neil said.

The guy rummaged in the bag he was carrying. 'I have a present for the Craig! He will like this!' he said.

At this point I should have caught on that something was up, because normally if a male 'fan' went to pull something out of a bag, security would jump right in front of him, just in case. Now, though, they were being surprisingly lax.

Hang on a minute, I thought. I've seen them overreact in less worrying situations. Yet here was this character behaving very strangely, and they weren't doing anything about it. But there wasn't time to question it properly or think it through. There was so much going on around me.

Out of his bag came the white-label version of my single, which I'd only recorded about a week previously. Even I didn't have a copy of it.

'Whoa! Where did you get that?' I said sharply.

'I got it out of a bin.'

'A bin? Where?'

'In a very cold part of the country, Craig.'

'Cold?' I said.

'Yeah, Fort William.'

My stomach turned over. 'Fort William?' I repeated.

'Yes, it is amazing what you find rooting in the bins of Fort William.'

How the hell does he know about Fort William? I wondered. The video wasn't out yet. It had been filmed in strict secrecy: even my mum didn't know where we had filmed it. Underneath the table, my legs began to shake with nerves. I thought about celebrities I knew who had police protection outside their houses because of problems with stalkers.

Bloody hell! I thought. I've heard about this happening, but I never thought it would happen to me. You expect it to happen to pretty young girls, but I'm a fella!

The shop had gone quiet and everyone was looking at this strange guy. Three security guards were attempting to move him along, but he kept shouting, 'Do not touch me, I'm hurting, I'm disabled!'

At that moment, I noticed two little metal pins on his shirt. He's got a radio mic on, I thought. This is really weird! Why would he want to record me?

'Excuse me, just come here one second,' I said. I leaned over the table and wiped my hands across his shirt, because I knew this would mess up his recording. 'Got a radio mic on there?' I said.

He sniggered, as if to say, 'My cover's been blown!' I began to wonder if he was delusional.

He wasn't finished yet, though. He turned to leave and went straight over to Claire. 'I love you, Claire, let me touch you!' he said as he very obviously made a lunge for her boobs, emitting a noise like a horn. Claire didn't respond. She wouldn't rise to it.

Now security had a valid reason to lift him up and carry him out of the shop – not least because there were children everywhere and he was beginning to upset them. But even outside the shop he didn't stop harassing me. He pressed himself against the window, kissing and licking the glass, and shouted, 'I love you, the Craig! I love you, the Craig!'

I felt a bit freaked out after he'd gone. One of the Hamleys staff asked me if I was all right. 'Would you like to come into the back for five minutes and have a cup of tea?' the manager offered.

I looked out at the sea of people still waiting to see me. 'No, I can't leave all these people waiting,' I said weakly.

The manager stood up and said, 'Craig will be back in five minutes. Please be patient. He's just having a little break.'

Later, I phoned up John Noel and told him that I thought I had a stalker. 'He's a real freak,' I said, going on to describe him.

'Don't worry about him, Craig,' John said, sounding quite unconcerned. 'There are lots of freaky people out there and they can find out everything on the internet nowadays. You were right not to react to him. Try not to worry. You've got security there. Just let them do their job; you stay quiet and you'll be fine. Just be aware that this is the world you live in. It could happen again, either with the same person or other people. But remember, you're safe.'

I had to take his word for it. After all, he was responsible for running my life.

Sometimes it was hard letting someone else guide me and make decisions for me. I had run my business for eight years and was used to being the one in charge, with staff working for me. Since many of the people working on my sites were older than me, I would never tell them what to do but rather ask them in a way that meant they couldn't refuse. I respected the fact that they were more experienced than I was and I got by quite well that way.

All of a sudden someone was telling me what to do in no uncertain terms. They were instructing me which jobs to take and, to some extent, how to behave. Fine, I accepted it, but all the same it was very difficult. John even negotiated the price I charged for the work I was doing. That was a hard one to get my head around because I felt out of control.

Every evening, my security would receive an itinerary. After dinner they'd say, 'Right, tomorrow we're leaving the hotel at six twenty a.m. We're on a breakfast show at seven forty and then at eight thirty-five you're going on to do a photo shoot. We'll probably eat after that and check in to a hotel in the area to get ready for the awards ceremony where you're presenting the second award. Then there's a party at Elton John's house we can go to if you want? OK?'

'Yes, fine,' I'd say. I couldn't really say no; I just had to go with the flow.

Sometimes I managed to let my hair down, though. Later that week, I had a drunken night out with Chris Moyles and Comedy Dave in London. When it got to about 3 a.m., Chris started telling me about a song that he and Dave had recorded. 'But the BBC aren't letting us release it,' he said.

'What's your song like?' I asked.

'Tell you what, I'll play it to you!' he said.

So they sneaked me past BBC security at Broadcasting House and we crept into Chris's little studio booth, where they played the song and sang along, drunk as lords. If I remember right, it was a rap song . . . Like me, they should probably have stuck to the day job.

It was obvious to me by now that my singing career wasn't going to last. There were two reasons for this: firstly, it would be only a matter of time before I had to perform live and look stupid, because I couldn't really sing; secondly, it wasn't worth my while.

When Warner Music had said that they would pay me £47,000 for a day in a studio, it had sounded like a good deal. I didn't realize that the fee included six weeks of promotion as well. Since John was able to negotiate £5,000 for some of the personal appearances I was making, and I was often getting booked for three personal appearances a day, suddenly £47,000 for six weeks' work didn't seem like quite such a good deal. Plus, I was getting confused with what I was doing for free for promotion, and what I was actually getting paid for.

Over a six-week period, I had done interviews with 170 radio stations and appeared on twenty TV shows, including *Top of the Pops*. I also did a road tour of the major radio stations, stopping in to meet the DJs and do countless interviews and stunts. It was incredibly tiring!

My final mimed performance of the single was on *Live and Kicking*, on Christmas Eve. This seemed like a particularly nice end to the promotional build-up, because Joanne came on stage with me and she loved it. Meanwhile, I couldn't wait for the next day, which was due to be my first day off since I'd left the *Big Brother* house in September.

After the show I flew home to my mum's, feeling totally run down and exhausted. All the family and my friends wanted to come and see me, but I turned my phone off and said to my mum, 'Please, Mum, we've got to limit who comes to the house. I've got no energy left to talk to anyone.'

Seeing my friends and family was just like doing another

round of interviews: they had 101 questions that they wanted to ask me. It wasn't their fault – they were just curious and so excited for me – but I couldn't escape the fact that they wanted to know all the same things that the journalists and presenters asked about.

In the end, just Bev, her girls and about four other family members came for Christmas Day. Yet, even with the best intentions, every conversation still turned into an interview. Then, in the afternoon, someone from Warner Music rang on my personal phone number, which only a very few people had. My heart sank. What now?

'An order for twenty-six thousand copies of your single has just been placed in Germany!' said a girl from the International Department. 'So we're sending a car tomorrow to pick you up and then we'll fly you out to Germany for three days to play with the Sugababes on the final night of the German *Big Brother*. Isn't that great?'

I held back a groan. 'Look,' I said, 'I've absolutely had it! I've already done a hundred and seventy-odd radio shows, interviews with every magazine and newspaper and personal appearances all over the UK. Now you're asking me to go to Germany on Boxing Day?'

In the end I agreed to go; I was still in the mode of doing everything I was told. But when I got back I decided that I didn't like being dictated to and I didn't want to be racing all over the UK and Europe doing any more free promotion. Recording pop music had lost its appeal and I certainly didn't want to be locked into a £500,000, five-album deal.

That was the turning point for me. I needed to focus on what

I knew best, and that was building. So when John mentioned a new live makeover programme called *Housecall* and said that there was a possibility of a year's contract with the BBC, I didn't hesitate to accept. It was time to drop my pop career.

On 2 January 2001, I started work on *Housecall*. On 3 January, the BBC put forward a proposal for me to sign a two-year exclusive contract. I ended up with a £16,000 solicitor's bill after parting ways with Warner Music, but it was the right decision!

With *Housecall*, I was on much safer ground. A live daytime lifestyle show, it was probably the most enjoyable programme I've ever worked on. I went on to appear on 235 live episodes, along with the presenter Suzi Perry, Colin McAllister and Justin Ryan, the Scottish boys, James Martin, the resident chef, and Gordon Whistance, who have all since become good friends and gone on to be big TV names.

Filmed in Birmingham, *Housecall* aired from 10 to 11 a.m. every day. Each series lasted between nine and twelve weeks and it ran for nine series in total. My role on the show was to give a room a complete makeover in just one hour. Every morning, a driver would pick me up from my hotel at 6 a.m. and take me to the house, where I would discuss with the designers what needed to be done. A couple of hours later, live on air, I'd make or build whatever was required.

Being on the show was such fun and so frantic that filming each episode seemed to last only about ten minutes. Suzi Perry, the presenter, would spend the hour running between our room, where I was building something with my team, the kitchen, where James was cooking, and the garden, where an exterior makeover was also in progress.

I also appeared in several other BBC DIY shows, including *Trading Up*, *Trading Up in the Sun*, *Big Strong Boys*, *Big Strong Boys in the Sun*, *Housetrapped!* and *Builders, Sweat and Tears*. I appeared on around five hundred shows, in all. When I was no longer under exclusive contract to the BBC, I made two series of *Boyz in the Wood* with a carpenter friend of mine called Rod Butler. It was a workshop-style programme for Discovery, Home & Leisure (now Discovery Realtime), where Rod and I made skilled carpentry items, like a rocking horse and a pool table. We filmed it at my garage workshop in Newport – yes, the one that the council wanted to demolish (they didn't!).

It wasn't long before I was producing my part of *Housecall*. The producers would send over some photographs of the interior of a house: 'OK, the designer wants a new fireplace built. What would you suggest, Craig?'

I'd advise what to build and which materials would be best. 'You could film me doing it in four different sections, giving a short explanation at each stage of the work,' I'd say.

It made life easier for the producers if I could put together and produce ten minutes of an hour's show for them, and I didn't mind doing it, either. It was easy for me and I learned a great deal about presenting and making TV as I went along.

I still keep up to date with current building regulations, because when you're advising people on television, you've got to do so correctly. Say one thing wrong and you can trigger two thousand phone calls! The channel won't be very forgiving about it, either.

Doing *Housecall* was fantastic. What's more, it left my after-noons free to race around the country and make personal appearances, which were a big part of my life in the year following *Big Brother*. I opened several DIY stores and did a lot of in-store building demonstrations at events like the Ideal Home Show.

I also agreed to some quite curious requests, which make me chuckle to look back on. One day in Downing Street, with the then Treasury minister Melanie Johnston, I launched a govern-ment campaign by picking up an actor who was playing the taxman and putting him in a bath of baked beans. The idea behind the stunt was to show employers that donating money free through the payroll was a much easier way of raising funds for charity than the old cliché of sitting in a bath of baked beans!

Another time I was approached by a magazine after it had run a rather unusual competition. The prize was the chance to ask anybody anywhere anything. The winner was a teenage girl and she chose to ask me a question. The magazine paid me £5,000 to answer it. No prizes for guessing what the question was: 'What was it really like in the *Big Brother* house?'

I went on to spend half an hour with the girl and her family, answering more questions and smiling for photographs. I was touched to find that meeting me was a big deal to them, but couldn't believe that that was the winning question!

Life was so busy that I didn't keep up with what was going on behind the scenes. One evening I was at another awards ceremony when Chris Tarrant came up to me and said, 'What's wrong with your agent?'

I was totally taken aback. 'Why?' I asked.

'I've had a great idea for us to do a primetime show on ITV, but he won't entertain it at all!'

I gulped. 'To be honest, Chris, I know nothing about this,' I said.

When I mentioned it to John Noel, he explained that if he had pursued the project with Chris then it would interfere with the DIY shows. 'We thought it wasn't right for you,' he said. I trusted his judgment and advice, but I would have liked to have known about the proposal before it was turned down. In fairness, things were busy and that happened a few times.

However, to my delight, my TV career as a DIY presenter was shaping up well. 'This looks like it could be your job from now on,' John kept saying. 'If you work hard and listen to what I say, and if you keep your profile clean, it could become your career.' I was and always am well behaved in public. I certainly didn't want to ruin things by getting photographed doing anything stupid like collapsing outside a club.

My social life was as lively as ever in the months after Christmas and I was still being invited to attend a raft of awards ceremonies and charity dinners around the country. One night Davina McCall invited me as her guest to a dinner in aid of Focus, a charity she was supporting. The table was filled with some of John Noel's other clients, including Dermot O'Leary, Tess Daly, John Leslie – and Davina, of course.

At one point, John Noel leaned across the table and said, 'I've got a surprise for you in a minute, Phillips.'

'Oh right, what's that?' I said.

'You'll see.'

A few minutes later, a guy with ginger hair approached me and, in a Leeds accent, said, 'Hello, Craig, I'm Leigh.'

Wait a minute, I thought. There's something familiar about this fella. Suddenly it clicked. 'Oh no, it's *you*!' I yelled. 'You're that freak from Hamleys!'

It was my stalker. Only now he was being himself: his disguise had been the neck brace and the Romanian accent.

It turned out that Leigh Francis was also one of John Noel's clients. At the time he was trying to get his own show stalking celebrities as a character called Avid Merrion and wanted to call it *Bo' Selecta!* Since John wanted to help him, he decided it would be easiest to set him up with his own clients. So I'd been framed. Ah, that explained why the security guards had been a bit lax that day!

Some of the footage Leigh had shot as he harassed me in Hamleys actually helped him on his way to doing a set of adverts for Channel 4 and *Big Brother* – and he quite literally roped me in to appearing in them with him.

The aim of the ads was to attract applicants for the second and third series of *Big Brother*. They began with Avid Merrion asking people to send in a short video giving three reasons why they thought they should be a housemate in the *Big Brother* house. Then he sat on his couch 'at home', looked down the lens of a camera and said, 'My name is Avid Merrion. Why should I be in the *Big Brother* house? Well, number one, I am sexy. Number two, I like the chicken. And finally, number three, I should be in the *Big Brother* house because I have kidnapped the Craig.'

Next he carried the camera down the hallway to find me. I

was under the stairs, all chained up. 'If you want to see the Craig again, then pick me,' he threatened. Believe it or not, this was the big break that led on to his own show, the cult comedy series *Bo' Selecta!*

A couple of years later, I appeared on the *Bo' Selecta!* Christmas single 'Proper Crimbo', which reached number four in the charts. Leigh's plan was to get more celebrities on the record and in the video than Band Aid – and he managed it. There were forty-seven in all, including Bob Geldof, Chris Moyles and a couple of the Spice Girls. But I was the only one in the video with my top off! I was all chained up, too, just as in the Channel 4 adverts.

In all, I appeared in twenty-eight episodes of *Bo' Selecta!* and I enjoyed every minute. Funnily enough, I often got more recognition for my role as 'the Craig' than I did for some of the DIY shows I worked on . . .

13

Adrenalin Rushes

I felt very lucky and I was grateful for the opportunities I'd been given after *Big Brother*. This made me all the more keen to continue working on behalf of charities. Now that I had been catapulted into a position where I could be of help to different causes by drawing media attention to them, I felt a responsibility to carry on. It gave me a great sense of satisfaction that I was in a position to help.

Having so publicly helped to raise funds and awareness for the Down's Syndrome Association meant that I also had a strong profile as a fundraiser. As a result, I was inundated with letters from organizations hoping to get me on board. Reading through their campaign literature, I was amazed by the wide range and number of charities that exist in the UK. It may sound stupid, but I had no idea that there were so many people with so many different physical and psychological problems –

and so many organizations set up to help them. If I could help them all, I would.

As it is, these days I put in anything between twenty-five and fifty days a year supporting different charity events. Many aspects of charity work can really take it out of you, but you derive a great deal of fulfilment from it as well. Long meetings are taken up with discussing fundraising plans and policy, but you can't forget that you're making a difference to people's lives. That's what's important.

In 2000 the Department for Transport asked me to launch the government's national Think! drink-drive media campaign alongside the then transport minister, Lord Whitty. For the first time I spoke publicly about my dad's accident and how it affected my family and me, which wasn't easy. I've gone on to become a patron of the road-safety charity Brake! and I launch several drink-drive campaigns around the country annually. Obviously, it's a cause very close to my heart.

In early 2001, as if life wasn't fast enough already, I started training for the London Marathon with my sister Bev to raise money for the Down's Syndrome Association. Unfortunately, my schedule was so packed that I didn't have a lot of time to get fit. I managed to slot in four trips to the gym and a couple of half-hour runs through Birmingham city centre, where I was based for *Housecall*, but it wasn't enough preparation for a marathon, not by half. Having spent the previous few months eating out and being driven from door to door didn't help.

I decided that it would be silly for me to go ahead with the marathon without training properly. But then I heard that quite a few sponsors had pledged funds to the Down's Syndrome

Association if I completed the run. Well, I'd better do it! I thought. So I went ahead in April and it was a great experience. I finished in five hours and five minutes, only one minute behind Steve Redgrave!

That same month, I received a very special invitation, along with little Joanne Harris: we were invited to the Pride of Britain Awards, which honours the achievements of some of the UK's truly remarkable people, including tireless charity workers, unsung heroes from the police and armed forces, courageous adults and brave children, among many others.

Little Jo and I were sitting at a table with my friend, the amazing and beautiful Michelle Lewis, who has since been awarded an MBE. Although she suffers from a debilitating muscle-wasting disease, Michelle is so dynamic that she raised more a million pounds for charity before she was eighteen (and she's getting close to the two-million-pound mark now). She went on to come second in the wheelchair class at the London Marathon the following year. Now she was on the Pride of Britain board along with Tony Blair, Richard Branson and Lorraine Phillips, helping to decide the winners.

Robbie Williams was on the next table. I had met Rob a couple of times by this point, but little Jo had never been introduced. 'Oooh, there's Robbie!' she said excitedly, spotting him.

'Craig! Craig! Call Robbie over, we want to see him!' Michelle said. 'We want to get some pictures with him.'

I looked over at Rob and he nodded his head, as if to say, I'll be over in a minute. Good as his word, he came to see us a little bit later, in dazzling form. Giving little Jo a lovely hug and a kiss, he said, 'Your name's Joanne, isn't it?'

Her face just lit up. She gave him a lovely big smile and flashed her eyes. Then suddenly she came over all sheepish and shy. Fluttering her eyelashes, she said, 'Yes, I'm Joanne.' She could be quite the little flirt!

'I've seen you on television; you're famous!' Robbie said.

'Go away!' she said, giving him a little tap.

They started chatting and she began telling him about everything she'd been up to. Usually people bombard Rob with questions, but now it was the other way round. He was asking her all about her life and she was recounting a string of stories: whom she'd met; what she'd done.

'Wow, that's fantastic, you're such a lucky girl!' he kept saying.

About five minutes into their chat, she licked her fingers and started fixing his hair, because it was sticking out at all angles. (Of course, it was probably meant to be like that . . .) 'What are you doing with your hair?' she said, flattening it with her hands. And do you know what? He absolutely loved it!

Then she pointed to his stripy jumper and said, 'What are you wearing this for, Robbie? You shouldn't wear stripes like that. They make you look fat!' I couldn't help cringing, along with everyone else around the table. Little Jo pulled his jumper, to stretch it. 'You need stripes going the other way,' she added with a beaming smile.

Now, people always tell Robbie how fantastic he looks. They gather around him, saying yes, yes, yes to everything, sucking up like mad. Then all of a sudden he's got this girl telling it how it is. 'The jumper is awful! You look fat!' It was absolutely brilliant. His face was a picture.

I gave him a look as if to say, Sorry! But he mouthed back, 'Don't worry,' and just laughed. I think he appreciated little Jo's genuine honesty. I suspect he doesn't come across it all that often from the general public.

'You're lovely,' he told her, his eyes twinkling.

'Thank you,' she said with a giggle. 'So are you.'

I always have a special time at the Pride of Britain Awards. The following year I was introduced to Sir Paul McCartney and Heather Mills. It was the best feeling ever, because my mum was there and because it's every Liverpool lad's dream to meet Paul McCartney. He even knew my name! A member of the greatest band in the world knew my name! He and Heather had seen me in *Big Brother* and read about me in the papers.

'Oh, hello, Craig,' he said, as we shook hands. 'It's a pleasure and an honour to meet you.' I was totally made up.

I tried not to say all the usual things or mention the Beatles. It's like when I meet footballers; I try not to talk about football. Luckily for me, he and Heather asked me about *Big Brother* and what I'd been doing since the show, which made it a bit easier for me.

Tony Blair was at the awards that year and he also talked to me, which was nice. I had already met Cherie, his wife, at a charity event at Downing Street and I'd felt an instant affinity with her because she was from my city – she was brought up in North Liverpool.

Cherie and I had talked about little Joanne Harris. By now, the NHS no longer had the same policy of discrimination against people with Down's syndrome. Although there was still some headway to be made, health secretary Alan Milburn had promised within days of me coming out of the house that no one else with Down's syndrome would be treated the way Joanne had. University Hospital, Birmingham, had also changed their minds about operating on her. In 2001, Alan Milburn pledged heart scans at birth for all children born with Down's syndrome. Next, health minister Yvette Cooper announced screening for Down's syndrome to be made available to all pregnant women.

'The Down's Syndrome Association has been campaigning to get equal healthcare treatment for people with Down's syndrome for the last decade,' I said to Cherie. 'Why has the policy only been changed now?'

She explained that, since millions of votes had been cast for me in the final week of *Big Brother*, I obviously had public opinion on my side. I had helped to make the public aware of the injustice of NHS policy when it came to children with Down's syndrome and the government finally had to listen. Apparently, more votes had been cast over the course of *Big Brother* than Labour had received in the last general election! I'm not sure where she got her facts from or if indeed she was right, but it was very flattering to hear, of course.

I've also met my share of royals. I was honoured enough to give out the gold Duke of Edinburgh Awards at Buckingham Palace, along with my good friend Terri Dwyer, and to meet Prince Philip. Another time at Buckingham Palace, when I was giving out the silver Duke of Edinburgh Awards, Prince Andrew came into the room, drew up a chair and gave an entertaining welcoming speech, which made me warm to him. Sophie, Countess of Wessex, was also very friendly and charming when I met her at a garden party at St James's Palace once – I may even have been guilty of flirting a little! I also met the Queen's cousin Princess Alexandra when I went to St James's Palace to give out bravery medals to the three explosive-detector dogs and their handlers for the Metropolitan and the British Transport Police who risked their lives going into the London Underground moments after the July 2005 bombings.

Since *Big Brother*, I've done all kinds of crazy things to raise awareness and money for charity. Until then, bungee jumping had been the biggest adrenalin rush I had experienced. (I've actually got Shelley to thank for my first bungee jump, which she bought for my twentieth birthday.) Given the chance, I love to do anything a bit daring, especially if it's for a good cause – and after *Big Brother*, there were lots of opportunities for adventure.

I did my first parachute jump with Kate Silverton. I first met Kate at a party held by John Noel at London Zoo after hours and she and I clicked instantly. Kate's very prim and proper when she presents the *BBC News* and *BBC News 24*, but she's actually madder than I am in real life. I worked with her on *Housecall* and she's become a really good friend over the years.

In 2002, Kate, *GMTV* presenter Andrea McLean and I were among 180 people to break the UK record for the most tandem parachute jumps in twenty-four hours. Attached to an instructor, we each fell 10,000 feet and raised £80,000 towards helping the Cystic Fibrosis Trust in its attempts to find a cure for the disease, which affects 7,500 young people in the UK.

The following August we were among 225 skydivers doing it all over again.

Shortly after the first jump, Kate talked me into spending a weekend in Wales cave kayaking with her. I remember it well, because it's the nearest I've come to dying, I think! Kate was working in Manchester and I was working in Liverpool at the time, so we met up halfway and drove through the night to Wales, where we stayed overnight.

The next morning we got up early to catch the morning waves. We put on all our kit, including helmets and elbow gear, and went paddling out into the freezing cold seawater to join a group of Kate's pals. They knew the area well and told us to follow them. Off we set, with Kate a little way ahead of me.

Suddenly she veered off in a different direction to the guys in front. 'No, Kate!' I called after her.

By now the other lads were about 100 metres ahead of us, moving out of sight around a jutting rock. Meanwhile, Kate was making her way into the mouth of a nearby cave. 'Come this way, Craig, it looks great!' she called.

It looks dark in there, I thought. Perhaps it's not such a good idea to go in.

It was a dilemma. Do I follow Kate as she goes off on her own into a place she doesn't know, or do I go the other way and follow the rest of the lads, who know what they're doing?

Really, I wanted to go the other way, but at the same time I didn't want to let Kate risk going in there on her own. The more I shouted at her to come back and join the others, the further she went. 'No, let's see what's down here!' she said.

'It's OK. It looks fun!' She disappeared into the mouth of the cave.

So I reluctantly followed her. The further we went, the darker it got and I started to lose sight of Kate. 'Come out!' I shouted. 'I don't like the look of this.' My voice echoed around the darkness.

'No, come further in!' she yelled. She had found a little alcove around the corner.

Suddenly, I heard a howling noise. It sounded like wind rushing through a tunnel. The noise became louder and the water beneath me began to surge. I felt myself starting to rise and move further and faster into the cave. All of a sudden, a huge wave roared behind me and caught me in its current. From the safety of her alcove, Kate watched as I shot past at 30 miles an hour, my canoe vertical, with the bow pointing down into the water. She later said she'd never seen anything like it.

I zoomed towards a rough area of rocks. Dropping my paddle, I braced myself to hit the wall of the cave. I was expecting the worst, but it didn't hurt as much as I thought it would, probably because of all the protective gear I was wearing. What happened next was much more frightening. The water went on rushing in, everything went pitch black and I rose higher and higher towards the roof of the cave, where there was no light or air.

At this point I was out of the canoe, but it was still tied to my ankle with a tight strap. I could feel it being dragged down, towing me with it. No! I needed to swim upwards and try to take a breath. Just then, I honestly thought I was going to die. This is it, I thought.

You hear stories about people drowning or hitting their heads in caves all the time, don't you? So I was thinking, What the hell am I doing? I was certain that it was all over for me. The next twenty seconds felt like hours. The water dropped and with it went the canoe, pulling me down. I had to do something! Somehow I managed to rip off the ankle strap.

To Kate's consternation, my empty canoe surfaced without me attached to it. Now she started to panic. But thirty seconds later, as the wave receded, I reappeared, coughing and spluttering like mad. I was really shaken up and wanted to get the hell out of that cave. 'I'm not following you ever again!' I shouted angrily. Kate just laughed. She's always smiling and laughing, except when she's reading serious items on the news.

Now I had to swim all the way out of the cave in the freezing water, holding on to the back of Kate's canoe. Luckily my canoe was wedged against a jutting rock only a couple of hundred metres away in another alcove. I got back in and soon we caught up with the guys. They laughed when we told them what had happened, but I didn't find it funny until some time afterwards, when I'd stopped shaking with fear. Still, it hasn't stopped me going on adventures with Kate.

Once she even managed to talk me into sailing the Channel with her on a huge eco-friendly yacht that Mike Golding had sailed around the world in. She had somehow managed to charter it for a TV pilot we were making. Luckily, there were no near misses on that adventure, just lots of fun, drinking and plain sailing.

I suppose I'll always love taking risks – just not stupid ones. I mean, it sounds more dangerous to get strapped to the wings of a 1940s Boeing Stearman bi-plane than go cave kayaking, but as it turned out, it wasn't at all. I did my wing-walking stunt to support the Women's Royal Voluntary Service and draw attention to the amazing work they do providing meals on wheels for the elderly.

I've also zip-lined across a 180-metre open quarry, abseiled down buildings in London and Liverpool and even dived with dangerous sharks – all for charity. It gives me a thrill to be a bit of a daredevil, but most of all, it makes people sit up and think.

Amidst the chaos of work, promotion and fundraising my life was such a whirlwind during the first six months after *Big Brother* that I didn't have a chance to go home for more than a couple of hours at a time. When I did, my priority was to see my family, and this meant that I neglected my building business. I was making hay while the sun was shining – just as everyone was telling me to do – but as a result I took my eye off the ball, which was a mistake.

Maybe I should have been more cautious and remembered that some people are dishonest. But it just didn't occur to me that anyone would be tempted to take advantage of the situation – and certainly not fifty people or more, as was actually the case.

I have never spoken about this before, but here goes: while I was running my building company, I had business accounts with many different companies for fuel, stationery and tool hire. Having these accounts enabled my staff and me to go in and sign for what we needed when we needed it. Every month I received statements of what we had all spent; I'd check them carefully, settle the bill and send the paperwork on to my accountant.

However, I obviously couldn't check my statements or bills while I was in the *Big Brother* house – which was plain for all to see. While I was in the house, everybody knew where I was twenty-four hours a day, and it wasn't overseeing my accounts in Newport, that's for sure. And when I left the house, I was splashed all over the papers every day, so again it was easy to keep track of what I was up to and where I was – which was a long way from Newport. Christmas Day 2000 was my only day off, and the only day I spent back home. I had been away from my building company for more than six months.

It seems that some of the builders I had employed – some of them just for a few weeks or months – decided to take advantage of this information. Their thinking must have gone like this: Well, Craig's super-famous now. He's obviously earning loads of money, because we've seen him all over the telly and newspapers. So why don't we help ourselves to a little bit of what he's got?

Some of them were probably subcontractors who'd worked with me briefly, so once my jobs came to an end, they started getting their own work. But this didn't stop them charging tools and materials to my accounts. As they were going back and forth from the builder's yard, ordering stuff for their own work or someone else's, they would add a few bags of cement and or some hammers to the order and bill them to me, claiming that they were still working on my sites. In other words, they were stealing from me.

I had a good relationship with the building-centre managers, who would always phone me if there were any problems. But now, of course, they couldn't get hold of me to check anything. What's more, there were so many branches in the Shropshire area, with so many different people working in them, that it was easy for a builder to walk in and say, 'I work for Craig; put this on his account.' They'd give my address and other information and put a squiggle on a counter slip. Simple.

It didn't take long for one of the girls helping with my accounts to spot that there was something wrong. However, every time she called, I was in the middle of filming or doing a charity stunt and was completely distracted. With so much going on around me, it was hard to focus on what she was saying. 'This month, another six thousand pounds was spent on this account, Craig! But it can't be right, because the two smaller jobs are finished and there are only four staff left on the final job.'

'Right, I'll look into it the moment I get a chance,' I'd say.

Finally, my solicitor contacted all the stores and told them to freeze my accounts. After that, nobody was allowed to buy materials unless they were authorized to do so by my manager Barry.

We tried to track back over the months to find out who had been ripping me off, but the trail was cold. When I asked the shops to send me photocopies of the counter slips, they were mostly just signed with a scribble that didn't marry up with any of the signatures that my staff had provided when I had originally taken them on. Each slip was supposed to have a signature, a printed name, a job reference and a site address, but none of them were properly filled out. I couldn't help feeling that the staff in some of the branches had also let me down.

We tried chasing up each individual receipt. 'Who signed this counter slip for two hundred pounds for cement and tools?'

'It's hard to know,' came the answer. 'Sometimes ten of your lads come in at different times in a day.'

I didn't know for sure who was doing it; I had my suspicions but no evidence. I think jealousy may have played a part. Some of the older builders resented the way my company had expanded while theirs remained stagnant. As the years went by, I overtook many building companies that had originally been bigger than mine. We were tendering for the same jobs and I was getting them, which caused bitterness.

Eventually, I paid off all the outstanding bills and closed the accounts. I was earning a lot of money at the time and it seemed a quicker and easier option than paying my solicitor and accountant to chase up every receipt. It was becoming more hassle and trouble than it was actually worth.

But it ended up costing me a huge amount of money, about £60,000, which obviously plunged me into serious debt. As a result, I had a massive overdraft, which was partly why I was working round the clock. Added to this, it wasn't as easy as it seemed to earn big money, because the taxman was taking 40 per cent and my agent was taking 18 per cent, so more than half of what I was earning was gone before I even saw it.

It was disappointing and depressing to think that there was so much dishonesty in the world. The whole sorry affair made me sad. There was some good news coming out of Newport, though: the council had decided not to knock down the external garage at my house after all! I think they must have started to rethink things when I popped up each day on the front page of the *Shropshire Star* newspaper, a few days after going into the *Big Brother* house.

As the following month went by, they must have been very aware of my presence on TV and in the press because, to my knowledge, no one in Shropshire or Telford had been such big news in recent years. (Unless you count my great friend the bodybuilder Kevin Turner, who won Mr Britain and Mr Europe, or the champion boxer Richie Woodall, that is.)

Once the council realized I was building up a media profile, it must have occurred to them that I would fight the demolition order publicly. So they did nothing. When *Big Brother* finished, they even wanted me to parade around Telford in an open-top bus with the mayor! I wasn't so sure about that . . .

I didn't want to let my building business slide any more; in fact I wanted to expand. Starting small, I began to build up a portfolio of properties. My mum decided to sell the little house in Liverpool that we'd been living in at the time of Dad's accident, so I bought it for £20,000, partly for sentimental reasons. It was quite run down and she couldn't afford to do it up, so it was just ticking over as a rented property. I spent about £15,000 on it and it's been rented out ever since, but it's nice to know it's still in the family.

In January 2002, I bought a nineteen-room, four-storey mansion in Liverpool at auction for £45,500. Although it was structurally unsound and probably needed around £350,000 spent on repairs and refurbishment, it was a lovely Grade II listed building and I thought it was a real bargain. You couldn't really get a mortgage on it, but I had some money available and decided to buy it as an investment.

I knew it required about nine months' work, using a team of ten good tradesmen, but things were frantic at the time, because I was doing loads of work for the BBC, as well as building demonstrations at exhibition centres all over the country. From Glasgow to Ireland to London to Birmingham, from the BBC Good Homes Show to the Ideal Home Show, I was showing people how to use hand and power tools, pave and deck patios, build and tile walls and lay floors, fit laminate flooring – you name it.

So I left my mansion empty for a couple of years until I had the time and money to do it up. I was also thinking that it had enormous TV potential. How brilliant it would be to show it being transformed and restored, week by week, on television! It might take time, but I was determined to make it happen. But for now, I was having a great time working for the BBC.

The personal appearances were still going strong as well. In May 2002, Harrods booked me to do a live building demonstration. It was part of a promotion for LG Electronics that involved a family living in a state-of-the art virtual home in the Harrods windows for a week, in full twenty-four-hour view of the public and media. Every day the family was set a different task. Kim Wilde, Tony Hart and I all set them challenges.

I was asked to set up a demonstration that all the family could help with: the mum, dad and two teenage kids. My idea was to build some little tables using very basic materials. It wasn't a hard task, as I was going to prep everything in stages, so all they really had to do was assemble the bits.

I was all set the day before. Then Harrods' PR company called me.

'Are you using MDF in the demo?' they asked.

'Yes, it's all prepped,' I said.

'Oh dear! MDF has just been banned in some states in America, so we don't want you using it in the shop window.'

My heart sank. Great! 'Well, that's thrown a spanner in the works, but I'll probably be able to improvise with plywood and laminate sections,' I said. 'Are you sure the dad is confident with power tools?'

'Yes, absolutely,' they said.

Hundreds of people watched through the window as we went about assembling these tables the next day. Knightsbridge virtually came to a standstill as passing drivers tried to get a peek at what we were up to. We were wearing radio mics and there were speakers outside so that people could hear what we were saying. Cameras were filming our every move.

I'd had a hectic morning doing the preparation all over again – and I had an equally hectic day ahead of me, because I was due to appear on Graham Norton's show next and get to a Westlife concert in Birmingham after that.

Things didn't exactly go according to plan. Firstly, the father was obviously not accustomed to using power tools. Secondly, his son picked up a very dangerous circular saw and started to cut into the wrong pieces of wood. It was a horrible situation, because at any moment one of them could have had an accident, in full view of the audience. Thirdly, the build didn't go to plan and started running late. I had two hours to complete it in the show window, but an hour in, we weren't even halfway through.

All of a sudden, who turns up but Mohamed Al Fayed? This wasn't totally unexpected, but nobody had been sure whether he would appear or not. Even the shop security didn't know.

Earlier I had asked one of his employees what he was like and she told me that she had worked for him for two years and never met or even spoken to him! 'I've been in rooms with him,' she said, 'but the pecking order is such that I never get to speak to him.'

Surrounded by security guards, Mr Al Fayed gave a royal wave. Everything and everyone stopped for him. Then he came into the window area. 'What are you doing?' he asked.

I explained briefly about my demo and then asked Mr Al Fayed, 'Do you know any DIY?'

'Not at all,' he said, laughing.

'Come on then, I'll show you how to use a hammer and chisel.' I took off my work belt, thinking it would be fun to put it on him. But to my horror, as I went to put it round his waist, it became clear that it wasn't going to fit him. He was far too big!

Oh God! I thought. Why did I even think about doing that? All the press are snapping away!

You know how easy it is to say the wrong thing when you get nervous? 'Mr Al Fayed,' I blurted out. 'I'm afraid it won't go on. You need to get to the gym!' Oh no, did I just say that?

Luckily, he laughed.

'Never mind,' I said, throwing the tool belt to the floor. I gave him a wooden mallet and a chisel and started showing him what to do with them.

'You know what I do with these?' he asked.

'No, what do you do with them?' I said.

His reply was to get me in a headlock and pretend to bash me on the head with the big wooden hammer. 'Anyone mess with me and I bash their heads!' he laughed.

I laughed along with him, thinking, Yes, you can say and do what you want!

As the allotted time drew to a close, Mr Al Fayed asked me if the project had gone well. 'To be honest with you, it's the worst make I've ever done!' I went on to list the problems we were having.

'Oh well, it doesn't matter, we're all having fun,' he said.

But I was in a real hurry by now and panicking slightly. I needed to start making my way to the Graham Norton show. 'I'm a little bit pushed for time and I've got to get off quite pronto here,' I said. 'I should have finished five minutes ago. So is there any way you would let me squeeze my car up to your side entrance so that I can fill the car with all my tools? Your security won't let me park on the main road because of the red lines.'

'Yeah, no problem,' he said, waving his arm at a security guard.

Five minutes later, while my driver was loading up my tools and I was trying to persuade Mr Al Fayed to come on Graham Norton's show with me, a bus ploughed straight into the back end of the car and dragged it up the road past the shop window.

'No! That's my car!' I shouted as I watched it crash past. Mr Al Fayed thought it was hilarious.

Sadly, the photo that appeared in the newspapers the next day didn't show the demonstration or the shot of me trying to put the tool belt on Mr Al Fayed or of him hammering my head. Instead it showed my driver and me pulling out the caved-in wheel arch where the bus had hit it and dragged it.

Eventually, I raced away with a beaten-up car, which, luckily enough, was just about OK and legal to drive, and I arrived at the studio in a real rush. As I quickly changed into a dinner suit outside, I forgot to put on a different pair of shoes. So I made my appearance wearing a dinner suit and a pair of steel-capped boots! I was praying the camera wouldn't zoom in on them.

Afterwards, I bombed it to the Westlife concert at the NEC in Birmingham, as the lads had invited me up for one of their after-show parties. I got in through the backstage area and, as I peeped through the curtains to see what they were up to, they were just coming to the end of their finale. Too late! Oh well, at least we were going out to a party afterwards . . . and I'd already seen them sing live four or five times. They're nice guys and they always make a fuss of me. Usually they announce to the crowd that I'm there and beam a spotlight on me.

Being under the spotlight was something I had to get used to – because 2002 was also the year that I started going up on stage in my own right! On 21 December I made my pantomime début at the Royal Court Theatre in Liverpool, playing Buttons in *Cinderella*. Winning *Big Brother* brought me so many opportunities, but treading the boards in front of my home-town audience had to be one of the best.

I didn't audition, but I couldn't have had a better teacher than Paul Hendy, who put me through my paces one weekend before we went into rehearsals. Paul used to host *Wheel of Fortune* on TV and is now a prolific pantomime producer. He gave me some invaluable tips on how to engage with an audience and *Cinderella* went on to break box-office records.

I've since been in several pantos up and down the country. I love everything about it, especially the audience interaction. Hand on heart, I wish I could do it every day!

14

Making a Dream Come True

When I worked in the butcher's shop, I used to think that if I ever lost my job, I would join the army. But I thought again when I started presenting the British Forces Broadcasting Service show *Hung, Drawn and Quartered* in 2004 and saw how strict and disciplined soldiers really are. Maybe I would have adapted when I was a kid, but later on in life I don't think I would have been able to hack being shouted at by a sergeant major because I hadn't brushed my boots properly.

Hung, Drawn and Quartered was a British Forces morale-boosting show that went out to about seventeen countries worldwide, not including England. It was basically a makeover show in which the designer Carolyn 'Wob' Eeles and I spruced up UN barracks all over the world. Later, my business partner Andy Bennett and I became executive producers on the show, producing it through Avent Productions, the independent television production company I set up in 2004. I met Andy in

2001 when we worked together on a range of BBC shows. He's a skilled cameraman and director with a vast knowledge of TV production. The show took us to the Falkland Islands, Ascension Island, Kosovo, Bosnia, Germany, Canada, Cyprus and Gibraltar. The last show was filmed in 2006, but it's still being repeated today.

The Ministry of Defence wanted to show what life was like for army personnel and their families living and working in the barracks; the idea was to highlight the positive aspects of being in the forces and counteract the negative coverage that is so often seen on the news. So we thought it would be good to include people from all the various forces (army, navy, marines and air force) in the makeovers, along with their spouses and children. In addition, we would explore aspects of their work and training, to show what a difficult job they do.

The original concept was for me to compete against a group of soldiers or commandos in a particular challenge. But what if I won the challenges? That wouldn't look good! So the MoD and British Forces TV decided to rejig the format. Instead I became part of the group, the idea being that I was the weakest link, because they were all fully trained and I was a civilian.

This part of the programme was called Operation Upgrade. It offered, for instance, the chance to win a new plasma-screen TV for the gym that we'd just done up, but only if the group took me through a particular task and I completed it in the target time. Although we produced the show, and developed the challenge concept in the pre-production stage, the challenges always came as a surprise to me. I had no idea what they would be until we actually started filming.

The Royal Marine Commandos were by far the toughest of all the forces we worked with and I was expecting to be put through a seriously punishing exercise when we joined them at HM Naval Base Clyde in Faslane in Scotland, home to the UK's nuclear submarines; it was November and the temperature was minus 4 degrees.

I was given a T-shirt and a life jacket, which straight away told me that I was going to be in the water. A sergeant lined me up with ten marine commandos and said, 'OK, we'll be going across one of the lochs in a high-powered boat. When we reach the other side, we'll bail out, jump in Canadian kayaks and row the two kilometres back across the loch.'

There was frozen water in the bottom of the kayak; when I tried to get in I had to stamp it out with my feet. It was really hard work rowing back across the loch. Not only was it freezing cold, but several speedboats pounded past, containing our camera crew, press, safety officers and paramedics, and they completely drenched me several times. They had no mercy!

About 200 metres from the bank, someone shouted something and the marines started capsizing the kayaks. A split second later I found myself fully immersed in icy water. My life jacket automatically burst open; then there was a frantic swim to the shore. The cold water was so painful that I swam like mad and was the first back!

As I raced up the embankment, someone shouted, 'Get the water off you as quickly as possible so that you don't freeze up!'

'Pee on yourself!' someone else yelled. 'It'll warm you up.'

So there I was trying to wee on myself and wipe the rest of the water off me . . . but almost immediately it was time to run up the bank, where we picked up a heavy rifle and a 25-kilo backpack and set off on a 10-kilometre jog. When was this challenge going to end? We ran for so long that I completely dried off! Following us were the cameraman's car and a press vehicle; there was also an ambulance trailing behind in the distance, in case I passed out. The brief had been to run me into the ground, but although I came close to passing out, I made it to the finish.

Afterwards, we moved straight on to a rifle range for shooting practice. By the end of it all, I was absolutely worn out! It was one of the two toughest military challenges I've ever been faced with.

And the other one? The time I had to complete a gruelling task with the Royal Navy in a ship simulator was as difficult as the Faslane challenge, if not more so. It took place on the multi-million-pound sinking-ship simulator, known as 'Hazard', situated at HMS *Excellent* in Portsmouth. It is a middle section of a warship propped up on hydraulic stilts with a form of container around it. During the exercise the simulator fills with around 70 tonnes of water and can tilt up to 20 degrees from the vertical.

The ship soon fills up with icy cold water, which comes bursting through holes in the ship (known as 'wounds') at such a rate that if you were standing in front of one, the force of the water would knock you to the ground. My task was to mend the wounds in each compartment by hammering blocks of wood into them.

The simulator was rocking back and forth on its stilts to emulate what would happen at sea in this situation, so I was getting bashed around from one side to another with the water level constantly rising – and rising fast. It was very frightening and absolutely exhausting. There were floor wounds on some decks where the water was 1.5 metres high and the Navy lads had to push me down and put their feet on my back to hold me there while I hammered blocks of wood into gaping holes. Alan Hamilton, one of our producers, was in the simulator with me trying to capture underwater footage. I later found out that he couldn't swim, but he still wanted to do it; he reckoned that since he was in a wetsuit with others around him he'd be OK!

Next, to make things even trickier, they turned the lights out and filled the ship up with smoke – to simulate a battle situation, apparently. Luckily we had to keep most of the main lights on in order to continue filming, but all the same it was really, really scary. When I finally made it out after twenty-five long hard minutes of being thrown around in freezing cold water, I was so exhausted that I couldn't do a piece to camera. I couldn't even talk! They had to put towels around me and pour hot coffee into me before I was able to do anything. It took me five minutes to get my breath back and do the piece to camera, in which I pretended that I'd only just come out of the ship. Despite the physical hardship, though, it was an extraordinarily exciting experience. I often look back at that programme and think about how lucky I was to get involved.

Through my work with the BFBS, I've also had some brilliant adventures in helicopters, including Gazelles, which are the smallest forces helicopters. Gazelles don't have armoury on them and are generally used as 'eyes', for reconnaissance. They can fly at very low altitude to gather intelligence, before doubling back on themselves as the big boys go in for battle.

One time I was in a Gazelle in Canada and the pilot was showing me how to fly really low and fast. Then, once the cameras were turned off, he took it up about 400 metres into the air, turned the engine off and let it drop in freefall. As we plummeted, the helicopter gained speed – but since the propellers are designed to rotate the opposite way to the way they usually go as the craft descends, the faster it fell and cut through the air, the faster the blades rotated, and we ended up just gliding down to the ground, landing with no engine power. The whole manoeuvre (which is something pilots have to be taught) reminded me of playing with sycamore tree seeds as a child.

Another time, in the Falkland Islands, I was taken up in a Harrier jet and flew at about 750 miles an hour, just 60 metres or so above the ground. I was wearing a g-force suit that was plugged into a vent that pushed air around the suit to stop me passing out because of the speed. We were travelling at Mach 2, twice the speed of sound. It was an awesome, once-in-a-lifetime adventure.

Working and spending time with the forces and their families has given me an even greater respect for the difficult but vital jobs they do, and it's been a privilege. I've always been overwhelmed at the warmth of the welcome I have received from young and older forces personnel alike. Whatever stand you take politically regarding the conflicts our armed forces have been involved in recently, I feel, from first-hand experience, that they are highly capable of protecting our country.

Back on solid ground in the UK, I pitched an idea to Discovery, Home & Leisure to film the conversion of the 150-year-old nineteen-room crumbling mansion that I had bought in Liverpool in 2002. The city had just been shortlisted for European Capital of Culture 2008 and the odds on it winning were looking positive.

My idea was to fully renovate and convert the building into four luxury apartments, each based on a theme that reflected an important aspect of Liverpool history or culture. The themes were music and arts, industry, the sea and the future. It was a huge challenge to project manage it, finance it and oversee all the workers while producing the show for Discovery. I was still working for the BBC, so I was badly snowed under. I spent a lot of time juggling TV deadlines, staff timetables, building schedules, budgets – and the rest.

Conversion was my biggest TV production to date. My plan was to remove 250 tonnes of clay from under the building, underpin it and create a whole new apartment beneath the house. I was also going to remove the entire roof and rebuild it with eleven skylight windows. First, we completely stripped down all nineteen rooms to bare brick, insulated and soundproofed the walls, floors and ceilings, and laid solid oak flooring and under-floor heating. As well as project managing twenty-five builders over nine months, Andy Bennett and I produced, directed, wrote and filmed all the action to cut into a ten-part show for primetime Discovery to be seen throughout Europe.

*

The show turned out to be one of the best rated shows on Discovery, Home & Leisure and is still being repeated today. Although it was hard work, I particularly enjoyed it because it gave me a chance to put my full building skills to good use on TV. So often people see me on screen doing minor DIY tasks around the house, but this time I actually renovated the entire house from scratch.

I was so pressed for time that I began to neglect the social whirl of London and stayed away from all the awards ceremonies and parties. Instead of dating celebrities, I was making a big bricks-and-mortar investment and starting my own production company. This was the way forward, I felt. I was building a solid future for myself and didn't have time to miss the glitter and razzmatazz.

The conversion project took up a massive amount of time, especially as I was going through builders as if they were going out of fashion. Unfortunately, there seemed to be a real shortage of skills in the area. I'm very fussy about quality of workmanship anyway; in this case the project was my own personal investment as well as being televised, so I wasn't going to accept second best.

Now, I don't mind paying the right money as long as a high calibre of workmanship is there, but such excellence was proving hard to find. At first I assumed that some of the workers I was taking on simply didn't take much pride in their work, but it wasn't that; in fact, they didn't have the skills, experience or up-to-date qualifications. Either way, I was getting very concerned about my project. Lots of established companies and tradesmen around the city were finding themselves overloaded by the continuous growth the city was experiencing. Merseyside was undergoing a multi-billion-pound regeneration programme, but it struck me that we weren't producing enough homegrown tradesmen to deliver this expansion, or maintain it in the future. It was a big problem.

It was around this time that I met Steve Rotherham, who went on to be Lord Mayor of Liverpool in 2008. At the time, Steve was working for the Learning and Skills Council, an organization responsible for planning and funding workforce education and training.

'Why on earth is there such a serious lack of skilled tradesmen in this city?' I asked him.

Steve, whose background was in bricklaying, shared my concern. 'We've tried really hard to tackle this problem,' he said, 'but it's all down to education. Building companies aren't taking on students, so young people aren't getting an opportunity to do apprenticeships, which is reducing the number of qualified tradesmen. I'm afraid that if we don't do anything about this, a lack of training on site will mean result in poorer quality of workmanship and a reduced workforce.'

It seemed a real shame. I thought back to the bricklaying course I had done in Telford and how it had transformed my life. Being in the building industry had helped me in so many ways. I wanted others to have the same benefits. 'Is there any way I can help?' I asked him. 'I'd like to put something back. Would it be possible for me to set up a training centre in my name, to try to bridge the gap that you're talking about? Perhaps it would help to get young people employed and trained by small construction companies.'

'That's a fantastic idea!' Steve said, and it pretty much went from there.

Turning the idea into reality was a long and complex process. There was a great deal of research to do; I drew up business plans, attended numerous meetings with the Learning and Skills Council, visited other construction academies and community colleges, talked to local building companies and searched around for premises. I even found myself two business partners.

Within a year we had a good relationship going with the LSC and they offered us a work-based learning contract. By now we had also found suitable premises for the academy, with a whopping 25,000 square feet of space.

Frustratingly, Health and Safety regulations obstructed some of my plans. I had spoken to local builders who felt that the existing construction colleges weren't preparing students for what it was really like to be on site. Let's face it, a building site can often be a harsh environment – cold, rainy and dirty – and the work is often heavy and difficult.

I wanted our skills centre premises to replicate site conditions – within reason – but Health and Safety insisted that the temperature inside the building was too low and made me install big heaters. Not only did this mean that my students stayed warm and relatively cosy while they were training, which is just the opposite of what a real building site is like for most of the year, but the heat also interfered with what they were learning. It dried the cement out too quickly; it changed the timings for plastering. But what could I do? If a lady in a flimsy blouse came out of her nice, warm office to our site with a clipboard and a thermometer and said that the building had to be a certain temperature to comply with regulations, I couldn't argue – although I tried.

Along with my building team, I designed and built the academy interior to resemble as far as possible a real construction site. Using more than 100,000 bricks, we built 44 individual solid rooms for various types of wet trades, such as plastering and artexing, 48 carpentry bench workstations and a 9,000 square-foot open-plan workshop for brickwork – large enough to build several entire houses inside.

Local construction companies had also complained to me in the past that students were turning up on site with too much classroom-based learning and too few, if any, practical skills. I took on board their criticisms in designing the layout of the centre. I didn't ignore the need to learn theory, though. Along with the workshop areas, there were large IT classrooms equipped for theory and health-and-safety work, and various staff offices, and administration and reception areas.

In late September 2005, we opened the doors to the Craig Phillips Building Skills Centre, the largest independent construction-training academy in the North-West. After all our hard work, it was a thrilling moment. We took in our first 152 students and I felt proud to think that I was helping young kids to learn a trade. After all, where would I be now if I hadn't gone to college? I'm certain I wouldn't have been selected for the *Big Brother* house without displaying the skills in the selection process that I had learned as a builder and running my own company.

Originally, the plan had been to get the skills centre up and running and then leave it in someone else's hands while I kept my media career going. But it didn't work out like that. With so many students and twenty-two staff, the responsibility was huge. Since I had invested a vast amount of my own money, time and resources in the project, I just couldn't let go.

The centre grew much more quickly than I imagined and so it took up a lot more of my time than I thought it would. Really, I was running before I could walk. I ended up having to cancel personal and TV appearances and that inevitably led to a parting of ways with John Noel. John was a brilliant agent and he did a great deal for me, but unfortunately there was no time to go to London any more.

About a year before the centre opened, I had asked Cherie Blair if she would like to become involved. We had met several times over the years after our first encounter at Downing Street and she had always shown a strong interest in what I was up to. I had also been asked to give a speech about education and introduce Tony Blair on stage at St George's Hall in Liverpool in 2005, just before the General Election. No matter what your politics are, it's an honour to speak on the same stage and introduce the prime minister in front of your hometown audience.

After the speech, over a cup of tea, Cherie kindly said she would be delighted to open the skills centre. It still took six months to arrange a date, though. We had to go through all the official channels and there's loads of bureaucracy. I thought I was busy, but Cherie Blair's schedule was absolutely choc-a-bloc.

Nevertheless, after being security-checked, we managed to get a date for January 2006.

That Christmas, I appeared in panto again, this time in *Aladdin* in Torquay with a great cast that included Syd Little, Jane Omorogbe (Rio from *Gladiators*) and Frank Williams, who played the vicar in *Dad's Army*. We also did a short New Year's run straight after Torquay at the Brindley Theatre in Runcorn, Cheshire, a little bit closer to home.

I was doing a personal appearance in a shopping centre promoting *Aladdin* and signing autographs when I heard a man's voice behind me, laughingly saying, 'Can I have your autograph?' I instantly knew who it was, even though I hadn't seen him for something like twelve years.

I turned round to see John Watson senior give me the same smile that had greeted me on the day I went back to tell him I had left his butcher's shop with too much change, more than twenty years previously. His face was redder, his hair was greyer and he looked older, but it was unmistakably him. I gave him a big hug. I was so pleased to see him.

When I'd finished the personal appearance, we had dinner together and a good chinwag that lasted about four hours. It was a fantastic catch-up, although I was sorry to hear that his wife, Betty, had passed away and that he was now living in some kind of sheltered accommodation. 'I'm so proud of you,' he told me, going on to say that he had kept lots of newspaper cuttings about me.

'Have you heard about my skills centre?' I asked him.

'Yes, it's all over the newspapers. I think it's a great idea.'

'I'm having a launch and Cherie Blair's coming up,' I said.

'It's all a big secret from the press at the moment, but give me your address and I'll send some passes out to you. Make sure you come and bring your John.' I also invited them to see *Aladdin*.

On 13 January 2006, Cherie Blair officially opened the skills centre. Alan Hamilton had by that time become my personal assistant and did a great job arranging for members of the press, the Lord Mayor of Liverpool, some of the city's key developers and education officials to be there, and a whole host of friends came along to support me – Dean Gaffney, Scott Wright, Dean Sullivan, Mark Moraghan, Louis Emerick, Tony Barton, panto co-star Syd Little, my old DIY presenter pal from BBC days Jake Robinson and footballer John Aldridge. Last but by no means least was my good pal Ricky Tomlinson, who talked to all the students and even gave them some plastering tips! The moment the launch event finished, I had to rush off to do a panto performance in Runcorn. Life was still as hectic as ever.

I hadn't spoken to young John Watson since the day I confronted him about the Liberty Life policies, but I was glad that he came along to the skills centre opening with his dad. I was so busy escorting Cherie Blair and her bodyguards every-where that I didn't get a chance to see them, but I got a lovely letter afterwards from them to say that they'd had a wonderful day, they were proud of me and they wished me all the best with it. The centre launch received great press in the national newspapers and in building-trade publications.

The work-based learning contract that the Learning and Skills Council had awarded us required us to find our students a job by the nineteenth week of their training. If we didn't meet this requirement, the LSC would stop the funding. Since we only had a small team of staff compared to other colleges and training centres, all our tutors were tied up training the new students, which left just my sister Beverley, our employer-engagement officer, with the task of finding jobs for the students.

There was another problem, too: the facility was new and couldn't achieve full centre approval (or accreditation) until the students had completed NVQ levels one and two, which usually took up to about twelve or fourteen months. Without centre approval we were unable to draw down various grants and funding that most colleges are entitled to. So things were tight.

Bev worked around the clock forging relationships with various building companies, large and small, local and further afield. I don't know where we would have been without her sheer determination and concern for the students' wellbeing and the future of the skills centre.

The centre thrived from the moment it opened. Within three months, about 100 out of the 152 students had work placements pencilled in or guaranteed, and some had the promise of trainee apprenticeships, largely thanks to Bev. My very small enterprise was making waves. The local construction companies had either seen or heard about our skills-based premises and courses and they had faith in what we were doing. In fact, a lot of building materials were donated to the centre, because they really wanted to see us do well.

I was flattered that various MDs from large national companies travelled from all over the country to visit me at the skills centre and offer their support. One MD, David Seymour, went a step further and asked me if I would consider endorsing three of his flagship products at Everbuild. I had been offered endorsements before, after finishing *Big Brother*, and John Noel had capitalized on offers that were made, but back then no one was sure just how long I would stay in the spotlight. Now, six years and hundreds of TV shows later, I was finally being recognized for being a builder!

Before we knew it, David and I had entered into a three-year endorsement deal – my face and signature appeared on his three brands in nearly four thousand building-trade counter outlets throughout the UK. I was proud and flattered to be informed by David's company that within the first three months of sales all the three products that I endorsed had increased sales by up to 70 per cent.

Back at the building skills centre we had one girl initially sign up alongside the 152 lads; she wanted to do a plastering course. Fantastic! we thought, because building is a very male-dominated industry. We immediately informed the Learning and Skills Council.

When the girl came for a chat about the course, we walked her around the building and assured her that we would look after her, even though she would be the only girl on the course. 'Don't be put off, because you'll have all the support you need.' All the teachers were told to keep an eye out for her.

Her uncle owned a building company, so she had an idea of how hard it was on site. 'I know it's dirty and cold and full of builders shouting their mouths off,' she said. 'I can handle that, no problem.' We never found out why, but at the last minute, to our disappointment, she pulled out.

Bricklaying can be heavy work for strong lads and even more so for ladies, especially if you're lugging bricks around all day. It's rough work, too; you scrape your hands to pieces. When I was a full-time bricklayer myself, my hands were like sandpaper.

You can't really wear gloves all the time when you're laying bricks. I didn't even wear them one freezing December back in the early days of my building career, when I was building two pillars at the gates of a Chinese restaurant. It was so cold that my fingers kept sticking to the bricks and pulling them back off the mortar. It was incredibly frustrating! However, it was a precision job, so I left the gloves off right up until Christmas Eve, when I finally finished. Then I got a phone call on Boxing Day to say that a Range Rover had knocked both of the pillars over and I had to build them again!

I shared my experiences with the students at the skills centre. More often than not, the talks I gave were totally informal. I often spoke about the obstacles I had overcome as a child, from losing my dad to being mildly dyslexic. I like to think that I helped the lads to know that you can overcome difficulties and make a success of yourself, as long as you're determined and prepared to work hard. This is part of what I say when I'm asked by the LSC and Construction Industry Training Board to hand out awards to construction apprentices and give motivational speeches to those in construction education. It gives me a great feeling to put something back into the industry which has given me so much. I realize only too well that it is my trade skills which have been key to my TV career and if you have a skill it is with you for life. Even those who achieve construction apprenticeships but then for whatever reason don't choose to pursue a career in the industry, if they have the get up and go they stand a good chance of being taken seriously by other employers. They have shown the dedication and motivation to start and finish a course.

As you would expect, there were a few lads at the skills centre who dragged their feet, but most of them seemed very keen to learn. There was one kid who looked scruffier than the others. We knew a little bit about his situation – he just wanted to get on, learn a trade and escape from his family, which was sad, but necessary, because his mum and dad apparently had problems with drink and drugs. He worked really, really hard and did well on the course.

Soon we noticed that his appearance had started to deteriorate. One of his teachers came to find me and said, 'He looks awful today, like he's been sleeping rough.'

So we called him in for a cup of tea and a little chat in my office. It turned out that he had been sleeping in his old banger of a car in the car park for three weeks. So that's why he was always the first in the college in the morning and the last one out in the evening! He often stayed behind to help clean up.

Well, you think you've got everything covered, and then something else crops up. We went to the LSC. 'We've got a problem,' I said. 'What do we do?'

We couldn't let him stay on the premises for insurance reasons, and it was alarmed anyway, but we didn't want to leave him outside either. Should I find him a room in one of my houses? I wondered.

The LSC advised me not to get too personally involved. 'He's not the only one. There are ten thousand youngsters with problems like his,' they said.

In the end we decided that the best thing would be if all the teachers were made aware of his situation and encouraged to support him in any way they could. We also helped him find out what social services could do to help him find temporary accommodation. He went on to complete his level two NVQ and later got a job, so I hope he's gone on to be successful. I admired his spirit – with so much working against him, he definitely had to have something extra to rise above it.

Meanwhile, I was having problems with my business 'parents'. The LSC said that my building centre would first have to 'hold someone's hand', or be parented in a business sense, before we could get full centre accreditation awarded by the Construction Industry Training Board.

The big daddy that we were allocated was Knowsley Community College in Merseyside, one of the largest providers of further education in the country, catering for twelve thousand students a year. Funding for my school came from the Learning and Skills Council through Knowsley Community College; they were supposed to support us with all the paperwork and bureaucracy to process our funds, grants and general running of the business.

As time went on, though, there were frequent glitches in the paperwork and transfer of money from Knowsley to us. This was a nightmare for me because there were staff wages and student grants to pay every month, not to mention premises rent, utilities, building tools and materials. If the money from the LSC didn't get to us through Knowsley Community College in time to pay all of these overheads, staff and students could go unpaid and our landlord would chase us for the rent. In other words, the delays were threatening the future of my skills centre.

Why was Knowsley College making life difficult, even though they were apparently receiving a fat fee to process our funding and hold our hand? Despite having a staff of six and a huge budget dedicated to finding their students work placements, Knowsley weren't placing anywhere near as many building students as my sister Bev, my staff and I were. Admittedly, it helped that I had a bit of a celebrity profile and lots of contacts, but the main thing was that I'd designed the school to be very hands on and teach the lads what employers wanted them to know.

Local businesses were starting to snap up my lads because they were crying out for students with useful, practical on-site skills. I couldn't help but suspect that my very small enterprise was making the mighty Knowsley look bad.

To make matters worse, my business partners were being very unhelpful and never put their money where their mouths were. Some months I found myself tearing my hair out over financial problems. It seemed so unfair! I believed that the centre was doing good – in fact, that the local community desperately needed it. But in spite of all I'd done and all the staff's hard work and dedication, the future was looking bleak.

Once again, the money didn't come through on the right

date. This time I knew there would – understandably – be a staff mutiny if people weren't paid on time. I had to do something, and fast. So, once again, I covered it by drawing on one of my credit cards and paying cash into the skills centre account – this time it was £25,000. The staff and students received their money.

But as usual, I never saw that money again, because the funding never came through, even though our school had delivered as promised. Before long, the business was almost insolvent and I was on the brink of bankruptcy. What the hell was I going to do?

15

Goodbyes and New Beginnings

For weeks I agonized over what to do. How could I continue to keep my building school going without the additional financial support? All I cared about was giving the students the skills to go out there and get jobs, but now I was bogged down in a financial mire that was getting in the way of my dream. I was hugely in debt to the bank and had personally guaranteed the overdraft along with a year's rent to the landlord if we closed; as the flow of money kept being interrupted, it felt as if I could go under any day.

The overdraft we were running at the bank was already huge and now we needed to extend it. Naturally, the bank required further security against the lending, so one afternoon the bank manager called us in to see him. Now, in the early stages of planning the centre, my business partners and I had discussed that when the time came to add serious money to the business, we could put down deeds to properties we owned outright as a form of security. However, when that moment came, I arrived with two deed titles for different properties but my business partners didn't. They either would not or could not release any equity or deeds to the properties they owned. I had a serious problem: should I surrender my properties to a company under financial strain when my business partners weren't willing to do the same? Just thinking about the finances made me so anxious that I was hardly sleeping.

In the spring of 2006 I employed ten students from the building skills centre to help me and my building team convert another nineteen-room Victorian mansion next to the one I had bought and renovated for *Conversion*. It was just a shell, so it needed a huge amount of work doing to it and, to my delight, the students had the skills to do it well. My heart swelled with pride at the thought that they had learned their trades at my school. This was what I had worked so long and hard for. The school was really making a difference in the industry.

But I couldn't go on supporting it financially on my own, not with the kind of funding problems I had encountered. I had to make a decision: either I ran a very real risk of total bankruptcy and losing everything I had worked for my whole life – or I sold the school.

It wouldn't be hard to find new owners, I knew. It was more than a going concern. Its reputation as an innovative, effective independent training centre was already established and it had an excellent infrastructure and staff. I talked things over with Councillor Steve Rotherham at the Learning and Skills Council, who was now a good friend. 'I think I might be able to help,' he said.

True to his word, Steve put me in touch with Peter Marples, the business development manager at Carter & Carter Group plc, which was the UK's largest independent training provider at the time.

So, in late May 2006, my assistant Alan and I went to meet Peter at Derby County football ground, where he was a member of the board. It was a rushed meeting, because half an hour later he was due at a press conference to announce Derby's new manager.

Alan and I took Peter through the skills centre's assets and liabilities. 'Yes, we want to buy it,' Peter said without hesitation once he had heard us out. 'We'd also like to keep you on board, if possible, Craig. You're definitely one of the assets!' He looked at his watch. 'Now, if you'll excuse me,' he said. Twenty minutes after the meeting had begun, we shook hands on the sale.

I felt very shaken as Alan and I walked away from the ground. 'I've worked for three years on this project,' I said, 'and it's all over in a twenty-minute meeting.' I wanted to weep with disappointment. In fact, I was crying inside.

'But think about it this way,' said Alan. 'We've just saved the school, twenty-two people's jobs and hundreds of students' careers.'

He was right, but I still took it badly. Then, just before the ownership transferred to Carter & Carter at the end of June, we were awarded full accreditation by the Construction Industry Training Board, which increased the value of the school substantially. In many ways, I had achieved my dream. I had established a school of excellence for builders that gave young lads a trade and a step up in life.

But there's no denying that I felt pretty depressed after Carter & Carter took over. It felt as if there was a big gap in my life. The school had become so all-consuming that it was hard to know what to do with myself once it was out of my hands. At least the anxiety had gone, though, and it helped knowing that Carter & Carter would keep my dream going.

In spring 2007, the managing director Phillip Carter visited the centre and requested a meeting to discuss me coming back on board at the centre. Then the unthinkable happened: Phillip, his son and two others died in a helicopter crash on the way home from a Liverpool v Chelsea game.

This was a tragic loss, not only to the Carter family, but also to the construction-education industry. Less than a year later, Carter & Carter went into administration. Fortunately, however, the future of the building centre and many other training centres was secured when Newcastle College purchased them and formed the National Construction Academy.

I decided to concentrate on my work for the British Forces Broadcasting Service and the day-to-day management of my property portfolio and building projects. 'When was the last time you did a series on terrestrial TV?' Alan asked me in early 2007.

I thought back. In 2004–5 I had been filming *Conversion* for the Discovery channel; I'd presented *Hung, Drawn and Quartered* up until 2006 for the BFBS. But terrestrial TV? 'It must be about two years ago,' I told him.

'Perhaps you need new representation,' Alan suggested.

He was right. Since John Noel and I had parted ways, I had

been so involved with the building school that I hadn't even thought about getting another agent. So Alan started research-ing agencies to approach.

One afternoon in January, as I came through the door of my office, he said, 'This one sounds interesting ... Debbie Catchpole at Fresh Partners.'

'Debbie Catchpole?' I said. 'If it's the same Debbie Catchpole I'm thinking of, I've worked with her before.'

Debbie had managed me for a while at John Noel, until she decided to take time out of the industry and spend some time in Australia. She had been an excellent agent back then; she had come up with the idea for a workshop-based series I presented for Discovery in 2002 called *Boyz in the Wood*. I knew that I would enjoy working with her again.

I went to meet her at Fresh Partners, which had been set up by someone I hugely admire: the chef Jamie Oliver. It was great to see her and we agreed we wanted to work together again. Not long afterwards, she suggested me for *60 Minute Makeover* on ITV1, working with my great friend Terri Dwyer. I filmed my first episode in March 2007 and I've appeared on nearly 150 episodes since then. In other words, I became madly busy again, racing up and down the country, and that's the way I like it! I even managed to squeeze in the renovation of another four-storey house.

The year 2008 was a great one to be living in Liverpool. We kicked off the city's European Capital of Culture celebrations with lots of high-profile events, including the Number One Project, a concert at Liverpool's new £160-million Echo Arena.

The Number One Project was a music-based charity event that marked the city's fifty-six number-one hit singles, more hit singles than any other city in the world has produced. Thirty different Merseyside acts and bands performed that night, including Gerry and the Pacemakers, the Searchers, Ray Quinn, the Christians, the Swinging Blue Jeans, the Scaffold, Sonia and Atomic Kitten.

Believe it or not, I took to the stage along with a group of stunning Hollyoaks actresses and sang Britain's first official chart number one, the 1952 hit 'How Much Is That Doggy In The Window?' in front of 10,600 people! It was enormous fun. The best part of the evening was gathering on stage along with the rest of the performers for the finale: Gerry Marsden's 'You'll Never Walk Alone'. I thought back to that moment outside the *Big Brother* house when the crowd had sung it to me and I was blown away all over again by the way my life had panned out. It was hard to believe that it had been eight years since that night.

Sometimes it seemed like only the day before and sometimes it seemed like a lifetime since I had come out of the *Big Brother* house, thrilled to have survived the full nine weeks and even happier to have won the money for little Jo's operation. So far, Jo hadn't needed either the money or the op. She was still bouncing back from her bouts of illness, although it was taking her longer to recover these days, and she had slowed down quite a lot. She needed oxygen at night while she was sleeping, which made life more difficult for her. As time went on, it became risky for her to spend even one night without oxygen and so she wasn't really able to visit London any more.

She and the family took to spending more time in Cyprus, because Joanne always felt better there. The atmosphere was healthier: the air was cleaner and the weather warmer. However, travelling took it out of her, especially flying, so Marion would try and spend a good two or three months on the island at a time. Jo always came back much improved and I think Marion was planning to spend up to six months a year there.

As the years passed, I often wondered whether Jo would ever go to America for the operation. Would she go through with it? Sometimes I would visualize her flying to America and return-ing triumphant, smiling her lovely warm smile, the quality of her life substantially improved. At others, well . . . in my heart of hearts I think I knew that that outcome was too good to be true. My hopes slowly faded as I began to fear it would never happen. A heart and lung transplant is a risky operation and the survival rates are low. There was around an 80 per cent chance that Jo wouldn't wake up afterwards, so no one wanted to contemplate operating until the situation was desperate – basically, if Jo wouldn't survive without it. We had the funds in place, but it was a matter of waiting for the specialists to let us know when they felt it was the right time to take her to America and suitable donor organs being available.

Jo was monitored by doctors at Birmingham Hospital every three months. Her condition was fairly stable most of the time and neither the doctors nor her family wanted to jeopardize that stability. She was leading a reasonably happy life so, as yet, the operation wasn't absolutely necessary.

For the last couple of years, she had been going to college to learn hairdressing, and now she was working part-time in a hairdresser's. She spent much of her time at work just talking, I think. She could talk for England; in fact she was a proper little old lady the way she chatted on! The oldies loved her – she'd make them a cup of tea or coffee, or comb their hair and help to wash it, gabbing all the while. Everybody knew her off the television and from her connections with me, so she was a little star. She even had a boyfriend, a boy with Down's syndrome whom she had met at college. He was a nice, funny character and well suited to Jo.

Then, out of the blue, Joanne fell really ill. Lee's mum Viv phoned me with the news. 'She was taken into hospital in Birmingham yesterday,' Viv told me. 'They've kept her in overnight and it's not looking good. She may only live another week.'

This was devastating news. I tried to keep my emotions in check and be practical. 'Can we take her to America?' I asked, my voice cracking.

'The doctors say she's not strong enough, love,' said Viv. 'She wouldn't make it. They don't even want to move her to London.'

So this was it. My mind filled with the inevitable. It was tragic and there wasn't a single thing I could do.

I was filming in London at the time and unfortunately on my one day off in weeks I was due to do something in Liverpool, so Marion arranged for me to visit Jo at around 11.30 p.m., long past official visiting hours, on my way to Liverpool from London. Little Jo's face lit up when she saw me, bless her, and she burst into happy tears. They hadn't told her I was coming, in case for some reason I couldn't make it, so it was a surprise for her – a nice one. Marion was pleased, because Jo had been miserable and very poorly for nearly a whole week now and this was the first time she had seen her looking animated.

Carefully trying not to dislodge the many tubes and wires that were connected to her, I gave Jo a lovely big hug. Then I tried to move away, because I could see the needles pulling on her skin. But she clung on and wouldn't let me go.

We had a good long chat once she had calmed down, though. She had her photo albums with her and so we went through all her pictures. I was in many of them, as were all the famous people she'd met, including Tina Turner, Robbie Williams and various other pop stars. It was as if she was recapping her life and I was very touched to see how happy it was making her.

After a couple of hours, she fell asleep and it was time for me to go. I leaned down to give her a hug and say ta-ra, love, when suddenly she woke up again and got very upset. It tore me up, but I had to leave.

Deep down I knew that I probably wasn't going to see Joanne again, even though I was planning to come and visit again at the weekend, if I could get time off.

After we had said our goodbyes, Marion walked me out, while the nurses stayed with Jo. We spoke at length and I realized she had already accepted that Joanne wouldn't be coming out of hospital this time. There can't be anything worse in the world than having to watch your daughter decline like that. It was so sad. But Marion had experienced so much heartache with all of Jo's ups and downs in health over the years that now she was really strong.

Little Jo died in her sleep a couple of days later, on 10 April 2008, aged only twenty-five. Everyone in the family managed to see her before she died.

Lee McCarthey called me to break the news. It's hard to put into words exactly how I felt at that moment. My emotions were mixed; I was devastated because she was almost like a member of my own family and always will be, yet I was also relieved that she would not be suffering or in pain any more as she clearly had been when I had last seen her at the hospital.

I felt privileged, too, that I had known her throughout her life, as she was truly unique. She never failed to put a smile on the faces of those around her, whether it was the first time they had met her or the hundredth.

I was with Bev when Lee called. We were both more or less silent for some time, and then we began to reminisce about Jo and how she made us all laugh. It helped.

People often become sentimental about loved ones that they've lost, but Joanne honestly did have a special glow about her. It's impossible to put into words, really. She had that lovely big warm smile and she was so affectionate, always hugging and kissing you. She was very touchy feely, particularly with people's faces, and it was so innocent, so loving. Absolutely beautiful, it was. She was priceless. Despite the odds she battled day to day, she shone with life. There's a huge hole in the family now. We all miss her very much.

I had a few days off around the time of Joanne's funeral on 23 April. It was a beautiful ceremony in a church in Shrewsbury and there was a massive turnout. They played her favourite song by Tina Turner, 'Simply The Best', and it felt completely right. All her friends and family were there to pay tribute to the best little girl that you could ever meet in your entire life.

Afterwards we went to a hotel bar in Shrewsbury with a large function room, where big screens showed footage of Joanne singing, doing an impression of Tina Turner, and loads of lovely photographs from her life. Joanne's boyfriend was there. I don't think he had fully grasped that Joanne had died and that he wasn't going to see her again, though. When I gave him a big hug and said I was sorry, he said, 'Today's the best day of my life!'

'Why's that?' I said, surprised.

'Because I've finally met Craig from *Big Brother*!' he said. 'I've seen all the pictures and Joanne's told me all about you,' he added. He had the biggest smile on his face.

The funds raised in 2000 for Jo's operation have now been distributed to a range of charities that are close to Joanne's family's hearts.

Little Jo was the original inspiration for all the work I do for charity now, so I was glad when my good friend Councillor Steve Rotherham became Lord Mayor of Liverpool in May 2008 and promised to break records for raising money for charity. His aim, he said, was to raise at least £208,000 for the Lord Mayor's Charity. Well, he's raised over £500,000 and that's more than any other lord mayor in England – ever. I'm one of the celebrity figureheads for the charity, along with Kenny Dalglish, comedian Sean Styles and Gerry Marsden, and I've done my best to support Steve in every way I can. I feel I owe him, after all, because he gave me a lot of help, advice and support with my building school and he was the link to its successful sale. I'm glad to say that it's as busy as ever and has so far seen hundreds of pupils graduate successfully.

The money raised by the Lord Mayor's Charity Appeal has been allotted equally between four charities: the Alder Hey Children's Hospital Imagine Appeal; the Liverpool Heart & Chest Hospital appeal 'Merseybeat'; the Marina Dalglish Appeal (breast cancer); and the Liverpool and South Sefton branch of the Alzheimer's Society.

Steve Rotherham's mum suffered from Alzheimer's before she died and, sadly, my mum is also suffering from it. I picked up on it about three to four years after *Big Brother* and she has slowly been declining for the last four or five years.

I first noticed it because I was talking to her every day or two, keeping her up to date with what I'd been doing, where I'd been and whom I'd been working with. But two days later, she would say, 'Ooh, what have you been up to?'

'The same as last week, Mum. I'm with the same presenters, you know – the Scottish boys, Colin and Justin.'

'Who are they? Have I met them?'

'Yes, Mum, you met them at the Ideal Home Show; they've been on *Housecall* and *Trading Up*.'

'Oh yes, of course I've met them,' she'd say. 'I know which ones they are.' Then, two days later, we'd have exactly the same conversation.

I started to get concerned. Mum had only just turned sixty, which is far too young to be going senile. I kept it to myself for a while; I didn't want to alarm everyone just yet without being sure of my facts, but began making a note of when and what time I spoke to her and what she was forgetting. A pattern began to emerge: she could remember everything from twenty years before, but was forgetting the more recent things. In other words, her long-term memory was OK, but her short-term memory seemed to be failing her.

I mentioned it to Beverley, to see if she had picked up on it. She hadn't, so I explained and showed her my notes. After that, Bev kept a lookout, too. It sounds bad, but we had to start testing Mum by telling her about things and then asking her questions about them a week later. We felt guilty about it, but we needed to know if a real problem was brewing.

Bev soon agreed that there might be. We then monitored her for a whole month and made more notes. During the month we decided that there was definitely a major problem, so we talked to Robbie.

At first, he refused to accept there was anything wrong with Mum. He was with her every day so it was less obvious to him, I suppose. He was a bit upset when we shared our thoughts with him but after we had explained, he agreed to keep a close eye on Mum. After a while he agreed with us that she was becoming quite forgetful.

How do you tell your mum that you think she's got some sort of degenerative illness? We called on the doctor who looked after Bev and me when we were kids and is still the family's GP. He has known Mum for more than thirty years and was really good: even though doctor-patient confidentiality dictates that you're not allowed to talk about your clients, he listened when we explained Mum's symptoms and how we had been monitoring them. He called her in for a check-up and did some tests of his own. Next he sent her to the specialists. It took about eighteen months, all in all, before they would confirm that Mum had Alzheimer's. Most of the time she's great and you can have a normal conversation with her, even today. She has good days when you can hardly tell she has Alzheimer's, but some days she appears lost.

We all know that the years to come will be harder for Mum and all the family, so Bev and I are really pleased that Mum has Robbie there full time to care for her. She also has a brother and sister close at hand. In difficult times, we all stick together. I'm glad that we've been raising money for the Alzheimer's Society and I intend to get more involved in the future.

So far I've managed to raise over £500,000 for different charities. Let's hope I can go on to make it a million before too long.

One of my other ambitions is to appear in a thousand TV shows. It would be a real achievement. By the close of 2008, I had appeared on over eight hundred DIY, property and construction shows and ITV have commissioned a further 140 shows of *60 Minute Makeover* for 2009, so I won't be far off my target by the end of the year.

One day I will seriously think about slowing things down and starting my own family. I often look at my sister Beverley and admire how well she's brought up Kelly and Lauren on her own. They are both in performing arts colleges and have blossomed to become beautiful talented princesses.

Who knows, I may even get married one day. I just need to

become a little bit more settled. Unfortunately, my relation-ships since *Big Brother* have generally crumbled because of my lifestyle. It's a difficult one, because it's hard for someone who isn't in the public eye to understand the demands and responsibilities that it entails.

It quickly became clear during my first year out of the *Big Brother* house that dating the kind of girls you see on TV wouldn't work for me, anyway. It wouldn't have been easy having a girlfriend and going public about it, especially if neither of you were settled in one place. I was racing up and down the country, staying in different hotels each night – at one point I was filming two *Trading Up* shows a week in different locations across the country – so sustaining a steady relation-ship was out of the question.

Plus, I have to say (and it probably comes as no surprise) that I found that a lot of the women in the public eye to be fairly bonkers! Some are insecure, always worried what they look like, and a lot of them are permanently trying to attract press attention. I certainly wouldn't want that going on all the time.

A little less than a year after *Big Brother*, I decided that I would be better off going out with someone I had known before I went on the show. So I called up a girl I had dated a couple of times in early 2000. 'I'm going up the wall here!' I told her. 'Can we meet up?' We went out on a few dates and then she became my first proper post-*Big Brother* girlfriend. When the press took pictures of us I was able to say, 'This is my girlfriend, Laura.'

Laura and I dated for about a year or so, nothing too serious. When the relationship faded, I started to date a Liverpudlian girl called Sharon. We had met when she did some modelling for a slot on a BBC *Housecall* shoot. Like Laura, she was beautiful-looking (far too good for me!). A trained teacher, she was also a very sensible and homely girl and we went on to live together on and off for a number of years. But sadly once again things didn't work out, because Sharon wanted to settle down and firm up our relationship, while I was still a bit all over the place and finding it difficult to juggle the different aspects of my life and career. I often think, Did I make the right choice by letting her go?

Then came Celena, a tiny little blonde professional singer who sometimes does a Kylie Minogue tribute as part of her act. Celena and I met on a P&O cruise liner in the Caribbean. She was a resident singer on the ship and I'd been employed by P&O to do a personal appearance that involved talking about my life and career to an audience of passengers.

As time went by, Celena and I started living together. We had loads of fun, but then history repeated itself and familiar cracks started to appear. I was doing four shows of *60 Minute Makeover* a week, sometimes staying away for five nights on the trot. Then at weekends I tried to maintain my other business interests, do personal appearances and even fit in a social life. Like Sharon, Celena was at a point in her life where she wanted to settle down, get married and have children, so it didn't work out.

Each time, I do believe I've been the problem. I'm the one who is too busy for commitment – or maybe afraid! I do know that I love kids so much and they are probably the only things that are missing from my life, but at the moment I don't think it would be fair on any woman or our children, for that matter, if I were to bring them into this world while I carried on pursuing the businesses and media career I have today. Hopefully that will all change in the not-too-distant future. Still, all my relationships both before and after *Big Brother* have meant a huge amount to me and each one has taught me more about love, life and myself.

I know I will never again be as famous or as recognized as I was when I came out of the *Big Brother* house. That was the peak for me and there was only one way to go after that. Still, my fame has come down to a nice sort of level now, where I can do normal things, when and where I want. I have experienced the sort of adulation that my musical heroes, like the Beatles and Oasis, must encounter every day and although it was great, I am grateful that, unlike them, I don't have to face it any more, although my work still enables me to dip in and out of the celebrity lifestyle (or whatever you want to call it).

As Robbie Williams and I once discussed, he has worked his way up over many years to where he is today, whereas I was catapulted into public view overnight, entirely unintentionally. Thankfully, though, there are many people who didn't even watch *Big Brother* who now know me as a celebrity builder from my TV work. I've made regular appearances on shows on all five terrestrial TV channels, many of the top satellite channels, and even done TV commercials, all things I could never have dreamed of before *Big Brother*.

The fame game has never been something I've thought about too much; I've just lived from day to day. It's not a big deal for me to be in the newspapers. Luckily, I don't have to earn a living by providing exclusives on my diet! I like to think I have just adapted my original profession and it's a great feeling to know people can learn how to do something from my TV work. It gives me a kick when people meet me and thank me for showing them how to build or repair something at home. I feel privileged to be on their TV screens – of the 150-plus *Big Brother* UK contestants, it is often said that I was the only one who turned my original profession into a sustainable media career.

I've got a really good balance now. I definitely wouldn't have liked that first year after *Big Brother* to go on: the security, the press and the mobs of people. It was very exciting but at times intimidating and certainly very tiring. However, I reckon I made hay while the sun shone, like all those successful people told me to, and I'm still making hay in the sunshine, nearly ten years later. I've had my ups and downs, lots of happy times and some very sad times – but despite the lows, I have a great family and friends around me, so I count myself very lucky. I like to think that my dad is watching over me some-how, guiding me through the hard times and (I hope) enjoying the good times. Either way, I know he'd be proud of me.

I would like to thank you for taking the time to read about the journey of my life so far. Whether you've met me personally or know me from TV, I hope that I have inspired you. Remember: you can achieve anything you want to with hard, honest work, dedication and, most importantly, by just being yourself. If I had to do it all again, I wouldn't change a thing.

Index

283